Literary Theory and Poetry

Literary Theory and Poetry
Extending the Canon

edited by David Murray
for
The University of Nottingham Critical Theory Group

B T Batsford Ltd. *London*

© David Murray 1989

First published 1989

All rights reserved. No part of this publication may be reproduced, in any form or by any means, without permission from the Publisher

Typeset by Deltatype Ltd, Ellesmere Port
and printed in Great Britain by
Billings Ltd, Worcester

Published by B. T. Batsford Ltd
4 Fitzhardinge Street, London W1H 0AH

A CIP catalogue record for this book is available from the British Library

ISBN 0 7134 58143
ISBN 0 7134 58151 Pbk

Contents

List of Contributors   *vii*

Introduction   *1*
David Murray

1 **Unity and Difference: Poetry and Criticism**   *4*
David Murray

2 **Cultural Coherence and Contradiction in Yeats**   *23*
Patrick Williams

3 **The Imperfect Librarian: Text and Discourse in *The Waste Land* and *Four Quartets***   *42*
Mick Burton

4 **Frames of Reference: The Reception of, and Response to, Three Women Poets**   *62*
Elaine Millard

5 **No Poetry For Ladies: Gertrude Stein, Julia Kristeva and Modernism**   *85*
Sara Mills

6 **Difficult Subjects: Black British Women's Poetry**   *108*
Patrick Williams

7 **Blake in Birdland: Displacement and Metamorphosis in the Poetics of Ishmael Reed**   *127*
Shamoon Zamir

8 **Image, Text and Performance: Inter-artistic Relationships in Contemporary Poetry**   *149*
Hazel Smith

**9 On Misreading Mallarmé:
The Resistance to Modernity** *167*
Bernard McGuirk

Further Reading *191*

Notes and References *193*

Appendix *211*

Index *214*

Contributors

David Murray teaches American Studies at the University of Nottingham, with research interests in modern poetry and North American Indians. Like most of the other contributors to this volume, he has been actively engaged in the Critical Theory Group at Nottingham, which involves an MA course, supervising for research degrees, and an extensive programme of seminars.

Patrick Williams is teaching at Strathclyde University, and has research interests and publications in literature and imperialism, literary theory and modernism.

Mick Burton teaches English at Worcester College of Higher Education, with research interests in Bakhtin, Lacan, and the use of literary theory in teaching.

Elaine Millard teaches English and Communication Studies at Bilborough College, and has written on feminist theory and literature.

Sara Mills teaches in the literary Linguistics programme at the University of Strathclyde, and has research interests and publications on feminism, linguistics, and colonial discourse.

Shamoon Zamir is completing a Ph D on ethnicity and writing at King's College, London, and is currently a Fulbright scholar at Yale.

Hazel Smith is a professional musician now based in Sydney, Australia, who has been extensively involved in performing and researching contemporary music and sound-texts. She has done research on Frank O'Hara, and has published several volumes of poetry.

Bernard McGuirk teaches Hispanic Studies at the University of Nottingham, with research interests and publications on French, Hispanic and Luso-Brazilian literatures. He is writing a book on post-structuralist approaches to Latin-American literature.

Introduction
David Murray

At present, it would be difficult to find any consensus about either an agreed critical approach to poetry, or an established body of twentieth-century poetry to which such an approach should be applied. This collection of essays, which can be read as a complement to Douglas Tallack's earlier Batsford volume *Literary Theory At Work*, on prose, is intended as an introduction to some contemporary theoretical issues by showing them in application. In dealing with problematic and distinctly non-canonical poems, as well as some established and well-known ones, though, there is also an intention to demonstrate both the *range* of available poetry, and the similarities of concern between recent developments in criticism and poetry. While no attempt has been made to argue explicitly for a new or alternative canon of criticism or poetry, certain themes and attitudes do inevitably recur throughout many of the essays, and can be briefly outlined.

We take our starting point from what is already a widespread dissatisfaction both with the version of literary history which gives Eliot and Yeats an unchallenged authority, thereby marginalizing all other, more radical, aspects of Modernism, and with a critical approach to individual poems developed in New Criticism which requires a demonstration of certain sorts of unity and coherence. My opening essay develops these general points, and uses Ezra Pound's *Cantos* as a way of showing counter-tendencies within Modernism, but also of demonstrating parallel and interacting developments in modern poetry, and the critical move from New Criticism to deconstruction. Both Patrick Williams writing on Yeats, and Mick Burton writing on Eliot, are concerned to show how a certain level of discourse, used and developed by the poets and accepted by the majority of their critics, can be challenged and historicized and thus shown to carry with it a whole series of cultural assumptions, about race and civilization in Yeats's case, and about the gendered self and about language itself in Eliot's. Thus one discourse implicitly excludes or marginalizes others, and this theme is taken up again by Elaine Millard, but in terms of readership and the reception of poetry. She demonstrates the ways in which her chosen poets, Emily Dickinson, Sylvia Plath, and Marianne Moore, have been read within a framework which distorts and limits what they are saying by stressing the life and not the operations of language within the text. Her use of recent French developments of Freudian models of the self to describe the way women are situated as subjects in language, is taken up and developed by Sara Mills; she in turn uses Julia Kristeva to re-read Gertrude Stein's experiments in language, as a truly revolutionary modernism in their destabilizing of the position of the subject as reader.

A different approach to the role of the poet in destabilizing or undercutting the dominant discourses of a society, is taken in Patrick Williams's account of Black British women poets. Using Deleuze's and Guattari's idea of a minor literature he demonstrates the resources open to those writers, as well as the cultural limitations. Shamoon Zamir also uses Deleuze and Guattari – though for different ends – as well as Jean Baudrillard, in his essay on the Black American poet Ishmael Reed, whose constant shape-shifting and linguistic displacements he sees as a way of refusing any fixed cultural identity. One of Reed's refusals is of any claim for the authenticity of an *oral* Black culture, and Zamir links this with the recurrent debate in recent criticism over the general privileging of speech over writing. Jacques Derrida has influentially demonstrated how written language in the West has come to be seen as *secondary* to speech, but has insisted that, in fact, writing should be our model of how language operates, rather than speech: in this way, we are made aware of the generation of meaning within the structures which make up language, and which are prior to the individual speaker, rather than seeing meaning as created by the speaker in an unmediated and spontaneous expression of self. This argument has important implications for concepts of self and spontaneity which have clustered around poetry, and also for the renewed interest in oral performance. In terms of race, for instance, it can be found here in the difference of view between Zamir and Williams, the latter arguing for the localized usefulness of the resource of the oral and denying that this involves any larger essentializing claims. However, the relation of structure to oral performance also raises fundamental questions about the nature and boundaries of the text.

Hazel Smith's account of Frank O'Hara and Jackson Mac Low shows how, by looking at the interface of poetry with modern music and painting, we are better able to understand both the problematic issue of representation in poetry, and also the complex and exciting movement between systems of meaning in intermedia works. In the performance of such works, performers and audience are involved in an indefinite deferral of any fixed or conventionally totalizable sense of form or meaning. Rounding off the collection, and reminding us of the truly international context of recent developments, Bernard McGuirk returns us to the issues raised in the first essay. His focus on Mallarmé alerts us to the radical *disjunctions* which characterize both the language of modern poetry and its development, but which have been covered over by a criticism concerned to reconstitute the unity of the text and of literary history itself. His use of Harold Bloom to demonstrate the problematic relation of later writers Rubén Darío and Cesar Vallejo to Mallarmé continues this sense of disruption and discontinuity, and his final citation from Derrida returns us to what, I hope, has been a recurrent theme throughout the collection: that of the play of meanings within poetic texts, to which recent criticism has tried to be responsive while at the same time demonstrating the various social discourses in which they are inevitably involved.

1 Unity and Difference: Poetry and Criticism

David Murray

Why do so many people who feel at home with novels feel uneasy when confronted by a poem, and especially a modern poem? If we explore this question in terms of the changing expectations of poetry, it may be possible to isolate some of the contradictions within which poetry criticism has to work. On the one hand, poetry is popularly associated with spontaneity and emotion. It 'just comes' and is an expression of the (higher) emotions. In this way, it is an outpouring like a cry or a bird-song. On the other hand, a great deal of poetry, especially modern poetry, is difficult. There is no evidence of its being either spontaneous or emotional, and yet there is the feeling that being poetry it must work differently from prose. Our uneasy reader will be told by teachers and critics that these poems cannot be entirely explained, by translating them to their prose meaning, because what is distinctive about them *as poems* is that all the elements combine together in a whole which is greater than the sum of its parts. This can provide the irritating and debilitating feeling of being left out, of hearing the story but not getting the joke, or worse still, of then having to have the joke laboriously explained by a commentary. This stress on the special 'whole' of poetry, with its accompanying exclusiveness, is, of course, not universal, and the importance of performance in much contemporary poetry indicates one possible way of changing attitudes to poetry as an *activity*, but in order to understand fully the implications of contemporary developments in poetry, it is necessary to understand just how fundamental and how potentially misleading ideas of unity and coherence have been, both to poetry and to criticism.

Judged in these terms, a successful poem would be one which created and sustained its own form, differentiating itself from what was around it, transforming materials taken from the world into elements within the poem, and giving them meaning by its underlying unity. It would communicate, ultimately, through that totality, rather than by any of its elements. Only when we conceived it spatially, as a whole, rather then sequentially and bit by bit, would we see it as a poem rather than as its separate ingredients. This could apply to a Romantic lyric, but it could also apply to a Modernist work like *The Waste Land*, or a poem by Seamus Heaney or Robert Lowell. The role of the critic would be to point out and underline the organic unity which was there, to reveal the totality of the poem beneath the discrete elements. A critical reading would be useful to the extent to which it demonstrated this unity, since in doing so, it would be showing how the poem really worked and affirming in the process that it was a successful, because unified, poem. This approach need not exclude poems that are not immediately regular or unifiable; in fact, this can act as a spur to the reader or critic to find the unifying elements beneath the contradictions and irregularities. Thus *The Waste Land*, for instance, can be shown to have thematic unity, and poems in so-called free verse can be shown to exhibit just as much unity of form and content as a sonnet.

The problem arises with those works which, in spite of their best efforts, critics are unable to see as unified. Are these works failures? And even with works that can be shown to be unified, against all appearances, *need* they be seen as such to gain critical approval? Need Gertrude Stein, Concrete poets, and the recent American 'language' poets be dismissed as incoherent, or Ezra Pound's *Cantos*, David Jones's *In Parenthesis*, or a poem by John Ashbery only be approved of to the extent that they can be shown to have achieved an underlying unity or coherence? While no one would deny the importance of what Wallace Stevens called the 'maker's rage to order' as both a major theme and a persistent formal concern in twentieth-century poetry, I want to show in this essay that, contrary to the views of New Criticism[1] which have for some years sustained and prioritized this concern for order and coherence, recent developments in criticism question fundamental assumptions about the extent to which any system can be closed or unified, and thereby sustain a distinction between inner and outer, and the extent to which meaning can be guaranteed and fixed within any linguistic or semiotic system.

Looked at in the light of post-structuralist critical theory, all sorts of aspects of modern poetry cease to look like failure or wilful and eccentric dead-ends, and a great deal of earlier poetry can be seen to be considerably less unified than it was seen to be by the New Critics. It would be wrong, though, to see the radical and innovatory aspects of modern poetry as only being discovered or fully made operative by critical theory. It is rather that recent critical developments have brought to the fore issues and techniques in modern poetry that had been marginalized by a New Critical approach. In juxtaposing Post-Structuralist ideas with aspects of modern poetry, my aim is not to elevate one over the other, but to show their complementarity. It is difficult, though, to see the significance of these developments without first appreciating the force and pervasiveness of a view of poetry which underlies both Romantic and New Critical approaches, and it is to this that we must first turn.

Frank Kermode has demonstrated the power and persistence of a view of poetry, running from German Romantic writers and critics onwards, which differentiates it from prose by virtue of its affinity with the material world. Where ordinary discursive prose was *about* the world, descriptive of it, the poetic image was also *of* it. Words used in poetry took on extra qualities by virtue of the whole they created, which became not an account of something, but of the same order of being as the thing itself. Within Romantic theory and poetry, this was conceivable by means of an affinity established between nature and the poet, whose imagination discovered the principles of nature and created according to those organic laws. The relation between poem and nature, then, was more than analogy or representation, was that of symbol. A symbol, here, is not an arbitrary sign standing for something in nature. It represents it best because it is part of what it represents. The ability of a poet actually to achieve such harmony with the forms and patterns of nature is, of course, problematic, and is one of the major issues in Romantic poetry, and recent criticism has questioned the adequacy of this as a description of what is actually happening in Romantic poetry.[2] Nevertheless, the stress on poetry as epistemologically and ontologically separate from prose (i.e. we can know different things and in a different way by means of it), can be seen continuing long after both the confidence in the poet's communion and harmony with nature, and the stress on the individual subject of the poet himself, disappears.

In Romantic poetry, the status of the poem was created and validated by the presence of the poet and his unity with nature, but even when he (and it usually is a 'he') fades from the scene in Modernism, and the poem is seen as separate from the poet and from the natural world, the claim for the poem's special status remains very similar. The language in it is seen not primarily as representational (about the world), but as made up of elements which refer to each other within the poem. The organicism developed when the poem was seen as gaining its coherence by virtue of its participation in the pattern of nature, is now continued, but without the connection to nature. Now the poem itself stands alone, and if its form is part or symbol of anything, it is an underlying order known only to us through this means. What is important for our purposes is that this view of the poem separates it off by its form from direct reference to the world, and also separates it off from the direct intentions of the poet. The impersonality of modern poetry is, therefore, reflected directly in a rejection of intentionalism in criticism. The meaning of the poem is to be guaranteed not by what the poet intended, nor by what the words refer to in the world outside the poem. Whatever the ostensible meaning, the essence of the poem is to be found in its self-referring totality.

What continues, then, behind the large changes from the Romantic lyric to *The Waste Land* is a critical claim for a special holistic way of knowing. As a result, not only has poetry often been judged ultimately by its ability to communicate and express this unity, but readers have judged their own experience of poetry by this, and failing to feel unified, have felt that either they or the poem must have failed. The development of Practical Criticism involved a new emphasis on what was on the page, rather than the reader's own presuppositions about either the subject matter or the author. By isolating the poem (and it is significant that it usually was a poem rather than a prose work) from its context, the intention was not only to screen out the reader's prior assumptions, but to lay bare what the poem really was saying. This, though, begs a very large question, in assuming that the poem has a meaning of its own which is entirely separable, rather than being given its meaning by context, whether explicit or implicit.

One of the effects of Practical Criticism has been the entirely salutary one of showing how the language of a poem works in detail, and discouraging the premature slotting of the poem into an established cultural and social context. This *could* well lead to a democratization of the reading-process. The words before us need not be seen as part of a pantheon about which we are to feel the proper reverence, and instead we are forced to ask what they are really doing. It could also lead to a greater openness of interpretation and an awareness of what each reader brings to the poem. In fact, though, the New Critical formulations put a crucial block on many of these developments precisely by their implied assumption that there is, underlying any surface ambiguity of meaning, a unified whole, a coherent form which is the poem. It could be argued that this is highly productive as an approach to poetry which actually works like that, and shares New Critical assumptions (though recent critics have questioned even this, as I shall show), but the effect of approaching modern poetry in such a way has been the inevitable suppression or marginalization of all those poems, or elements within poems, which specifically threaten or reject the inevitable subordination of part to unified whole. It is in dealing with these hitherto overlooked elements that later critical developments have been useful.

Recent critical approaches have built in different ways upon the structuralist demonstration that meaning is generated by, and dependent on, structures, systems, codes, whether of language, literary convention, or ideology, rather than being inherent in any element of that system. A poem, then, in structuralist terms, is made up of elements which together constitute a special and circumscribed system, and this system itself gives a meaning to those elements which is different from the meaning of the same element if it was operating in a different system.[3]

To read a poem we need to be aware, though not necessarily consciously, of the system, which is a sort of micro-system within the larger systems of language and ideology, from which it takes its elements and uses them for its own purposes. Clearly, this approach has strong affinities with New Criticism, and could be said to share many of its limitations. Later developments of (or away from) structuralism, though, have raised crucial questions which revolve around whether any semiotic system can be seen as closed and, therefore, stable. Post-structuralist questionings of oppositions like open/closed, inside/outside, and part-whole, have the effect of undermining the fundamental assumption that underlies the idea of structure itself – namely, that it is somehow prior to, or outside of, its constituent elements. In this way, Derrida has argued, the idea of structure fulfils the same purpose as earlier ideas of a generative centre or teleology in questioning a fixed point, whether origin or end, from which all other elements ultimately take their meaning.[4] This belief in underlying structure is the equivalent of the New Critical belief in the work of art as existing beyond the variability and ambiguities of its elements. If within a system, though, there are, as Saussure insisted, no positive terms, that is, no elements that are self-sufficient in meaning, and do not take their meaning from the other elements with which they are connected in a relation of difference, then the question of where the centre or essence of the text is becomes a difficult one. Derrida points out that

... whether in the order of spoken or written discourse, no element can function as a sign without referring to another element which itself is not simply present (i.e. itself takes its meaning from referring to other signs). This interweaving results in each 'element' – phoneme or grapheme – being constituted on the basis of the trace within it of the other elements of the chain or system. This interweaving, this textile is the text, produced only in the transformation of another text. Nothing, neither among the elements nor within the system, is anywhere ever simply present or absent. There are only, everywhere, differences and traces of traces.[5]

If, as we look more closely at a text, we find not a fixed anchor-point or centre from which the text gains its unity, but instead an endless deferral of that finding of centre and a system of differences which themselves unravel into other systems, then the activity of criticism as demonstrator of unity is thrown into question. Rather than seeing the poem as a set of oppositions and interplay functioning within clearly defined boundaries (that is, free play guaranteed by a final limit or generative centre, whether we call this structure, or organic unity, or authorial intention), it becomes necessary to see it as a fundamentally unstable collection of elements which, operating as a system, can create *effects* of unified meaning and coherence.

The exploration of these ideas in deconstructive criticism is not by any means confined to modern poetry, and it could be argued that most deconstruction has tended so far to work best by exposing instability and contradiction precisely where it seems most unlikely, by unravelling a whole system through picking at a previously ignored loose thread.[6] In this way, it depended upon previously-established orders, remorselessly breaking them down, leading hostile critics to see it as parasitic and entirely negative, a declaration of war on meaning itself. As a leading post-structuralist critic, Barbara Johnson, has put it:

... deconstruction has sometimes been seen as a terroristic belief in meaninglessness. It is commonly opposed to humanism, which is then an imperialistic belief in meaningfulness.

A way round this false opposition is to stress what deconstructive reading actually does: 'deconstruction is a reading strategy that carefully follows both the meanings and the suspensions and displacements of meaning in a text', as opposed to the previous method which encouraged the reader to 'stop reading when the text stops saying what it ought to have said'.[7] Loose endings, such as meanings from other contexts which are suppressed in the context of the poem, are followed up so that the whole begins to unravel. In particular, figures of speech are shown in their operation to be suppressing as well as supporting and producing meaning; the best way to illustrate this is by looking at metaphor, which has since the nineteenth century become increasingly not only the figure of speech seen as most fundamental to poetry, but almost the only rhetorical figure which is generally recognized and understood.[8] It is useful for our purpose because of the play of difference and similarity, or unity, within which it operates.

Metaphor is based on the recognition of similarities, and can be seen as a process of viewing one object 'through' another, aligning one with another, so that the similarities are brought out. This means emphasizing those characteristics that are alike, and ignoring those that are different. If we describe a man as a hawk, for instance, we emphasize those aspects of him which are like certain well-known characteristics of a hawk (fierceness, keenness of sight, etc.), and we automatically exclude the manifest differences, as well as subordinating the independent existence of the hawk. This process depends on us limiting the role of the hawk to the instant recognition of similar features. We see through it in order to bring out characteristics of the man. If we pull back from this proccess and start to bring the various characteristics of a hawk into play, we find ourselves not with a metaphor, but a series of differences that cannot be subsumed under metaphor or totalized.[9] The operation of metaphor is thus very similar to the New Critical reading of a poem, whereby what connects up and can be brought into unified patterns is privileged over what remains discrete and different. It is, therefore, highly significant that so much discussion of poetry chooses to focus on metaphor.

Many modern poets, most notably perhaps William Carlos Williams, have rejected metaphor precisely because of its ruthless subordination of difference in the name of a single unified focus. Rather than finding similarities, he prefers

> that power which discovers in things those inimitable particles of dissimilarity to all other things which are the peculiar perfections of the thing in question.[10]

Accordingly, Williams's poetry avoids metaphor, and even explicitly draws attention to this:

> Rather notice, mon cher,
> that the moon is
> tilted above
> the point of the steeple
> than that its color
> is shell-pink.
>
> Rather observe
> that it is early morning
> than that the sky
> is smooth
> as a turquoise.[11]

Francis Ponge, too, concentrates on the qualities of objects, rather than the using of objects, to illuminate qualities of our state of mind or to build large general patterns:

> Poetry itself does not interest me, in the sense that raw analogical magma is called poetry today. Analogies are interesting, but less so than differences. What is important is to grasp through analogies, the differential quality.[12]

Deconstruction adopts a similar strategy in exploring the ways that figures of speech like metaphor make demands on us, without our being aware, to see the world in a particular configuration and obliterate other possible configurations from view. The deconstructive answer is to reinstate the differences that have been covered over in these rhetorical figures, and to make what was apparently coherent and unified incoherent and multiple. So far, this is what a great deal of deconstructive criticism has in fact done, which has often meant it operating on the same canonical material as New Criticism, and deconstructing the sets of ambiguities in tension which New Criticism characteristically finds in a poem, into elements in an ultimately *undecidable* relation to each other.[13] This openness to the displacements of meaning, to the absences as well as the presences of the text, should make a deconstructive approach at least as suitable for contemporary experimental poetry with which New Critical approaches are unable to cope. The difference, though, is that there is no self-evident order to deconstruct, so that criticism has to engage more in a parallel activity. When Derrida engages with Francis Ponge, for instance, he is not engaged in tracking down the unnoticed gaps and breakdowns of meaning, so much as weaving Ponge's texts into his own meditations. By punning on his name (Signs/Ponge or Sign/Sponge) Derrida forces us to look more carefully at the relation of signs to proper names as a way of engaging with the problem of concreteness and specificity in Ponge, but there is no suggestion that he is revealing an area that Ponge himself had not already explored.[14]

Barbara Johnson's warning about the dangers of presenting the change from New Criticism to deconstruction as a simple move from order to anarchy needs to be repeated in relation to modern poetry, in that it is equally misleading and self-defeating to see innovation in twentieth century poetry as a 'terroristic belief in meaninglessness', though this is often the way it can come out if approached through New Critical methods. As Derrida himself has always insisted, though, there is not a once-and-for-all move from 'false' unity to 'honest' difference, but a recognition of the endless intertwining of these two ideas, and of the fact that we cannot deconstruct metaphysics without using the language of metaphysics. Nowhere can this recognition of the inextricability of order and disorder, and the instability of any system of signification, be more clearly seen in twentieth-century poetry – both formally and thematically – than in the development of the long poem. The next section will concentrate on some of the issues raised by these poems, in particular the *Cantos* of Ezra Pound, in the light of the deconstructive concerns already outlined.

Primarily an American rather than a British phenomenon, the

modern long poem finds its clearest expression in Ezra Pound's *Cantos*, William Carlos Williams's *Paterson*, Louis Zukosky's *A*, Charles Olson's *Maximus Poems*, and Robert Duncan's *Passages*, but the issues of formal organization and subject-matter raised in these works are fundamental to modern poetry in general. Having rejected the traditional organizational options of a sequential narrative of action, or lyric meditations linked by the presence of the poet in the poem, and wanting to include a wider range of material than nineteenth-century poetry had encompassed, the problem poets faced was how to present and organize this material in such a way that it gained new meaning from its new context *without* totally losing the meaning it had had by virtue of its original context.

Discontinuity and fragmentation become of special importance in attaining their end, since the recognition of something *as* a fragment, as discontinuous with what is around it, alerts us both to its connection with the former context and to its own specificity, as we try to relate it to its new surroundings. What is underlined in the process is the fact that meaning is a contextual and relational matter, as William Carlos Williams's description of his own approach in *Paterson* indicates:

> a mass of detail
> to interrelate on a new ground, difficultly,
> an assonance, a homologue
> triple piled
> pulling the disparate together to clarify
> and compress[15]

One of the ways to 'interrelate' is by means of similarities and analogies, thus creating a unified structure, a 'homologue', and this could be used to project a view of the world, and the work of art as ultimately unified. Next to the word 'homologue', though, Williams has placed 'assonance' which directs us toward a recognition of similarity *and* difference. To interrelate 'difficultly' is to be aware of connections and similarities, but not to let them effect a closure and a unity which obliterates the concrete and specific qualities which make for difference.

The aim, then, is to give due weight both to relationality – the play of meanings within a system – and to concreteness and specificity, but to do this without recourse to the most easily available and 'poetic' device, that of symbolic or metaphoric connection, since this would close off the movement between the two poles. This can be seen most clearly in the complex movements within Ezra Pound's *Cantos*. In his concern for concreteness and visual clarity as an antidote to what he saw as the vagueness and subjective indulgences of lyric voice to be found in his nineteenth-century predecessors, Pound came to value and utilize what he called an 'ideogrammic' method. This seemed to offer the 'direct presentation of the thing' in a clear visual image, and so corresponded to the requirements of poetry already outlined in his development of Imagism, but it could also allow for complex interrelations between its elements, since these are not fixed in rigid grammatical and syntactic relations. Instead, the elements are juxtaposed, without the connectives of syntax. Presented with disparate unconnected elements, the mind searches for relationships between them based on similarity or association, and according to Pound, builds up abstractions. Ideas come into being which are all the more vivid by being held 'in solution' by the details to which they apply, and out of which they have arisen.[16]

Pound wanted the *Cantos* to be inclusive of all sorts of non-poetic elements neglected by his predecessors, and his technique of collage-like juxtaposition of materials was chosen for its ability to allow the readers to see the relations between the materials for themselves. His aim was to find a form and a means of organization that would both include the materials of history in their specificity, and allow for the emergence of a coherence and an order which he could not find in modern culture, but the problems arise when the materials of history fail to yield up pattern or overall meaning. In this case, we, as readers, are left with disparate elements, having meanings in other systems not known to us, and without any overall system into which we can put them. The poem then works more like a hieroglyph, where we are faced with elements which resist effacing themselves as transparent signs of something else, and insist on their own concreteness and specificity.

Pound's method of assembling discontinuous fragments – a method towards which he also pushed Eliot, temporarily, in *The Waste Land* – since it deliberately problematizes the connections between the disparate elements, is always potentially about to break down. In other words, there is a tension between the centripetal force of the poem as a system giving its elements meaning, and the centrifugal scattering of the fragments back into the systems from which they were pulled, and in which they had another meaning. The usual defence of a Modernist work like this would be to stress the idea of *tension*, and judge the poem by its ability to sustain it – the recurrent idea of an ultimate unity which can contain contradictory forces in balance or equilibrium. Certainly, Pound himself explicitly dramatizes this tension in his struggle to find meaning in, or impose meaning on, the flux of the material of this huge poem written over the space of half a century, and his final sections could be seen to contain an admission of his own failure – but need we accept these criteria?

Pound referred approvingly to the epic form as a 'poem including history', but his own attempts to 'include' history by weaving it into an overall pattern run the constant risk of failure, and his difficulties can be illustrated by what happens when he insists on presenting fragments of documentary evidence. Inevitably, they refer us back to the whole from which they have been torn, as well as taking their place as signifying elements within the new context of the poem, so that they face both ways, eroding any distinction between inside and outside the poem. In this way, we have a 'poem including history', but we are also led along the trailing loose ends of the poem to recognize the connections to a history which includes a poem including history. This, then, is not the tension of elements *within* the poem referred to earlier, but a radical undecidability about the status of the elements inside or outside it, and it is this undecidability, as opposed to the play of ambiguity *within* a system, which Derrida has stressed. This has often been recognized at work in techniques closely allied with Pound's, those of collage and montage, where the dislocated element, when put into a new context, still takes with it associations with its former context. At the same time, experience of the range of the collage and montage innovations of Modernism helps us to see that the processes here at work, those of selection and combination, are, as Gregory Ulmer says, 'characteristic of all speaking and writing. Moreover, as in language usage, the operations are carried out on preformed language.'[17] In other words, the discontinuous cuttings and graftings of collage and montage can make us aware that all the elements which make up something that we think of as a whole, such as a work of art, can, in fact, be reinstated as fragments of other systems. This awareness of intertextuality alerts us to the multiple functioning of any element in a work of art, both in that work and also as an element of other wholes. While in general this point may seem self-evident, taking it seriously involves a breaking down of those boundaries of a text which guarantee the distinction between inner and outer, and this is one of the effects of a deconstructive reading. The clearly-designated systems of signification which apparently control the play of meanings within the text, and to which a New Critical reading tries to be obedient, are, in a deconstructive reading, undermined.

Pound's *Cantos* both enact and explicitly thematize this whole issue. In the appropriately named *Drafts and Fragments* which was the last part to be published, Pound acknowledges an ultimate lack of coherence in the poem:

> I have brought the great ball of crystal;
>   who can lift it?
> Can you enter the great acorn of light?
>   But the beauty is not the madness
> Tho' my errors and wrecks lie about me.
> And I am not a demigod,
> I cannot make it cohere[18]

But whereas both he and his critics have seen this as a mark of its failure, his own summing-up can be read differently when he laments

> That I lost my center
>   fighting the world.
> The dreams clash
>   and are shattered –
> and that I tried to make a paradiso terrestre[19]

Losing his centre can be seen as the effect of the centrifugal forces activated by the form of the poem, as well as the events of Pound's life. The sheer contingency of the world thwarted Pound's efforts to find a coherence, a congruity between past and present (his insistence that Mussolini was like Jefferson and, therefore, represented durable values, was conclusively undermined by the actual dissimilarities and difference evidenced in the historical events which led to Pound's imprisonment by the Americans at Pisa). Thus, in the *Cantos*, when he puts disparate materials together, the very method involves the setting-up of relations of similarity and congruity, but also the setting-free of the elements to combine or contrast with other elements elsewhere in the poem. More or less

Unity and Difference: Poetry and Criticism 17

'meaningful relationships' are therefore being set up throughout the poem, *and* with elements outside the poem, in what Derrida has called 'dissemination', a scattering of seed, rather than the regulated and controlled productivity of a closed system – a promiscuous mingling, rather than a system of marriage. The trouble with promiscuity, though, is supposed to be that 'you never know where it will lead', but it is this movement between regulation and free play, and the idea of a form which is open enough to allow for this double action, which has been crucial for modern artists in many areas. Seen in this light, losing one's centre is an *enabling* event which allows for a complex movement between the poem and its contexts. Joseph Riddel describes the effects of using historical materials in collage-like conjunction, rather than concentrating on the poet's subjective expression:

> Documents decenter the lyrical voice, the centering or narrative subject. But the poet's performance (method) also decenters the documents. Affiliation maps and demythologises the fiction of narrative or filiative order.[20]

Another way of exemplifying this movement between original context (filiation) and the new ones created by the artist in the new structure (affiliation), is to look at the widespread use of what has been called assemblage in the contemporary arts as a whole, and the next section will explore this idea by relating it to another closely-related idea, that of bricolage.

William Seitz has located the first clear example of the principle of assemblage when

> finally and with authority – and for the first time in Western thought – Dada substituted a non-rational metaphysic of oppositions for a rationalised hierarchy of values.[21]

This is different from cubism where

> the ambiguously beautiful device of *passage* – a final attempt to soften the shock of discontinuity – tends to bridge disassociations of image. The method of assemblage, which is post-cubist, is that of *juxtaposition*. (p. 25)

Assemblage brings together objects and images, but does not de-nature, de-sign them:

> The assembler is especially akin to the modern poet in using elements

which (unlike 'pure' colors, lines) retain marks of their previous form and history. Like words, they are associationally alive. (p. 17)

Crucially, though, they are torn out of any full context to be put into this new space, and the idea of filling a space whose boundaries are defined only by their existence, rather than being already delimited or shaped, is important. John Cage expresses it well, when he talks about Robert Rauschenberg's work: 'this is not a composition, it is a place where things are, as on a table'.[23] The provision of a space which does not in itself organize or shape the materials used can be an attempt to create work which obliterates or, at least, changes the usual distinctions between art and life. Cage quotes Rauschenberg to this effect:

> Painting relates to both art and life. Neither can be made. (I try to act in that gap between the two.) (p. 105)

The result of this reluctance to shape or design/de-sign is, as Cage says, that 'there is no more subject in a combine than there is in a page from a newspaper. Each thing that is there is a subject. It is a situation involving multiplicity' (p. 101). It is the acceptance of multiplicity without the discovering or imposition of an overall unity which is relevant for the discussion of poetry through the crucial idea of forms. As Cage says, 'were he [Rauschenberg] saying something in particular, he would have to focus the painting', but as it is 'each minute part is at the center' (p. 103). Decisions made about the final shape or form of a painting, then, involve not so much an overall intention or design as a responsiveness to each new entity that is found and assembled, and a sensitivity to finding a way of combining which does not de-nature it. Chance and randomness, therefore, begin to play a part. As Seitz says, 'the pre-condition of juxtaposition is a state of total randomness and disassociation', and the assembler, in putting materials together, 'discovers order as well as materials, by accident'. The order or form grows by testing, and

> the artist must cede a measure of his control, and hence of his ego, to the materials and what transpires between them, placing himself partially in the role of discoverer or spectator, as well as that of originator. (p. 39)

This idea, then, of the creation of the orders of the work from the inside out – from the possibilities presented by the ingredients as they are encountered and assembled, rather than by the total mastery of the form by the artist – once again refers us to the movement between inside and outside, and Seitz describes assemblage as 'a method with disconcertingly centrifugal possibilities'.

But if one pole of assemblage is the extinction of the artist in the ceding of control to the random play of meanings amongst the elements of the work, the other is always the specific putting-together of these elements in form – and meaning-creating acts. It is important to stress this role, given the tendency in deconstruction to stress the role of language itself, or any semiotic *system*, at the expense of any individual act of meaning. This is not the same as arguing for creativity as a creation out of nothing, an act of absolute freedom, and one way of describing this creation of the new out of preformed elements is Levi-Strauss's idea of bricolage. Used originally to describe the way that mythical thought is built up out of pre-existent elements, it has been recognized as capable of broader application. The 'bricoleur', according to Levi-Strauss:

> 'speaks' not only *with* things, as we have already seen, but also through the medium of things: giving an account of his personality and life by the choices he makes between the limited possibilities. The 'bricoleur' may not ever complete his purpose, but he always puts something of himself into it.[23]

The link with the concerns of modern poetry can be demonstrated by using a poem by Robert Duncan which deals with the constructions of Simon Rodia in Los Angeles. Rodia's improbable structures were built literally from the debris of the society around him:

> three spires
> rising 104 feet, bejewelled with glass,
> shells, fragments of tile, scavenged
>   from the city dump, from sea-wrack,
> taller than the Holy Roman Catholic Church[24]

Threatened by city planning ordinances and breaking all the rules, Rodia's work is used by Duncan as an instance of the form-making activity of modern art. Here, Duncan stresses the creation of the structure as an act or expression of self, but this needs always to be seen in the context of his awareness that 'the great art of our time is the collagist's art, to bring all things into new complexes of meaning'.[25] What is involved in this creation is the taking of objects or images, and by juxtaposition, combination, building them into a larger design or structure, without totally effacing the *origin* of the elements. Within his poem, Duncan quotes from a fellow-poet, Charles Olson (itself an act of grafting, of collage), to stress the expression of self in form-making acts:

> There are only his own
> composed forms, and each one
> the issue of the time of the moment of its creation,
> not any ultimate except what he in his heat
> and that instant in its solidity yield

Rodia's construction fulfils this requirement for Duncan, and his description of it chimes very closely with the idea of bricolage:

> an original, accretion of disregarded/splendors,
> resurrected against the rules,
> having in this its personal joke . . .
>   an ecstasy
> of broken bottles
> and colored dishes thrown up against whatever
>   piety, city ordinance, places
> risking height

His celebration of what seems to be the individual creative spirit, 'risking height', needs to be balanced both by the awareness of the limits within which Rodia, like all artists, works and also, in Duncan's case, by a countervailing stress on the way that orders in art seem to be found as well as made. To use a characteristic word-play, if the artist has individual responsibility, this involves the responsibility to respond to what is there, to be passive as well as active. This final uncertainty or ambivalence about whether the making of forms is really a creation or a revealing of what is always already there, is never to be underestimated, particularly in American poetry, and it does mean that the notion of self, while not necessarily given up, is always being negotiated anew.

In this chapter I have tried to show the complementary nature of developments in modern poetry and criticism; but it could be argued that, in its continual recourse to ideas of essence or origin, either in the self as form-creating, or in the idea of transcendent forms which are already present to be found, or the idea that objects can be presented in their concreteness without the mediation of language, modern poetry has not, in fact, taken the step of radical scepticism involved in deconstruction. I would want to argue, though, that it is precisely in moving *between* these areas of potential essentialism, without being too fastidious to entertain any of them, that modern poetry is most interesting and saves itself from sterility. Derrida himself has acknowledged the impossibility of *not* using the language of metaphysics in order to undermine it, which seems to me precisely what poets are themselves acknowledging.

One final instance of this is oral performance. There has been a sustained attack within deconstruction on phonocentrism (the pervasive belief that speech is direct and unmediated, as opposed to the secondariness of writing), because it blinds us to the fact that *any* use of language involves us in the same play of differences which generate meaning within language. Speech seems to offer presence and unmediated meaning, since it is part of a unique instance, whereas writing can be repeated, read in different contexts, and the dependence of the words for their meaning on *other* words and on context, rather than on original intention, is revealed. For deconstruction, emphasis on writing rather than speech reveals what speech *is*, but is seldom recognized to be. Although a great deal of modern poetry, in reaction against the excesses of the lyric expression of self and subjectivity in nineteenth-century poetry, has stressed impersonality and objectivity, the written text rather than the speaking voice, the issue of the *performance* of poetry has raised in several different contexts the role of the text. Although there is always the possibility of the reinstatement of a claim for the presence of the poet and for unmediated expression, much more important is the way in which performance throws into question the boundedness of the text. Rather than seeing the performance as the original of the text, and as therefore having some priority over it, it becomes a dispersing of the authority of any single or unified text. In the reception of an oral performance we are without the ability to glance back, re-collect and re-constitute the whole. The fact that there may be recordings of the performance still does not make it like the written text, in that no one performance is definitive. There is, therefore, no authoritative text, either written or recorded.

Several of the essays which follow deal with the implications of this, either formally in the relations of sounds to words, or socially in the special issues raised by oral performance within a society where written texts are culturally privileged. It may be therefore that in restressing the role of speech as well as of writing, modern poetry in performance, far from sliding into the appeal to unmediated presence suspected by deconstruction, is in fact engaged in an undermining of textuality – an undermining with which criticism, in its emphasis on texts of the past, has yet fully to come to terms.

2 Cultural Coherence and Contradiction in Yeats

Patrick Williams

> ... Yeats's two great passions – Ireland and Art.
> LOUIS MACNEICE[1]

MacNeice's comment, with its accompanying warning not to accept Yeats's own blinkered concepts of either, is particularly appropriate to Yeats's late poem 'The Statues'. While 'The Statues' is clearly about Art – with all the implications and problems connected with that initial capital letter – it is not until the final stanza that it is seen to be, indeed to have been all along, about Ireland, too, and not least among the poem's sources of interest are the remarkable claims made on behalf of both. In addition, however, the poem reveals itself to be concerned with another of Yeats's enduring interests – perhaps worthy of being considered a passion also – the East, and one of the reasons for choosing to analyse it here is that it represents the final form of Yeats's reflections on a subject which occupied him from childhood onward.

If the poem makes great claims for Ireland and Art, then, equally, great things have been claimed for the poem:

> ... an astonishing and masterful revaluation of past and present.

> ... perhaps the most difficult poem that Yeats wrote.

> The poem is the most complex in the collection, perhaps the most complex Yeats had written since 'Byzantium'. Its suggestivity radiates in every direction, and the reader never comes to the end of trying to understand it.[2]

Whether or not a difficult poem calls for a difficult critical method is by no means certain, but it is proposed to use here one which, at least at first sight, would appear unpromising. The work of Mikhail

Bakhtin is almost exclusively concerned with prose fiction, and, as more of it becomes available through translation, is increasingly recognized as one of the most important critical oeuvres on the subject. Bakhtin has very little to say on poetry, other than in the short section 'Discourse in Poetry and Discourse in the Novel' in *The Dialogic Imagination*. Poetry, and particularly lyric poetry, is seemingly constructed in this essay as the locus of negative qualities and restrictive practices, in an opposition whose positive term is the open, accommodating novel. The relevance of Bakhtin for present purposes lies in the fact that, as is true of his thinking as a whole, this apparently static binary opposition is nothing of the sort, and the novel and the lyric merely serve as literary instances of two tendencies within discourse and language in general, tendencies which are, however, never fully realized. These two tendencies or forces in language Bakhtin calls, firstly, the centripetal or monologic, and secondly the centrifugal or dialogic. The former strives towards the creation of a closed, unified, static language, while the latter works with linguistic diversity in open, relative, interactive forms. These have their literary correlates, not in the novel and lyric as such, but in what might be termed 'novelistic' and 'poetistic' tendencies.

In addition, discourse is, according to Bakhtin, the materialized form of social interaction; thus, on the political level, we find the traditional ruling class typically monologic in its desire to impose its own meanings on the rest of the population, and to silence opponents or deny validity to their utterances. Conversely, the dialogic is pre-eminently the realm of the oppressed classes in society, whose regional and class varieties and oppositional discourse undermine the official form and its pretence of universality. Similarly, the struggle between these two tendencies is both an image of, and a concrete element in, social struggle. As such, it is a perhaps extreme example of a central fact about language, that it is by nature dialogic, however much certain groups may attempt to repress or deny this. Among other things, this means that any utterance is actively or implicitly oriented towards an audience and its potential response. Also, although Bakhtin believes in a form of intentionality on the part of speaker or author, this is not the absolute guarantee of meaning: the fact that language pre-exists us and is not wholly ours, that words never come to us in any pure state but already overlain with numerous actual or potential meanings or inflections, that, as Bakhtin says, 'The word in language is half someone else's . . .',³ results in meaning being a social phenomenon – negotiated, potentially conflictual, dialogic. Textual meaning is dialogized – made plural rather than singular –by a number of factors. These include the inherent dialogism of language just referred to, the number of different discourses in dialogue within a single text, the relation of the text to other texts, and the relation of the text to the extra-textual, including what Bakhtin calls heteroglossia, the ensemble of social and historical elements which condition any utterance. All of this applies to the lyric as well as to the novel, though to a lesser extent, given the latter's unparalleled ability to incorporate diverse discourses and endlessly dialogize itself. As a result, the monologic aspirations of the lyric can never be fully achieved, though the attempt, for all that, never ceases:

> Poetry comes upon language as stratified, language in the process of uninterrupted ideological evolution, already fragmented into 'languages'. And poetry sees its own language surrounded by other languages, surrounded by literary and extra-literary heteroglossia. But poetry, striving for maximal purity, works in its own language as if that language were unitary, the only language, as if there were no heteroglossia outside it. Poetry behaves as if it lived in the heartland of its own language territory.[4]

In applying some elements of Bakhtin's theories to Yeats's poem, the present essay will not attempt anything resembling a line-by-line exegesis, especially since many critics have already done so; nor will it concern itself with an aesthetic valuation of the poem. It is, however, proposed to examine some of the discourses in dialogue within Yeats's poem and with which the poem as a whole is in turn in dialogue, including those of culture, class, gender and race. (Inevitably, the present essay will also be in dialogue with other critics on Yeats's work.) As Bakhtin points out, however, such discourses are far from neutral: they are on the contrary variably but inescapably ideological (as indeed one might expect from their implication in social struggle), and they will be approached here not with any sense of their ultimate truth or falsehood – regardless of claims Yeats himself might have made in this respect – but precisely as ideological representations, the reproduction, or re-working of pre-existing ideological discourses. I feel that the emphasis on the pre-existing is important, since a persistent tendency in Yeats scholarship has been to regard his ideas as self-produced – springing Athena-like, fully armed from his labouring, but self-contained and self-referential brain. While there is no doubt that Yeats devoted a great deal of time and effort to the production of a personal system of beliefs, the stress on the autogenous nature of such production is dangerously misleading.

A particular form of dialogue is created within Yeats's own work by the relation of 'The Statues' to other poems in the collection, and to earlier poems on similar subjects, among which the decline of civilization, the exalting of Irishness, and the relation of Europe and the East figure prominently. For the former, the re-ordering of *Last Poems*, rectifying the confusion caused by the Macmillan edition, is significant: the re-insertion of 'Under Ben Bulben' at the beginning acts almost as a table of contents, setting out areas which poems such as 'Long-Legged Fly', 'A Bronze Head', and 'The Statues' will debate, and carrying on from their immediate predecessors such as 'The Gyres', 'Lapis Lazuli' and 'The Curse of Cromwell'. In particular 'Under Ben Bulben' adumbrates all the central concerns of 'The Statues', especially the task of the artist, his power and cultural or social responsibility, the ancient lineage of the Irish and the problem of contemporary racial degeneration, and the necessity of violence. In fact, the relationship is so close and symmetrical that it seems almost one of echo and amplification rather than dialogue.

Bakhtin's work is very much concerned with the relationship to the Other and how this affects our own discourse, and before approaching 'The Statues' in detail it is necessary to mention another theorist who has analysed this relationship from a perspective which is particularly relevant here. In *Orientalism*, Edward Said examines Europe's relation with the Orient, and the way in which a particular negative image of the latter has been created and repeated endlessly, in texts ranging from the fictional to the scientific and philosophical. This representation of the Orient has, in turn, formed the basis for European activity involving the Orient, from travel, to commerce, to war and outright imperial annexation. Said describes the phenomenon of Orientalism as follows:

> Thus Orientalism is not only a positive doctrine about the Orient that exists at any one time in the West; it is also an influential academic tradition . . . as well as an area of concern defined by travellers, commercial enterprises, governments, military expeditions, readers of novels and accounts of exotic adventure, natural historians and

pilgrims to whom the Orient is a specific kind of knowledge about specific places, peoples and civilisations. . . . Orientalism can be discussed and analysed as the corporate institution for dealing with the Orient – dealing with it by making statements about it, authorising views of it, describing it, by teaching it, settling it, ruling over it: in short, Orientalism as a Western style for dominating, restructuring, and having authority over the Orient.[5]

Far from simply encountering the Other, which is what Bakhtin's model would seem to suggest, the West has for centuries systematically *constructed* its Other in the shape of an Orient which is exotic, backward, cruel, superstitious, decadent, treacherous, aggressive and dirty (by turns or simultaneously). What is important in this is not the possible truth of the assertions (and they are always justified as the height of objective veracity by their proponents), but the fact that, whatever the context – philosophical, moral, technological, religious – they guarantee the West a position of unassailable superiority *vis-à-vis* the East. More importantly, they provide the legitimation for economic, political or military intervention.

In the images of culture which it offers, 'The Statues' is, it would appear, classically, inescapably, Orientalist. It represents the putative triumph of the West in terms frequently encountered elsewhere in Orientalist and colonialist discourse: the defeat of Asiatic formlessness by European form, of Eastern chaos by Western order. An indication of the way such ideas constitute a staple of Orientalism can be gained by comparison with works such as *A Passage to India*: when, on his way home to England, Fielding reaches the Mediterranean, he experiences cultural, even geographical, difference as evidence of Western superiority:

> The buildings of Venice, like the mountains of Crete and the fields of Egypt, stood in the right place, whereas in poor India everything was placed wrong. He had forgotten the beauty of form among idol temples and lumpy hills; indeed, without form, how can there be beauty?

More importantly, Europe offers

> . . . the harmony between the works of man and the earth that upholds them, the civilisation that has escaped muddle, the spirit in a reasonable form, with flesh and blood subsisting.[6]

'The Statues' takes such ideas a stage further. Not merely are the beauty, harmony and measure of European culture, as established in the first verse, placed in opposition to the vast, formless insubstantiality of the East, but, in a somewhat radical departure from the norm, it is these very cultural forms which are, in verse two, credited with having secured the triumph of the West – rather than, as one might have supposed, the skill and courage of the Athenian sailors, or, for those who prefer a vision of history as the deeds of the great, the brilliant generalship of Themistocles:

> No! Greater than Pythagoras, for the men
> That with a mallet or a chisel modelled these
> Calculations that look but casual flesh, put down
> All Asiatic vague immensities,
> And not the banks of oars that swam upon
> The many-headed foam at Salamis.[7]

The defeat of Xerxes' fleet in 480 BC and his army the following year, which ended the threat of extensive Asiatic colonization of Europe, is apparently of secondary importance compared with the power embodied in Greek statuary.

With its power established, European culture takes its revenge on Asia, in an act of imperialism which is not thwarted: the third verse shows it crossing the sea to Asia and imposing European form on indigenous formlessness. In a letter, Yeats said that he envisaged this as art spreading in the wake of Alexander's conquests, but the lack of specificity in the text allows a potentially greater applicability. It is important to note the effects of this interaction of East and West, however. In a manner reminiscent of the theories of climatic influence current in the eighteenth and nineteenth centuries, once *in* Asia the vigorous European 'image' sits down in the shade and becomes fat and lazy – in other words thoroughly Oriental. Although, therefore, according to this view European art may succeed in giving the Orient something which it had never previously possessed, a proper sense of form, the value of the gift is rapidly eroded as the form is Orientalized and inevitably degraded. The assertion of Eastern cultural sterility and inertia is, unsurprisingly, another of the mainstays of Orientalist discourse as analysed by Said.

The poem also figures as an intervention in an important cultural debate which had continued for over a century, and one whose significance it is all too easy to overlook today – the attempt by intellectuals to construct a purely European, autogenous Greece, free of contaminating influence either from 'African' Egypt or 'Semitic' Asia Minor. Indeed, in many ways, 'The Statues' echoes terms from Matthew Arnold's *Culture and Anarchy*, where true civilization depends on the successful outcome of the struggle between the Hellene and the Semite, the heroic, cultivated spirit versus the bourgeois and the philistine. The latter provides a fascinating illustration of Bakhtin's views on struggle at the level of language: the one word articulates the disabling lack of culture (philistine as cultural barbarian), the wrong race (philistine as Semite), and the unavowable historical influence (philistine as Asia, whose effect on Greece must be denied). In addition to creating the deepest divide possible between Greece and the East, intellectuals set about trying to de-Semitize Asia, exaggerating or inventing non-Semitic explanations for cultural developments, and minimizing the obvious Semitic contributions. This bears out the point which Said makes in *Orientalism* about Semitic culture (and particularly Islam) being construed as the great and abiding antagonist of the West, but it is at the same time an aspect of the general rise of anti-Semitism in Europe from the late nineteenth century onwards. This type of dual focus is both cause and effect of the ideological imprecision of the term Semite, which allows it to stand for Jews, or Jews and Arabs, or (unspecified) Orientals in general.

In the final verse, in what appears as a bold gesture, the poem claims the Irish as direct heirs of the Greek cultural tradition. Such a linkage has important implications which are not, however, spelt out – perhaps, in the circumstances, not needing to be. The choice of Patrick Pearse and his invocation of Cuchulain during the Easter Rising of 1916 to embody the connection between Greece and Ireland establishes Ireland as one of the line of 'gallant little' states resisting a brutal foreign oppressor. The Greeks established this lineage in the Persian wars of the fifth century BC, and rejoined it in the nineteenth century with their war of independence against the Ottoman empire (which also gave rise to the intellectual movement to construct a European Greece). The most recent instance was that of 'gallant little Belgium' in 1914, symbol of why the war against Germany had to be fought. The poem's claim of a rightful place for Ireland in this tradition is doubly significant therefore, not simply for its retrospective valorizing of the events of 1916, but also because it casts the unnamed England in the role of brutal (Oriental) oppressor. Interestingly enough, in the nineteenth-century dialogue of Hellene versus Semite, both Michelet and Renan, from their standpoint on the Continent, were happy to ascribe 'Semitic' qualities to England, some of which Matthew Arnold was prepared to accept – commercial-mindedness, for example, but others which he was not –including arrogance and greed. The unspoken relation with England is one to which we shall return. For the moment, however, it is important to bear in mind 'the fact that Irish nationalism in whatever form fundamentally sought to define itself in relation to England and Englishness'[8], as well as the Bakhtinian stress on the inextricable interconnection of the linguistic and the political.

In terms of resistance in the face of enormous odds, the Greek-Irish parallel established here also accords very well with the ancient Irish tradition of heroic, possibly (even preferably) self-sacrificial, valour, something which is no less important in *Last Poems* than in earlier works ostensibly more concerned with the heroic past. The newly-inflected version of this, with culture as the source and power of resistance and salvation, also continued Yeats's meditations on the ability of culture and the producers of culture to influence political or historical events. The theme appears, most famously, later in the same collection, in 'The Man and The Echo', with its series of rhetorical questions on possible sins of omission or commission, questions which remain unanswered either by Self or Other.

Given Bakhtin's use of a term such as dialogue, it is easy to imagine that he is referring to something like unconstrained verbal intercourse between equals. Such, however, is not the case. As Bakhtin makes clear, relations in discourse are structured by power relations such as those existing between classes. As such, discourse is certainly not unconstrained, and equality rarely obtains. Said is also concerned with discourse and power. As he sees it, differences in power determine both who speaks and what is said. Particularly within the colonial context, the disparity between Europe and the Orient is so great that the latter is effectively silenced, the supposed dialogue turning to monologue – which, Bakhtin reminds us, is the aim of dominant or hegemonic groups. In this position of unassailable power, Europe not only speaks to the Orient, but about it, and on behalf of it, representing it both to the world and to itself – the

West telling the East what the East is *really* like is one of the most notorious and persistent traits of colonialist and Orientalist discourse. The Orient is not the only silenced or marginalized interlocutor in the poem, however; others include women and the working class, and to these we shall return in due course.

It should be clear by now that within the terms of a well-established discourse, that of Orientalism, 'The Statues' sets up a typically unbalanced and value-laden image of two cultures. In the past, critics have, when not ignoring this side of the poem altogether, felt constrained to attempt to explain it away, usually by its enforced removal to a transcendent realm of pure Art or Platonic forms. While this type of manoeuvre would no doubt be rejected by any of the major forms of criticism to have emerged in the last twenty years, it is not even coherent within its own terms. To take just one example of the relentless de-politicization of Yeats's work – as central a critic as Richard Ellmann can write: 'His political poems for example are always complicated by his being above politics.'[9] Such a statement ignores not only the repeated interrogation of art's potential as a form of social action which we have already mentioned, but also Yeats's period as a member of the Irish government (unless that can be construed as putting you above politics), as well as what Yeats was writing about his work in this final period, for example: 'For the first time I am saying what I believe about Irish and European politics.'[10] While this sort of remark may suggest the possibility of having to review Yeats's entire previous literary output as less than truthful, it is not the attitude of someone disengaged from politics.

F.A.C. Wilson's lengthier exculpation of Yeats in his essay on 'The Statues' is typical of the transcendentalizing tendency mentioned above. He acknowledges the problems caused by 'what seems to be the intransigence and race-prejudice of the last period'[11] but then goes on to dissolve them away by positing a transcendent perspective. Thus, for example, of the vitriolic condemnation of modern society in the final verse he has this to say: 'The "modern tide" in "The Statues" is judged transcendentally and therefore purely.'[12] – though he neglects to mention what such an all-purifying transcendent position would consist of. The following section is worth quoting at length as an illustration of the contortions which result from the effort of absolution:

The issue is complicated by the terminology Yeats uses, as when he contrasts subjective or 'Aryan' culture (by 'Aryan' Yeats means 'Indo-European', the Hindu as well as the Graeco-Roman civilisation) with the inferior and objective non-Aryan, or as he confusingly terms it 'Asiatic', ethos; terms which may seem to imply ugly racial theories. And indeed I cannot dispute a fascist influence on his *nomenclature*; but his *meaning*, which is entirely pure, is simply that the major subjective religions have owed their inception to the Indo-European race, while his 'Asiatics' – the peoples of Asia Minor and the steppe and desert country beyond – have normally thought of God objectively, and have not been able to rise above the 'many', 'the multiplicity of the generative universe', to a sense of the 'One' or of the archetypal world.

He adds in a footnote: 'This makes Islam objective. But I have no space to dissect Yeats's sweeping generalisation.'[13]

There are various points to note. The first is, once again, the assertion of absolute purity – despite all appearances to the contrary – on the part of Yeats. The second is the attempt to divide 'nomenclature' from 'meaning'. From a Bakhtinian perspective, if no other (though others would in fact make the same point), this is entirely unacceptable: words may be, indeed are, inflected differently in the different concrete situations in which they are used, but that in no way relieves them of the ideological weight they carry, and to suggest that the sort of overburdened terms and comparisons Yeats uses can somehow be disengaged from their contemporary context (particularly national and racial tension and the rise of Fascism), as well as from the larger historical or cultural discourses which we have already mentioned, is, at the very least, to be dangerously perverse. (This is one of many points on which the type of approach adopted here, which emphasizes the production of meaning within discourses, would differ from, for example, New Criticism, which assumes that meanings are in fact isolatable within a poem, indeed that, in a sense, meaning only exists within the terms established by the work.)

The third point is the terminological slippage which occurs: in the first sentence we move, with parentheses and qualifying clauses as a smoke-screen, from ' "Aryan" *culture*' to ' "Asiatic" *ethos*'. This allows you to have your cultural cake and eat it: on the one hand, to continue to vaunt Western civilization as such, but on the other, if pressed too hard on the racist implications of the terminology, to assert, as Ellmann for example does, that what is in fact being discussed is simply differing 'ways of regarding experience', and not real cultures at all. By the second sentence, we have slipped to religion, and then race, by which stage the reader – if not the critic – might be forgiven for becoming thoroughly confused about what exactly Yeats was supposed to have said (or meant). There is also the problem of Islam. It is not at all clear, either from Yeats or his explicators, how, as one of the great monotheisms, Islam is unable to rise above 'multiplicity' and embrace the concept of the 'One'. On the contrary, there are obvious grounds for suggesting that, lacking a triune deity, Islam has a better sense of the One than Christianity. We are left with the conclusion that it is simply the fact that Islam is the product of an inherently inferior – Semitic – culture which makes it an inferior religion. It is not surprising that Wilson feels unable to dissect Yeats's generalization.

However, even if such attempts to absolve Yeats on his or their own terms were coherent or convincing – which, I would suggest, they are not – they would risk missing altogether an important point, acknowledged by Bakhtin but made even more forcefully by Said, that what matters is what the text legitimates, the kinds of positions, attitudes, actions in the real world which it authorizes, and at this level (i.e. of textual effects in the real world) – which is, to repeat, one to which Yeats's writings return time and again – it is difficult to see what form of argument in mitigation might be advanced.

The aim of the type of criticism we have just examined, and indeed the aim of the poem itself, is to create coherence out of the different discourses which it articulates, but if such a thing is established it is a false, precarious, contradictory kind of coherence. The poem constructs a model of Greek culture as autonomous, self-generating and powerful, but this nostalgia for supposedly pure origins is seriously flawed, both culturally and ethnically. Although the poem contains no hint of it whatsoever, Yeats acknowledges elsewhere that both Africa and Asia played a part in the development of this 'pure' Greek culture. The Pythagorean numbers which are taken as the basis of it all came originally from Babylon, while artistic techniques (and many other things besides) were learned in Egypt. This much may just be admissible; what remains unmentionable, in spite of evidence to the contrary, is, as Martin Bernal points out, the possibility of Egyptian or Semitic settlement or colonization of Greece.[14] Artistic culture might admit of influence and borrowings but race must remain inviolate. Further, the positing of Greek art as a conqueror of the 'Asiatic vague immensities' is undermined by the knowledge, similarly unspoken within the text, that cultural triumph could at best only follow in the wake of military conquest, as the 'One image [which] crossed the many-headed' did so merely as a camp follower of Alexander's victorious armies.

The 'silencing' of the Orient to which we have already referred is an example of an even more deceitful and ungrateful denial of (cultural) indebtedness – since according to Bakhin it is frequently the 'alien word' of the older culture (here, the Orient) which forms the basis of the conceptual development of the new vital hegemonic culture (here, Greece).[15] Thus, for example, Bernal argues not simply for a far greater Greek linguistic debt to other cultures than anyone has previously been prepared to acknowledge, but, perhaps more significantly, for a Phoenician origin of that (apparently) quintessentially Greek invention, the *polis* or city state.

Despite the effort to achieve what Bakhtin would call 'authoritative discourse', the text's powerful cultural assertions are undermined. The claim to authoritativeness is two-fold: firstly, in asserting descent from the Greeks (probably the single most powerful point of cultural reference available), and secondly, in the poem's aligning itself with the discourse of Orientalism. In both cases, the contradictions inherent in the very attempt serve to undermine the project. Firstly, there is the difficulty of defining oneself as *central* (i.e. heir to the classical artistic tradition), while knowing oneself to be consistently radically *marginalized* by the most powerful of actual cultural influences (i.e. England). To the extent that the construction of an Irish identity is here dependent – not to say parasitic – upon the prior existence of a stable Greek identity, any flaw in the latter is bound to have serious repercussions on the former. Also, the very terms used to assert Irishness could be used against it – which reveals the inherently ideological nature of the debate. Such a reversal, as we might expect from what we have seen of Bakhtin's theories, is a function of the inequality of power relations. Yeats was not the first to see a connection between Ireland and Greece. As Martin Bernal points out, the Cambridge classical historian and member of the Protestant Ascendancy, William Ridgeway, saw a likeness between Spartans and Ulstermen, and between the way the Northern (putatively Germanic)

Dorians ruled over the indigenous Pelasgians and that in which the 'Teutonic' English governed the subject – 'marginally European' – native Irish. This same marginality affects the attempt to annex the power of Orientalism on behalf of Ireland. Although this represents a bold, if not necessarily laudable, cultural gesture, its effectiveness is undone by the marginal status of the Irish, resulting in their ending up on the very side of the cultural binary opposition from which they had supposedly escaped – the wrong one. Especially during the period of colonialism, they were the nation most likely to be compared to 'natives' by the English. Lord Salisbury, for instance, Prime Minister at the end of the nineteenth century, notoriously remarked that the Irish were as fit for self-government as the Hottentots.

The desire to distance oneself from unacceptable contemporaneity – 'the filthy modern tide' – by a stated closeness to antique tradition is also vitiated by the fact that for a certain type of English person the Irish have always (or at least since the sixteenth century) been 'the filthy tide'. Even someone like Engels could, in *The Condition of the Working Class in England*, describe them, in typically Orientalist fashion, as an example of inert, degraded humanity, in comparison to the English working class whom he wanted to praise.

Further, after all the problems with the construction of a 'Western' identity, the accompanying model of nationalism is no more stable either. Ernest Gellner, for example, states that Irish nationalism is an 'Eastern' form.[16] This may be why (although, as D.G. Boyce says in the passage quoted above, Irish nationalism seeks to define itself against England), in the present circumstances, it may only be possible to do so implicitly.

Women, the poem would seem to suggest, are largely irrelevant to the serious business of cultural struggle and transmission. Although they figure in the text as aetiolated adolescents on a par with the males, thereafter they rate mention only as consumers of dreams given form by male artists. F.A.C. Wilson has this to say:

> Woman had not been able to evolve, out of the shifting, indefinite, 'multiform' sea of Asiatic consciousness, an 'image' towards which to adapt herself, but after Pheidias [*sic*] she could. His masculine archetype could give her 'dreams' and provide those dreams of the ideal manhood with their concrete 'objective correlative', while his

feminine archetype, the lines may also imply, would provide her with the idea of a new and perfect femininity towards which she could evolve.[17]

Woman is then the analogue of the Oriental in her total dependence on the European male sculptors for the gift of proper form – and this type of identification should come as no surprise, since, as Said points out, the Orient has been continuously represented as 'feminine' – to the detriment of both. Gobineau, generally regarded as the founder of nineteenth-century 'scientific' racism, thought that history was the story of the conquest, by white 'male' races, of black 'female' ones, and that the tragic irony of history was that the 'male' races were, in the end, corrupted and brought down by the 'female' ones.

This problematic femininity, I would suggest, is one of the keys to the Grimalkin passage in the third stanza which has caused critics so much difficulty in the past. It seems to be significant, in view of what we have said so far, that we have here the second juxtaposition in the poem of a statue and an exemplar of femininity. As befits the awful Orient, both statue and woman are degraded examples of their kind: woman as withered old witch (or witch's cat) crawls to the feet of the bloated Buddha, whose emptiness contains no substance to body forth her dreams, unlike the properly formed, properly sexual creations of Europe. This is clearly only part of the meaning of the passage but is perhaps no less important for that.

The implications of the gender–culture relationship are extended by the fact that Yeats seems to have regarded the work of Pound, Joyce and Woolf as Asiatic in its formlessness.[18] Such stigmatizing is interesting in the light of recent work on Woolf by Pam Slaughter,[19] where she examines the male drive to divide, separate, and impose order at all costs, and the corresponding female tendency to include, to unite, to achieve a form of wholeness rather than a rigid ordering. This is important, since in Woolf's terms such male drives, far from being laudable as Yeats would contend, are responsible for patriarchal repressiveness, political oppression, war, and all manner of contemporary horrors. The other important difference is that, whereas Yeats would see these as eternal, immutable characteristics, both Woolf and Slaughter stress that they are socially constructed subject positions, neither unchangeable nor gender-specific. (Though there may be a tendency in certain directions: Ellmann, for instance, talks of 'the exciting theme that man is never satisfied unless he destroys all he has created',[20] which assumes an assenting – masculine – readership under its guise of universality, and which participates in the reproduction of appropriate masculine responses.) The connections between art and sexuality are made clearer by a verse from 'Under Ben Bulben':

> Poet and sculptor, do the work,
> Nor let the modish painter shirk
> What his great forefathers did,
> Bring the soul of man to God,
> Make him fill the cradles right.[21]

The necessity to 'fill the cradles right' is also evoked in a famous passage from *On the Boiler*, published in the year of Yeats's death, which also paraphrases part of 'The Statues':

> Europe was not born when Greek galleys defeated the Persian hordes at Salamis; but when the Doric studios sent out those broad-backed marble statues against the multiform, vague, expressive Asiatic sea, they give to the sexual instinct of Europe its goal, its fixed type.[22]

The need to give European women a fixed sexual goal has another contemporary discursive resonance: particularly since the rapid expansion of Britain as an imperial power towards the end of the nineteenth century, one of the most persistent, if not always fully articulated, fears in the colonialist or Orientalist context was the threat of miscegenation. This was a disturbing prospect, whatever shape it took, and its inexpressible, traumatic form was sex between a white woman and a black man, since it was this combination which most fundamentally undermined (white) racial purity. Hence the importance of anything which might prevent deviant sexual behaviour on the part of white women.

Finally, the juxtaposition of statuary, physical ideal and fixity leads us to Bakhtin's remarks on the 'classical body' as the inherent form of high culture which 'The Statues' can be taken to symbolize. As Peter Stallybrass and Allon White remark:

> Clearly, as often as they are able, 'high' languages attempt to legitimate their authority by appealing to values inherent in the classical body. Bakhtin was struck by the compelling difference between the human body as represented in popular festivity and the body as represented in classical statuary in the Renaissance. He noticed how the two forms of iconography 'embodied' utterly contrary

registers of being. To begin with, the classical statue was always mounted on a plinth which meant that it was elevated, static, and monumental. In the one simple fact of the plinth or pedestal the classical body signalled a whole different somatic conception from that of the grotesque body which was usually multiple (Bosch, Breugel), teeming, always part of a throng. By contrast the classical statue is the radiant centre of a transcendent individualism, 'put on a pedestal', raised above the viewer and the commonality and anticipating passive admiration from below. We *gaze up* at the figure and wonder. We are placed by it as spectators to an instant – frozen yet apparently universal – of epic or tragic time. The presence of the statue is a problematic presence in that it immediately retroflects us to the heroic past, it is a *memento classici* for which we are the eternal latecomers, and for whom meditative imitation is the appropriate contrition. The classical statue has no openings or orifices whereas the grotesque costume and masks emphasise the gaping mouth, the protruberant belly and buttocks, the feet and the genitals. In this way the grotesque body stands in opposition to the bourgeois individualist conception of the body, which finds *its* image and legitimation in the classical.[23]

Here we see the congruence between those official centripetal languages mentioned at the beginning of this chapter, and cultural forms which might appear to be above such matters but are, on the contrary, profoundly implicated in them. In 'The Statues' we find the closure of the dominant discourses, the closure of the classical body, and the closure, as Bakhtin sees it, of the lyric form all acting in concordance, to silence and exclude. We can, for instance, be sure that the degradation of Grimalkin and Buddha consists at least as much in their distance from the (classical) bodily ideal as from the properly 'subjective' state. Beyond this, the (en)closed nature of the classical body, shorn of orifices and organs, gives it a disturbingly life-denying quality compared to the fecund grotesque body, and thus makes it a very strange symbol for European sexuality. Although there may be a Byronic echo in the final stated desire to 'trace/The lineaments of a plummet-measured [stone or bronze] face', it is difficult to see how these could ever be lineaments of *gratified* desire. The importance and the explanation of this seemingly contradictory sexual ideal appears when we see what is excluded, those characters and qualities in opposition to which it is constructed: these are precisely the fecundity and lack of restraint which typify the grotesque body, the 'formless spawning fury' of modern society. It is at this point that the discourse of sexuality slides into that of class.

The final silenced and disavowed Other whose exclusion the poem seeks is the lower classes, presumably the working class, since Yeats spends so much time elsewhere praising the peasantry. The 'many-headed foam' which Europe overcame in the shape of the menacing Asiatic hordes now returns in the guise of the 'filthy modern tide' – threatening society with destruction from within, rather than without. In the essay 'Words upon the Window Pane', written a few years earlier, Yeats talks of the 'tyranny of the Many', which means the end of liberty in society, and such an eventuality is presented as imminent. One reason why society has reached this position is its inability or unwillingness to hold to the classical sexual ideal. Yeats's desire to give the European sexual instinct its proper form in the end reveals its true nature as discriminatory, elitist, and above all eugenicist.

Although eugenics began in the 1860s with the work of Francis Galton, it reached its high point in the 1920s and 30s, when it managed to unite a remarkable political cross-section of British society, from the extreme right wing to the Fabian left. Its central tenet was that the race was degenerating dangerously through faulty breeding habits. (The fault was that the lower classes were breeding far too much and the upper classes not enough.) Although the discourse was framed in terms of the all-embracing good of the race, it functioned in rather more restricted and class-discriminatory ways. By the 1920s and 30s, eugenics had changed from its original 'positive' attitude of encouraging the breeding of 'healthy stock', to a frighteningly negative one – the elimination of the 'unfit' (which meant the working class). As Yeats says bluntly in 'Tomorrow's Revolution', published in 1939,

> Sooner or later we must limit the families of the unintelligent classes, and if our Government cannot send them doctor and clinic it must, till it gets tired of it, send monk and confession box.[24]

If this is insufficient, however, other methods are always available:

> If some financial reorganisation . . . enable[s] everybody without effort to procure all necessities of life and so remove the last check upon the multiplication of the uneducable masses, it will become the duty of the educated classes to seize and control one or more of those necessities. The drilled and docile masses may submit, but a prolonged civil war seems more likely, with the victory of the skilful, riding their machines as did the feudal knights their armoured horses.[25]

Eugenics was held by its numerous adherents to be the most advanced and scientific of doctrines, a form of applied genetics, but it is worth emphasizing yet again the utter irrelevance of the 'truth' of such discourses, in view of their ideological products and effects. As ideology, of course, they are open to appropriation or reversal, and so we find, at the same time as Yeats was expounding his views on the subject, Sidney Webb warning the English that, unless the decline in their birthrate was halted, the country would soon fall to the Irish and the Jews.[26]

In 'The Statues', it is a sign of the irredeemably fallen state of modern society, or that section of it which Yeats wishes to inveigh against, that it has no individuating features or symbols at all. The Greeks have the matchless line and form of Phidias's statues; the European-influenced Orient has its degraded, but still individualized avatars in Buddha and Grimalkin; the aboriginal Eastern horde is at least 'many-headed', whereas the modern working class is no more than a seething, amorphous mass which appears to have reversed the process of evolution and returned to the primeval slime. In this dissolution, the poem enacts that very elimination of the unacceptable working class body which eugenics hopes to achieve in society at large.

Such a denial of any bodily status, no matter how grotesque or repellent, to the lower classes is an indication of the absolute gulf which the poem attempts to place between them and the rightful position of the Irish as heirs of 'that ancient sect'. However, as we saw in the case of Greece and the Orient, this attempt to constitute a separate, sanitized Irish identity is doomed to failure: like it or not, the Irish are part of what they attempt to deny – 'thrown upon this filthy modern tide' – and it is part of them, irrevocably contaminating their sense of self-hood, dissolving their rigidly maintained 'form'.

The obsession with form is yet another place where, for Bakhtin, poetry and politics coincide. The romantic view of art as the imposition of order and formal coherence on the chaos of experience has its clear correlate in the desire to impose correct political order upon those formless, spawning, anarchic strata of society which might seek to evade such constraints. The monologic tendency of the lyric also repeats, at the formal level, that silencing or usurping of the Other's speech which takes place at the level of the larger discourse such as Orientalism. In turn, lyrical monologism is the appropriate means for the text to swim against the (filthy) historical tide as it strives for that unitary language which Bakhtin sees as the vehicle for myth. This, in a sense, is as it should be, since what we are concerned with here, in spite of the text's repeated invoking of history (Pythagoras, Phidias, Salamis, 1916, Patrick Pearse), in spite of Yeats's stated belief that his work was 'inside history and time',[27] is myth, a powerful ideological construct using elements of history as its basic material. The creation of myth may of course have a positive function, but this should not blind those of us who have not already climbed into 'our proper dark' to its inescapably ideological nature, to its discriminatory effects, nor to those acts of denial, repression and exclusion which are inseparable from its very construction.

3 The Imperfect Librarian: Text and Discourse in *The Waste Land* and *Four Quartets*

Mick Burton

> No matter how multiple and varied these semantic and accentual threads, associations, pointers, hints, correlations that emerge from every poetic word, one language, one conceptual horizon, is sufficient to them all.
>
> (M. BAKHTIN)[1]

Eliot's major poems have been recognized as incorporating a wide variety of voices from the literature of the past and from the received cultural traditions of European civilization in general. The aim of this chapter, though, is to demonstrate the limits put upon that variety and inclusiveness, by concentrating on the way the reader is directed by the structures of the text to produce meaning. This will involve looking at the poems both as texts and as a certain sort of discourse.

In a recent guide to *The Waste Land* the poem is proclaimed as 'a study of civilisation doomed to its own sterility'. This study is achieved through 'A chorus of voices, now individual, now subsumed in the blind and thwarted Tiresias'.[2] These remarks, in themselves unexceptional, herald the kind of reading that typifies responses from Cleanth Brooks to Walton Litz.[3] The end result in each case is to engage with the poem as text, and to avoid the more problematic engagement with the poem as discourse. An understanding of the difference between text and discourse as I am using them here is essential if we are to penetrate some of the blind spots and unacknowledged contradictions which criticism of modernist poetry embodies. These contradictions arise because modernist poetry itself blurs the dialectic of text and discourse, thus creating a power vacuum wherein the tendency to the centripetal, the authority of the text in its complex modes of structuration, develops by its apparent absence. Who will 'set his lands in order' at the end of *The Waste Land*? What voice hails us as 'Distracted from distraction by distraction' in 'Burnt Norton'? Text is, in Umberto Eco's words, 'a network of different messages depending on different codes'.[4] Roland Barthes enriches the notion by his category of 'signifying' work – 'that radical work . . . through which the subject explores how language works him and undoes him as soon as he stops observing it and enters it'.[5] From this perspective the reader becomes lost in textual pleasures as she or he reads. In the case of such a text as *The Waste Land* she or he is keyed into a mode of apprehension which finally cedes, to the cultural impressionist who underwrites its different voices, the last word. Such yielding is a function of the poem's authoritative power; as text it is generated from a core of allusions at which the reader's own sensitive antennae must buzz with recognition, recollection, and repetition. She or he is thus assimilated to the positions inscribed by the text through a process of contagion which seems inevitable, even though the text could have been (and was, before Pound's hatchet), other.

Its textuality inheres in associative clustering, the particularity of which seems natural and inevitable to one whose cultural memory is in concord with such associations. In any case, 'text is a new tissue of past citations. Bits of codes, formulae, rhythmic models, fragments of social languages etc. pass into the text and are distributed within it, for there is always language before and around the text'.[6] Thus to read *The Waste Land* as text entails submission to its accretion of allusion; the resultant pattern is then a vision built from fragments. For the reader saturated in fertility rites and/or Wagner, the ideological structure seems natural; it is right to read the poem as a critique of a sterile civilization.

If, however, the reader, after this empathic moment, can retain his or her otherness, she or he can then engage with the text as discourse. His or her subjectivity may be allowed to work dialogically with the text, not as a subsumed part of its structuration, but as an other. As Bakhtin has it, 'the first task is to understand the work as the author understood it, without leaving the limits of his understanding . . . the second is to use one's temporal and cultural exotopy'.[7] It is important to note at this point how being 'other' can be approached in psychoanalytic as well as sociolinguistic terms, and this chapter will use insights from Lacan to reinforce Bakhtin. Being other is a necessary condition of entering discourse for both writers, starting though they do from entirely different standpoints. By ignoring this condition, we remain in thrall to text.

Very little of the canon of criticism of *The Waste Land* moves from the first of Bakhtin's 'moments of understanding', but William Spanos[8] has produced a very complex and forceful analysis of the poem read against the grain of its textuality. His argument examines the shifting temporality of the discourse structures in *The Waste Land* in terms of the engagement with tradition. Tradition can itself be seen as a means of concealment rather than of information, and Spanos quotes Heidegger to this effect: 'When tradition thus becomes master (over ontological understanding) it does so in such a way that what it "transmits" is made so inaccessible . . . that it rather becomes concealed.'[9] We may recall Eliot's views on Tradition and the dialectical process of searching through the 'monuments' for the 'ideal order' that seems to be implied as a necessary condition for the writing of poetry in the twentieth century. For Spanos it is the search for a new beginning that is 'clearly what Eliot's great poem is laboring to enact'.[10] He uses Heidegger to underline the danger of this beginning; 'But we do not repeat a beginning by reducing it to something past and now known, which need merely be imitated; no, the beginning must be begun again, more radically with all the strangeness, darkness and insecurity that attends a true beginning.'[11]

Spanos's powerful essay does engage the text as discourse; it sets up a deconstruction, or in the Heideggerian term, de-struction, which entails radical questioning of the text's own methods of construction and self-validation. In contrast to the received critical view of *The Waste Land* as a complex verbal icon, enacting in its spatial disjunction the historical fragmentation of its motifs, Spanos discerns

> an emergent or open-ended plot, one discovered and appropriated by the poet himself, in the protagonist's sequential and cumulative discovery and appropriation of a more primordial possibility of being in the destroyed myths of the past, the myths, that is, which in their destroyed state, preserve their own unique historical integrity yet point towards the future.[12]

This analysis certainly removes *The Waste Land* from its state as the 'dead paradigm of the modernist poetics of ironic inclusiveness'.[13] Yet it is necessarily insufficient; for the new beginning so prized by Spanos and Heidegger is really, when stripped of its special language, an appeal to an ahistorical essence, a primal state. In destroying the logocentrism of all-inclusive irony, Spanos in turn privileges an absolute subjectivity, raised to the level of metaphysical origins. He is betrayed by the 'jargon of authenticity'.

In stark contrast to Spanos, Maud Ellmann argues that *The Waste Land* 'like any good sphinx, lures the reader into hermeneutics, too; but there is no secret underneath its hugger-muggery'.[14] Her strategy is to search 'in the silences between the words'[15] for meaning which 'flickers local, evanescent in the very "wastes" that stretch across the page. These silences curtail the power of the author, for they invite the hypocrite lecteur to reconstruct their broken sense.'[16] It would appear, then, that the text's project colludes with the death of the author, as the reader is born. But what reader? Pound? Students in higher education, for whom even World War Two is a myth? Ellmann's critique, for all its entertaining brilliance, still falls into the text's enchantments. She writes: 'a double consciousness pervades the text, as if it had been written by a vicar and an infidel. The speaker is divided from himself, unable to resist the imp within who cynically subverts his pieties'.[17] There lurks an uneasy conflation, in these two sentences, of the vicar/infidel writer, and the speaker, who as Ellmann remarks earlier, seems to have no identity at all. This blurring of the author figure and the speaker/s who offer the reader such disjointed subject positions obscures the ideological basis of the text. The author as presence may not figure in the poem, a method entirely in accord with Eliot's doctrine of impersonality, but the reader's reception is grounded in a horizon of expectations structured by associational clustering. She or he is placed, as subject of the enunciation, as producer of meaning, across a distinctly ordered range of narrative events, each with its cultural signifying work involving his or her participation.

No reader, for example, can escape the initial disjunctive pressure of the epigraph and the dedication. Latin, Greek and Italian signal an intertextuality beyond the reach of most common readers. They are pinned to its 'necessity' just as Prufrock is formulated, 'sprawling on a pin'. Likewise, the Chaucerian flickering of the opening lines mesmerizes the reader into a 'remembrance' of the tradition, skewed and deformed in the waste land. The use of the copula in 'April is the cruellest month' asserts, claims authority. As subjects of the enunciation we too are forced to agree that this is the case. We are then positioned as German aristocrats, then as Marie, who felt free. But this may well escape our notice, this continually sliding construction of ourselves as readers through identification, as the complexities of textual association bind us to exposition. A real dilemma for the reader of *The Waste Land* occurs in precisely this necessity to erect a scaffolding to hold in the unstable raw material of disjointed citation.

'The Fire Sermon' is the most concentrated section of the poem. An examination of the text's movement reveals the power of its structural devices. We should remember Eliot's note on Tiresias as a unifying persona of the whole catalogue of wretched humanity which characterizes the text. The reader begins 'The Fire Sermon' on the banks of the Thames, with echoes of Spenser, Marvell and *The Tempest*. Parallel to this literary detritus is the decay and decadence of 'cardboard boxes, cigarette ends/Or other testimony of summer nights'. The drowned condoms, fag ends, as it were, of sterile sexual relations, implicate the reader in a discourse about sex through images of waste, disgust and death (the rattle of the bones). 'White bodies naked on the low damp ground' is witness to the entropy of knowledge – 'Behold, the man is become as one of us, to know good and evil . . . and his knowledge was first of his nakedness.'[18] With the undertone of the Fall, the city directors' heirs and their women, Sweeney and Mrs Porter serve to underscore 'the horror' of the original epigraph of the poem. The implication of violence and sex as universal partners is signalled by 'jug jug . . .' and Mr Eugenides offers some dubious eroticism in Brighton. All this prefigures the sustained passage in which Tiresias appears, to watch an unpleasant couple copulating. He narrates, in tightly controlled, disgusted diction ('Endeavours to engage her in caresses') ('Her brain allows one half-formed thought to pass') a scene of monumental inanity. He gives it universal credence by his presence, and by his cadences of forlorn pessimism ('And I Tiresias have foresuffered all . . . lowest of the dead'). By way of Goldsmith the reader is led back to *The Tempest*, to the fragment of splendour in St Magnus Martyr, to the river; Wagner's Rhinemaidens make an entry, as do Elizabeth and Leicester, three Thames daughters lament wretched sexual encounters, and the section ends with traces of St Augustine and Buddha.

Where is the reader placed in all this? The sweep of the text is authoritative in its ordering of fragments into patterns of sexual failure, and in using this patterning as an allegory of the condition of being as one of stale recollection. The mythic method[19] works most intensely in 'The Fire Sermon', locking the reader into a perception of reality as universal sterility and failure. At this point she or he must invoke his or her own exotopy before this concatenation of horror. For *The Waste Land* is, as a text, constructed by apparently random disjunctions which never offer a stable position from which to read. Anthony Easthope discusses the way in which the canon of English poetry created the fiction that the reader and the writer were one, so that responsibility for producing meaning could be firmly attributed to the 'Poet'.[20] Eliot's impersonality technique seems to split the reader from any such personal identification, and forces the production of meaning, the mode of reading the text's enunciation, upon the reader's own associative powers. The pressure is on the reader to produce the same meaning that the concatenation of images seems to necessitate, its truth value as a critique of civilization in decay. But, to borrow from Foucault, 'what is at stake in the will to truth, in the will to utter this "true" discourse, if not desire and power?'[21] Given this hidden motivation of the text in its secondary moment as discourse, entry is at a price: 'none shall enter the order of discourse if he does not satisfy certain requirements, or if he is not, from the outset, qualified to do so.'[22] Thus the reader must emerge from his or her Barthesian *jouissance* (a touch of de Sade in this case) to realize his or her otherness, his or her distance from the text, to analyse the cost of entering the text as discourse.

If the reader is a woman she has been hailed as inferior throughout; she is invited to construct the discourse of her degradation. What is her glory? A moment in the hyacinth garden, as passive recipient in a romantic fling, ironized as fantasy by the bracketing effect of the citations from Tristan and Isolde, the closure indicating her as a sterile dead end ('Oed' und leer das Meer'). Thus even this apparent concession to female value, as valued anaesthetic, is merely scopophilia, like a Badedas commercial. For the rest of the text she is discursively labelled as follows. She is:
– drenched with 'strange synthetic perfumes' (her stench being 'so rank a feline smell');[23]
– raped, by Tereus; consider the profound ambiguity of the mythic

method here – rape is cast as the universal answer to female sexuality;
- neurotic, 'My nerves are bad tonight';
- a gossip, 'He did I was there.'
- needing to 'get herself some teeth';
- ill from 'them pills I took, to bring it off';
- a nymphomaniac, 'The nymphs are departed';
- a brothel keeper – Mrs Porter;
- a lower middle class typist, 'bored and tired';
- brainless, 'her brain allows one half-formed thought to pass';
- worse, unsatisfied, 'paces about her room again, alone';
- seduced/raped, 'Supine on the floor of a narrow canoe';
- completely disjointed, feet 'at Moorgate' heart 'Under my feet';
- mindless, 'On Margate Sands';
- lastly, devil in charge of 'bats with baby faces'.

Thus the 'great poem' of Spanos's essay labours to interpellate women as signifieds of disgust and terror. The woman reader is naturalized and universalized by the mythic method. Her material history, her story, is erased in this poem as she becomes traced by adolescent fantasies as both desired and hated object. Only as other, as exotopic interrogator, can she resist dialogically the text's misogyny. This critique has mined a vein of the poem's discourse structure which a New Critical reading, such as that of Brooks, would mask. It is not envisaged as a reductive strategy, but as productive of further discourses concerning the interplay of aesthetic and valuative norms evolving around literary canons. For too long masculine complacency and complicity have underwritten criticism of *The Waste Land* which thus has retained the authority, or 'auctoritas' associated with the author figure, the shadowy arranger of the patriarchal culture show.

At least, in *The Waste Land*, there are enough gaps in the text for the reader to interrogate its ideological saturation, since the syntactic patterns permit some prising apart. In the implied other of the poem, however, the reader's task is tougher. Some such text as *Four Quartets* is the projected trace of the lines in *The Waste Land* beginning 'Who is the third who always walks beside you?' This third, the super-receiver which (not whom) Bakhtin cites as 'a constitutive moment of the whole utterance' is the metaphysical fiction behind the 'gaze into chaos', the guarantee that somehow the assemblage of fragments from the past, the palimpsest of the now jaundiced present, is sufficient against contingency.[24]

The Imperfect Librarian   49

The ached-for centre is much more obvious in *Four Quartets*. Although the form of the text is frequently deconstructive the reader's ground of existence is finally more circumscribed, more restricted. The invitation to read *Four Quartets* is obscurely framed by the epigraph. The two fragments from Heraclitus may be translated to serve particular ideological positions. As Spanos points out, 'virtually all commentary on *Four Quartets* has been more or less uniform in beginning from the end, in using the complementary epigraphs from Heraclitus as absolute point of departure.'[25] The semantic field of *logos* in Greek is wider than word; it involves ideas of accounting, telling a tale, enunciating theories or principles. But its intertextual resonances always echo Liddell and Scott's final citation; 'the Word or Wisdom of God'. It is this resonance that Spanos attempts to minimize by privileging the phenomenological sense of *logos* exemplified in Heidegger. In *Being and Time* we find that '*logos* as "discourse" means rather the same as *deloun*; to make manifest what one is talking about in one's discourse . . . The *logos* lets something be seen, namely what the discourse is about; and it does so either for the one who is doing the talking . . . or for persons who are talking with one another, as the case may be.'[26] If we choose to ignore the privileging of the *Logos* in the Christian sense, for the present, we may see how the reader is invited to assess the organizing principle of the text. In 'Burnt Norton' 'the unseen eyebeam crossed' flashes a subliminal image of an Eden lost, in which human kind, unable to bear very much reality, confuses motes and beams. Yet simultaneously the voice of sexual ecstasy, from Donne's 'Our eyebeams twisted, and did thread/Our eyes upon one double string' creates a powerful split for the reader; sexual expression, the realization of desire, is implicated with the loss of a paradisal state of being. The metaphoric fusion, the stasis of two bodies become one, is deconstructed through the trace of St Luke: 'And why beholdest thou the mote that is in thy brother's eye, but perceivest not the beam that is in your own eye?'[27] Eliot's text uses the theme of sinful hypocrisy, which the Gospel continues in the next verse, to focus on the dilemma of the pull of sexual desire. As this slippage of signifiers moves in time across the literary and religious discourses of Donne and St Luke the reader is disenfranchized, unless she or he is attuned to such complex convergence as a mode of apprehension. The stasis of fusion, the sexual ecstasy, transforms to the stasis of guilt, the

Judaeo-Christian archetype, in the complex of associations built into the text. The intertextual references in the diction of 'Burnt Norton' at this moment appear to enact a post-structuralist diffusion; they hint at the expression of radical alterity, of sheer otherness, which the text develops as its judgemental positioning of its readers as subjects; they, as subjects of the enunciation, are compelled to produce the meaning of the text; it appears that a single meaning, given the intertextual web of allusion, is beyond reach.

The text, then, seems to be witnessing that form of the human condition attested to by Jacques Lacan. In his distinction between the Imaginary and Symbolic phases of psychic growth, he argues that the infant has in the Imaginary an illusion of wholeness, as in a mirror image. But the fragile self-image in the mirror is splintered by the invasion of language; words, in their spatio-temporal realization – sounds in the space between persons, marks on a page – urge the dissolution of the unified image of self by an articulation of 'differance'. Jacques Derrida's term covers the way language constructs subjectivity, being a person, as different and always deferred. There are no final meanings for the individual – she or he is positioned somewhere by the discourses she or he enters, or is forced to enter, but the location changes, and assurance fades. Thus it is through Lacan's version of a postlapsarian state that the reader may see how *Four Quartets* problematizes both a particular lived experience – the modernist view of life – and a concept of being which appears to be situated in a fragmentary limbo below the surface of the text. The variety of textual forms offered to him or her enact the strain, the cracking and above all, the slippage of the signifier in the modernist language game. Thus:

> Words strain,
> Crack and sometimes break, under the burden,
> Under the tension, slip, slide, perish,
> Decay with imprecision, will not stay in place,
> Will not stay still
> ['Burnt Norton' V, 13–17]

Hence as the text tries out new versions of itself, the problem of its registers becomes foregrounded. In 'East Coker' the reader is confronted by a sudden textual shift:

> That was a way of putting it – not very satisfactory;

> A periphrastic study in a worn-out poetical fashion,
> Leaving one still with the intolerable wrestle
> With words and meanings. The poetry does not matter.
> ['East Coker' II, 18–21]

Heidegger's *logos* appears to be at work here. The principle upon which the poem's project is grounded is made manifest for the reader: varieties of text are displayed, then discarded as fallible. As she or he reads, she or he becomes absorbed in the signifying work of the text. The Tradition creates a polyphony of voices in which the reader is positioned, often in many directions at the same time. It seems that only in the interstices of the infinitely complex text of the poem, and of life, is there a resting place. For in our entry into the world, we have little say:

> Footfalls echo in the memory
> Down the passage which we did not take
> Towards the door we never opened
> Into the rose-garden.
> ['Burnt Norton' I, 14–15]

The beat of 'Footfalls' echoes the pulse of the mother from whom we are expelled. Eliot's grammar is interesting: we do not take that first journey, that primal passage; we do not open the vulval mouth which ejects us into being. And yet the purpose of this initial mystery, as the text reminds us, is obscure. All we have are echoes: 'My words echo / Thus, in your mind'. Echoes are images of sound; sounds are the raw material of language. The poem seems to be yearning for a state of innocence in which the echoes are traces of an original wholeness uncontaminated by expulsion into an imperfect world. One powerful reason why this world is imperfect is that the individual subject is made to grow into a pre-existing world of language. As the poem at this point invokes Francis Thompson's *The Hound of Heaven* ('Halts me by that footfall'), so the reader, attuned to its particular harmonies, is seduced, echoically. For the reader not so attuned, this is hard graft. She or he has to take on board the massive burden of the text's intertextuality, or fail. Just as the child has to discover a place for itself in the discourses of others, so the reader of *Four Quartets* has to find a place in the polyphonic intertext that the poem seems to be. As she or he reads, the poem exerts a double bind; she or he moves along the spatio-temporal realization of linguistic structures which constitute *Four Quartets* with an increasingly saturated cultural memory. The ripples on the poem's surface, forcing the reader to follow the text's traces, conflict with the experience of temporality that the reading of the poem entails.

The opening lines of 'Burnt Norton' privilege presence for the subject and assert its denial. The closing lines

> Quick now, here, now, always –
> Ridiculous, the waste sad time
> Stretching before and after.

attempt to foreclose on the material, historical periodicity of experience mediated by words which move 'Only in time' by a resigned insistence – 'that which is only living/Can only die'. Thus the text resists the notion of being as 'extended temporal activity'. There seems to be an implied alternative state, which will manifest itself as the poem develops. However, 'East Coker' opens with a submission of subjectivity to cyclic encoding:

> Houses rise and fall, crumble, are extended,
> Are removed, destroyed, restored . . .

This impression is furthered by the correspondence with Sir Thomas Elyot:

> The association of man and woman
> In daunsinge, signifying matrimonie –
> A dignified and commodious sacrament.
> ['East Coker' I, 29–31]

The repetition of 'time' (lines 39–46) enacting in syntax and lexis the significance of the dance, seems, in its closure of 'Dung and death', to inscribe the subject in a pattern of universal structuration. But,

> Dawn points, and another day
> Prepares for heat and silence. Out at sea the dawn wind
> Wrinkles and slides. I am here
> Or there, or elsewhere. In my beginning.
> ['East Coker' I, 48/51]

The dislocation is a strategy to resist the pressure of time and space. The present tense signifies a privileged present time: 'Late November' disturbs the spring, 'Late roses are filled with early snow'; in the dissolution of linear time imaged by the unseasonal moments the subject/reader may be celebrated, as in an epiphany, or dragged down 'in a vortex'. There appears to be a powerful ambivalence here, recalling the exploration of corruption and dissolution in *The Rainbow* and *Women in Love*. But here, all the striving, all the attention to 'The trilling wire in the blood' and 'The dance upon the artery' is reduced by a deflationary tactic at the end of 'East Coker' II, since 'The only wisdom we can hope to acquire/Is the wisdom of humility; humility is endless'. In this text, then, the signifying work functions to show up the positivistic, empirical self as a fiction. Real subjectivity involves the rejection of a linear understanding of time, with all its material connotations. In this condition, the contingency of being depends upon acceptance of the moment of revelation, which acts to ground the time-less, ego-less mode of living that is humility. This is the inscription of the authentic, prefiguring the final surrender.

To arrive at this state, the poem develops a critique, in 'East Coker' III, of the inauthentic, 'The generous patrons of art, the statesmen and the rulers' which culminates in an apparent deconstruction: 'In order to arrive at what you are not/You must go through the way in which you are not.' The subject/reader has a very complex task at this point of the poem. She or he has already been made to feel insecure by the multiplicity of intertextual reference in the text. The task proposed in these lines involves the probing and finally dismissal of all those discourses which constitute the subject as a person. Because each discourse has been examined from within, as the text of *Four Quartets* shows in its wide range of allusion, it seems to be a liberating, deconstructive moment. The consequences of the deconstructive turn, however, should emphasize the metonymic, that is the horizontal patterning in language which both enables sentences to be made, and implies that their structures could be different. This is in stark contrast to metaphor, which involves substitution of one word for another, and by extension, a state of completion, of fusion. In Jacques Lacan's terms metonymy entails desire, the search for wholeness which entry into language denies and frustrates. The nearest equivalent to the primordial condition of completion is expressed in language by metaphor. 'East Coker' offers the stillness, the stasis of sickness: the 'faith and the love and the hope are all in the waiting' for the 'wounded surgeon', the submission to the hands of the 'dying nurse'. The text's way of metaphor extinguishes the metonymy of desire.[28] But as if to stress the provisionality of this position 'East

Coker' V opens with an ironic disclaimer, a carping, grumbling enunciation of the utter absurdity of all attempts at discourse, 'a raid on the inarticulate/With shabby equipment always deteriorating'. The text here works as a locus of signifiers signifying only their emptiness and inadequacy; it is hard for the reader to resist the authority of this textual positioning which seems so reasonable. But without such resistance she or he is then drawn cleverly to 'another intensity/For a further union, a deeper communion' in which as subject of the enunciation she is entrapped by a final, irresolvable metaphor: 'In my end is my beginning'.

As if to universalize the temporal as merely contingent, and therefore always eluding meaning in the traditional echo-chambers of English history, the text re-locates the reader of 'The Dry Salvages' within a New World. It is lapped by a sea that 'Tosses up our losses/The shattered lobsterpot, the broken oar'. The sea subsumes time as myth. Although the 'anxious worried women . . . Trying to unweave, unwind, unravel/And piece together the past and the future' do not, like the Norns in *Götterdämmerung* whom they evoke, feel the rope of the world's fate snap in their hands, they emblemize the inadequacy, as understood by this text, of temporal relations. The groundswell, with its eternal bell, mocks in its monotonous echo 'Attachment to self and to things and to persons' which form the basis of subjectivity in a material world, the world of the women. Yet even here, in this pendulum of world time beyond historical time, the agony of being a subject is recognized:

> There is no end, but addition; the trailing
> Consequence of further days and hours,
> While emotion takes to itself the emotionless
> Years of living among the breakage
> Of what was believed in as the most reliable
> And therefore fittest for renunciation.
> ['The Dry Salvages' II, 7–12]

De Man offers an interesting key to this difficult passage when he argues that 'A literary text simultaneously asserts and denies the authority of its own rhetorical mode'.[29] In the passage above there is a severe tension in the structure between the mode of metaphor and the mode of metonymy. This tension pivots round the word 'emotion', which is personified to operate the predication 'takes to itself'. The rhetorical figure which enables the grammar to function is synecdoche, in which 'emotion' stands for, or substitutes, as in metaphor, for the experiencing subject, who of course is subjected to the metonymy of desire. This strain and conflict of tropes enacts the striving towards totality and the resistance to its temptations which the varied devices of *Four Quartets* embody in the text's signifying work. The reader is embroiled in this conflict by having to take a stance towards the last two lines of the passage. Are they redolent of a weary nihilism, the last ironic fling at a tawdry universe of interpersonal insignificance? Or do they show the deconstructive paradox at the centre of the text, that all the discourse structures which construct the subject leave him or her in a deadlock, or 'aporia'? For the passage which has enacted in its dialectic of metaphor and metonymy the 'Years of living among the breakage' is disclosed as mere poetic gesture by the final assertive 'renunciation'. It is assertive because of the authority of its context and its syntactic placing, which is dismissive of all associated with emotion. In exhaustion, the reader is left with an act which refuses all action. The tensions of the subject in discourse are rendered selfishly egocentric by the contrast of the text's privileging 'an act of surrender', forsaking of worldly goods (and of all others, perhaps); repudiation, as of a false principle; the renouncing of the world, the flesh and the devil, as at baptism. As Carlyle asserts: 'it is only with Renunciation that life, properly speaking, can be said to begin.'[30] Thus the material, historical temporal being, which receives its constitution from the discourses of the Other, that which is not itself, is denied by the text's foregrounding of sheer intransitivity, the way of negation. The project of the passivization of the subject/reader begins to pervade the text's work upon his or her horizon of expectations.

Accordingly in Movement III the metaphors of the various journeys of the subject as states of suspension, of withdrawal from the spatio-temporal, lull the subject/reader into such receptivity as is required to accept 'the one action', the thought that each present moment is as the moment of death. Although this centrality of the present may be justified by reference to the *Bhagavad-Gita*, the reader may dimly see a construct arising from the renunciation of the mediated subject, which is the immanent subject, removed from the prison-house of time and the chains of the discourses of the Other. The text's sleight of hand is invested with the authority typical of its overall strategy by its employment of what appear to be dialogic devices. The seemingly casual opening 'I sometimes wonder' with its suggestion of disinterested, insouciant curiosity, invites the reader/subject to share a mild speculative chat about time and the real, only to reposition him or her as passive recipient of superior wisdom, underlining this by the imperative 'And do not think of the fruit of action./Fare forward.' At first the reader seems equal, a partner in the text's speculation, but then it is clear that this was a delusion: 'You are not the same people who left the station' and 'You shall not think "the past is finished" '. The text here takes on the semblance of a discourse which is in effect a monologue; the subject/reader is confirmed in absolute subservience to the words' voice. The answer to the rack of periodicity is the text's foregrounding of what Derrida has identified as 'The metaphysics of presence as self-proximity . . . giving a privileged position to a sort of absolute now, the life of the present, the living present'.[31] Derrida's focus in this passage is on Rousseau, who provides a useful intertextual gloss: 'The great remedy to the miseries of this world is absorption into the present moment.'[32] Elsewhere Rousseau celebrates the epiphany of the immanent subject:

> The night was coming on. I perceived the sky, some stars, and a little grass. The first sensation was a delicious moment. I did not feel anything except through them. I was born in that instant to life, and it seemed to me that I filled with my light existence all the objects which I perceived. Entirely given up to the present moment, I did not remember anything; I had no distinct notion of any individuality, not the least idea of what had happened to me; I did not know who I was nor where I was; I felt neither evil, nor fear, nor trouble.[33]

In Eliot's text this revelation of pure presence is formulated as 'The point of intersection of the timeless/With time'. At the centre, then, all discourses stripped away, is the subject spiritualized in an elusive immanence. The opening lines of movement V create a curious context for this paradox. A series of human attempts to solve the dialectic of alterity is catalogued, only to meet the imperious dismissal of 'all these are usual/Pastimes and drugs, and features of the press.' It would be easy for the reader to grant these activities an equivalence of value, on the basis of their syntactic isomorphism; they are strung together without differentiation. Even if the passage can be read as elephantine humour, the reifying effect of the nominalizations 'pastimes', 'drugs' and 'features of the press' must cause intense anxiety. How can this text reduce astrophysics and psychodynamics to a 'pastime'? The complex intellectual and material praxis which constitutes these disciplines is ridiculed as a frenetic neural itch, periodically inflamed by events in history. The real, then, is an activity of a most august imagination, 'an occupation for the saint' to which the reader of *Four Quartets* is admitted only as 'the music/While the music lasts.' Is the reader, then, incorporated in the text only through 'the unattended/ Moment, the moment in and out of time'? Effectively she or he has to yield to 'The hint half guessed, the gift half understood' which is 'Incarnation'. Yet this defeat by assimilation is not the only outcome; the text itself points to those 'Who are only undefeated/ Because we have gone on trying.' Before we attend to the reader's strategies of resistance, however, 'Little Gidding', in all its apparent polyphonic richness, remains.

The movement here is from tragedy to redemption; the origin of humanity's flawed character lies in the material world, subject to violent, entropic change as the condition of its being. Thus the opening is of a moment 'suspended in time, between pole and tropic'. So the speaking subject is caught between the solipsism of self-guarantee and the tropes of discourse that predicate difference and desire. At Little Gidding the material world's periodicity is shown as deceiving: significance is read against the grain of the seasons, through the epiphany of 'Midwinter Spring'. The sheer contingency of being is signalled by the foregrounding in the passage that follows of the conditional clauses: 'If you came this way . . .', 'If you came this way in maytime . . .', 'If you came at night . . .', 'If you came by day . . .'. What redeems this imprisoning grid of conditionality is the probability that 'It would be the same . . .'. Whatever the protean transformations of the subject/ reader caught in time achieve, the syntax of the conditional, its subordinate value and function renders ineffectual: 'It would always be the same'. The plurality of the possible is reduced by the weary predication of the probable.

This reductive exhaustion derives from the effect of the 'supplement of copula'. Derrida sees 'the formal copula function' as 'a process of falling, abstraction, degradation, as evacuation of the semantic plenitude of the lexeme "to be" '.[34] In less Derridean terms, when we use 'is' as a formal connective of two noun phrases, it does not have the full and final meaning of 'being'. The second of the phrases is a supplement to the first. Derrida argues that the supplement is on the one hand 'a surplus, a plenitude enriching another plenitude, the fullest measure of presence'.[35] But the deconstructive aspect of the supplement is this: 'It adds only to replace. It intervenes or insinuates itself in-the-place-of; if it fills, it is as if one fills a void.'[36] If we apply these notions to the text the results are shattering. Taking 'And what you thought you came for/ Is only a shell, a husk of meaning' the reader is blown apart. The original quest, in itself a full understanding riddled by doubt – 'you thought you came for' – is supplemented – conceptualized – as emptiness: 'a shell, a husk of meaning'. The search for ontological security, the goal of western philosophies, is dislosed by the text as utterly hollow. It is Conrad's 'The horror, the horror' in a text given supreme authority by its apparent polyphony. Worse, the project is universalized: 'If you came this way,/Taking any route, starting from anywhere/At any time or at any season'. Human subjects are in the deepest of aporias; from this dead end there seems no way forward.

The first two stanzas of movement II enact the nullity of plenitude as it is fondly imaged in human discourses and material endeavour: for stories end as 'Dust in the air suspended'; the earth itself suffers 'death'. The extensive assimilation to death is through the stasis of material transformed to endstates of insignificance. In the third stanza, however, the future tense of 'shall rot' signals the prophetic voice of doom at our complicity with the temporal in contrast to the eternal; the rot will affect 'The marred foundations we forgot/Of sanctuary and choir'. Yet there is some weakness here, for the text changes its discourse pattern to include us, and thus itself becomes implicated with precisely that temporality it has been striving to deny as valid. Such slippage is easily missed by the reader who at this stage of the poem is still caught in its interstitial grounding of his or her subjectivity.

And so the subject/reader is swept on into the next section of the text, the rhetorical embodiment of subjectivity as ultimate limitation. Here, as the Dante references hint, is Hell, the realm of the Other, that upon which being depends, yet which can only confirm its alterity. The linguistic structure of the text is curious and revealing at this point. In the opening of the section the syntax embodies a suspension of space and time in the eight lines of subordination before the main verb 'I met one . . .'; all the prepositional phrases offer a sense of location in their apparent function as spatial coordinates, with a hint of the temporal in 'After . . .' and the other embedded clause 'While . . .'. But each location slips aside, the force of the preposition lost in the paradoxes which complete the phrases, such as 'the recurrent end of the unending'. The stability of the sign is erased in the slippage of signifiers; the reader is drawn into a fluid, nightmare world of flux, stasis, displacement and condensation which surrounds the authoritative author in a dramatic embracement of intertextuality, the Tradition.

It is here, in this text, that the ground of desire is finally articulated; it is the search for a form of subjectivity without Desire[37] which has been the dominant motif and metaphysical frame of the text. For the reader, the Tradition is constructed, through the Dante references, as a set of traces in which the privilege of the signifier becomes more and more explicit. Latini, the Florentine scholar, the explorer of signification, is as a paternal image to Dante, the explorer of signification; so Dante stands to the text of 'Little Gidding' as *'miglior fabbro'*, an author with the authority of the *Logos*. As the text advises the reader, 'the words sufficed/To compel the recognition they preceded'. It is what Lacan called the 'passion of the signifier' that the text is celebrating here: 'this passion of the signifier now becomes a new dimension of the human condition in that it is not only man who speaks, but that in man and through man it speaks.'[38] It speaks our alterity, captured in the text as the split subject:

> So I assumed a double part, and cried –
> And heard another's voice cry, "What, are you here?"
> Although we were not. I was still the same
> Knowing myself yet being someone other
> ['Little Gidding' II, 97–100]

This splitting is the effect of the tension between the Imaginary and the Symbolic, the illusory state of wholeness of our pre-linguistic world, and the fragmented world of the subject constructed by discourse of the Other, who is never whole and stable.

Self-knowledge is therefore the infiltration of the discourses of the Other, a process whereby one's subjectivity is designated by selective entry. We may recall Foucault's remarks on societies of discourse, and on the entry requirements for particular discourses.

For at this point in 'Little Gidding' a version of discourse-mediated reality is emerging. It seems very insubstantial since 'last year's words belong to last year's language' and the 'crown upon your lifetime's effort' is 'bitter tastelessness of shadow fruit', 'the laceration/Of laughter at what ceases to amuse' and 'the rending pain of re-enactment/Of all that you have done, and been'. The project 'to purify the dialect of the tribe' begins to reveal emptiness as fundamental as Kurtz discloses in *Heart Of Darkness*, for all the pain of the 'intolerable wrestle/With words and meanings' dissolves in the lines of soothing hauteur, beginning 'And every phrase . . .' and ending 'Every phrase and every sentence is an end and a beginning'. ('Little Gidding' V) The plenitude of presence reigns smoothly here, guaranteeing the 'rightness', the being 'at home', the 'easy commerce', the precision, the 'complete consort dancing together'. This effect is created by the suspension of the lines from 'The word' to 'dancing together' from syntactic movement; they are joined in a nominative absolute apposition, pointing to a perfect text, nominative and absolute, out of reach except to those who 'kneel/Where prayer has been valid'. The screws are finally turned on the reader in the final line of the poem, after the gesture to its own complex strategies in 'We shall not cease from exploration'. The extinction is imaged in the perfect union of fire and rose; metaphor defeats metonymy, and the *Logos* awaits, to assimilate all.

To submit here is to accept the authority of the text and its author as given. Sharratt argues, 'Once we accept that *Four Quartets* is a major literary achievement we must be brought, inescapably, to a personal negotiation of its demands upon us as readers . . . but as readers of the poem we are defeated by it; we can never fully read it.'[39] The blindness of this insight is revealing. The adjunct 'fully' conceals an implied presence, the plenitude of some kind of superreader. Moreover the fate of such a monster is not articulated. It would, however, include a transcendent authenticity, an authenticity of stasis: conversion to the mode of monologue by submission to the signifier, the Word, with its entailment of subjectivity centripetally constructed by a cyclical circumvention of the dialogic.

We need to remind ourselves of the accuracy of the epigraph from Bakhtin cited at the beginning of this chapter. It is a 'perfect' account of the poem read as text. Reading the poem in the late Eighties however must involve strategies which disclose the praxis of the text as discourse, involving it dialogically, from the standpoint of exotopy. This is not to fall into the trap of imagining that from that position a superior metalanguage can be established; it is rather to heed Foucault's warning that 'the act of writing as it is institutionalised today, in the book, the publishing-system and the person of the writer, takes place in a "society of discourse" '.[40] Edward Said reinforces the necessity of criticism to remain in the world, and to avoid 'monocentrism',[41] but the last citation is Bakhtin's: 'There is no first or last discourse, and dialogical context knows no limits . . .'[42] We must not bow to the textual imperialism even of such complex examples of textual praxis as *The Waste Land* and *Four Quartets*. As readers they address us, urging us to produce their meaning; as readers in the world we must reply, and interrogate, through dialogue, not reverence.

4 Frames of References: The Reception of, and Response to, Three Women Poets

Elaine Millard

Tell Her I only said – the Syntax –
And left the Verb and the Pronoun – out
    EMILY DICKINSON[1]

What happens when we read is a continuing topic of interest, as relevant to primary teachers and educationalists as to critical theorists. Teachers of very young readers have, in recent years, been guided by the research of socio-linguists to switch attention from the processes of decoding grapheme to phoneme, whereby the reader is encouraged to build up words through sounding out individual letters, to methods that place greater emphasis on larger units of meaning. Frank Smith has called this process of making meaning from texts a psycho-linguistic guessing game, emphasizing the prior knowledge and linguistic competences that any reader, however young, brings to the reading task.[2] In the processes of learning to read, such operations of prediction from prior experience and intertextual knowledge are seen to be at least as important as the recognition of word shapes and patterns.

In the sixth form and beyond, students need to take this process one stage further, and be encouraged to become much more self-reflexive about the processes that shape their response to the written text. In teaching poetry at this level, I begin to focus their attention on the language of a poem, by presenting students with a poetry text photocopied in the centre of a large piece of paper on which I ask them to mark any patterns or correspondences they find, whether they believe these to have any particular relevance or not. As well as looking for the key words and phrases that pattern out meaning through imagery or thematic repetition, I also ask them to find patterns of repetition at the level of sound or rhythm. As the study progresses, they are asked to move beyond the words on the page to identify shared connotations with other texts, at first limiting this to those of the author in question, but rapidly moving on to other authors, other media.

My purpose in this is to train students in what amounts to careful habits of close reading, that open the text out onto larger fields of literary study. I teach what Stanley Fish called 'interpretative strategies',[3] and Jonathan Culler 'literary competence'[4] to induct them into a particular community of readers. These reader response theorists suggest that what the study of English teaches its students is shared practices of managing texts; both concern themselves more with the possibility of describing the systems through which these meanings are made, than with the interpretation of individual works.

Of those theorists subsumed under the general heading of 'Reader Response' criticism, Wolfgang Iser comes closest to describing the working practices important for the 'A' level student, in a method where the reader is summarized by Terry Eagleton as one who

> makes implicit connections, fills in gaps, draws inferences and tests out hunches; and to do this draws on a tacit knowledge of the world in general, and on literary conventions in particular.[5]

The strategies I am developing with students can be compared to critical practices of the structuralist or semiotician, whereby the text is seen to be part of a rule-governed system of signs and codes, producing meaning by combination and recombination of their formal elements, whether at the level of sound or of genre. I wish to establish in their practice that poetry is a 'system of systems' whose meanings depend on the interplay of the text with the reader's own 'horizons of expectations'. Texts do things to the reader because she approaches them in a particular way. Kate Millett approaches Henry Miller, for example, with a very different set of expectations from Norman Mailer.[6] However, by broadening the analysis to the chain of connotations and second-order meanings or myths generated in reading, the poem can also be seen not as a closed field, but as related to wider systems of meaning, through notions of intertextuality and with reference to the cultural practices of a whole society. This is where its approach differs significantly from

New Criticism, where the words on the page are all that are to be considered, and the poem is a discrete unit of meaning, 'the verbal icon'.[7]

Some colleagues are unconvinced by the argument that it is processes of reading they are working to encourage, preferring to describe as the 'personal response' what are, in effect, the result of learned strategies. To some, the concentration on formal properties seem an unwarranted limitation on the reader, excluding important questions of historical context and shared cultural practices. In fact, the very opposite is the case.

The work of the French writer, Roland Barthes, has, more than that of any other literary theorist, freed the creative reader from the obligation of reconstructing what might be supposed to have been the intentions of the author.[8] Along with structuralist theories of the text and the science of semiotics, his writing has done much to unsettle the general acceptance of a simple correspondence of art to life, work to experience. In *Image, Music, Text*, the liberated reader is described as an anti-hero, who works productively within the polyvalent codes with their intertextual resonances, from a wide variety of cultural discourses which are seen to be at play:

> We now know that the text is not a line of words releasing a single 'theological' meaning (the 'message' of an Author-God), but a multi-dimensional space in which a variety of writings, none of them original, blend and clash. The text is a tissue of quotations drawn from innumerable centres of culture.[9]

Barthes has also made the distinction between readerly and writerly works, using the former to describe those texts which allow the reader to determine the final synthesis of codes, while the latter encourage an awareness of its signifying procedures. The reader of such a text defers closure, or the acceptance of a single unified interpretation, and concentrates on the power of the text to interrogate its own foundations.

Although Barthes's own encoded readings are confined to fictional narratives, his method of opening up the symbolic field of a text, by following the threadwork of semes and symbols, seems equally productive in revealing the network of literary and cultural knowledge which a reader draws on to make meanings in reading poetry. A problem does present itself, however, if, by concentrating on teaching students how to read the formal properties of the text, the process of selecting what to read is ignored and choice is limited to those texts firmly established within the established literary canon, without questioning any of the presuppositions underlying the selection and the limitations it imposes.

In particular, the poetry presented in school anthologies and in university courses has been, and still often is, very much a men's club, where the norm is represented as 'a man speaking to men'. Poetry by women has received relatively little significant critical attention, and those women who have been read with any large-scale interest have tended to attract biographical speculation, rather than any acknowledgement of their particularities of style or form.

Teachers of literature frequently choose to teach individual poets as members of a particular literary group, or as inheritors of certain traditions. It could be said that a knowledge of such framing contexts is one component of the literary competence of any educated reader. However, when we turn attention to the way women poets are read by academics and literary critics, the common competences employed are more often predicated on reading strategies that foreground the poet's presumed experiences, than on formalist concerns or relationships to literary movements. Readings of women's poetry which treat writing as a form of disclosure, rather than composition, reinforce the link between the woman poet and the expression of self, particularly a damaged and pained self. Women's strategies for representation, it appears, work only to reinforce the double bind of critical formulations that imply either that her sex cannot write, or that those who do are exceptional only because they are able to reflect upon disadvantaged and damaged selves. Locked into readings that lock them out of any scene of writing other than their attics, drawing rooms and parlours, women who write poetry attract the kind of attention that sets the critic on a quest for personal relevance, rather than the play of intertextualities. Many feminist critics have seen it as their major task to uncover the frame-ups resulting from male readings of women's texts. In *The Madwoman in the Attic*, Sandra M. Gilbert and Susan Gubar suggest that John Crowe Ransom's comments, in a 1956 essay on Emily Dickinson, are typical of this tendency. He wrote that

> it is a common belief amongst readers (among men readers at least) that the woman poet as a type . . . makes flights into nature rather too

easily, and upon errands which do not have metaphysical importance enough to justify so radical a strategy.

They further cite, as evidence of male mis-reading of this poet, R.P. Blackmur's strictures that

> she was neither a professional poet nor an amateur, she was a private poet who wrote indefatigably, as some women cook or knit. Her gift for words, and the cultural predicament of her time, drove her to poetry instead of antimacassars.[10]

Similar examples can be found wherever women's poetry is under discussion. There is a predisposition to look for limitations, and even where praise is intended it is framed, as in the last example, to suggest deficiencies or oddnesses of personality, rather than the strength of achievement.

The Faber Book of Political Verse furnishes a different example of the way in which women's contribution to poetry is marginalized, this time by omission. Tom Paulin's definition of the political allows for the inclusion of a wide range of poetry by men, some of which might be considered to express personal conflict. For example, included is a poem in which Sir Thomas Wyatt bemoans his lack of advancement and neglect by his friends. This is included as a political statement when no space has been found for the voices of Emily Brontë or Emily Dickinson, who engage in a similar interrogation of their worldly circumstances. The underlying assumption, I presume, is that Wyatt speaks for 'mankind' in lamenting his state, being 'imprisoned in liberties', an interpretation which is supported by the recorded historical facts of his relationship with Thomas Cromwell, and subsequent fall from favour. On the other hand, through exclusion it is implied that these women poets are restricted to personal and individual statements, despite the fact that both Brontë and Dickinson belong firmly to the Puritan-Republican tradition of thought, from which a large proportion of the anthology is drawn.

Of the ninety poems selected by Paulin, only two are the work of women: one is the editor's own translation from the Russian, the other is likened by him in the Preface to 'Jane Austen incognito in America', employing the novelist's art of 'witty anecdotal formality'.[11] Moreover, room has been found for Linton Kwesi Johnson and John Cooper Clarke as part of a popular verse tradition, but Liz Lochhead, for example, who writes for a similar audience to confront the politics of gender, is omitted. The message taken away by the reader of this anthology is that women are only tangentially related to both poetry and politics, and can therefore be largely discounted from what Cora Kaplan has termed 'high language', that is the literary and rhetorical registers associated with public life and the arts. Kaplan argues that women are at a disadvantage in such discourses because of

> the intra- and trans-class prejudice against women as speakers at all which seems most likely to erode women's use of 'high' language. This preference is connected with the patriarchal definition of ideal femininity. 'Silence gives the proper grace to women.'[12]

In writing, and particularly in writing poetry, women are allotted personal, but not public, space, a private but not a political or rhetorical voice.

These disparate instances of the reception and subsequent selection of women's poetry furnish prime examples of the way the interpretation of women's writing, by those established in literary circles, works to create and reinforce the popular stereotypes of the woman poet. She is, according to such formulations, a poor, crazed creature, either abandoned or ignored by men, who turns to writing as a last means of expressing frustration and rage at the limited nature of her existence. Poetry for her, the story continues, is a compensation for emotional failure, and a question of self-expression. Situated always outside her contemporary literary institutions and artistic conventions, she can only be understood as a freak, an unusual sport of nature, whose mind is at odds with the body she inhabits. In *The Bloodaxe Book of Contemporary Women Poets*, Jeni Couzyn caricatures these stereotypes in her introduction, placing them into three categories: first, 'Mrs Dedication' who, like Elizabeth Barratt Browning, puts 'all mental and emotional energy into romantic devotion to a man', then 'Miss Eccentric Spinster', a sub-group that includes women like Emily Dickinson and Stevie Smith, who are presumed to be 'the victims of a love affair from which [they] never recovered' and, finally, 'mad girl', of whom Sylvia Plath is the prime example.[13]

Another strand of feminist scholarship has been to argue the case for women's tangential relationship with the literary values of their age, frequently locating the outcome of this indirection in a problematical relationship to their own work. This is the main argument of Gilbert and Gubar's *The Madwoman in the Attic*, where the writing woman's dilemma is characterized as an anxiety of authorship. They argue that the discourse of literature is one in which women find themselves confined and imprisoned by disabling images of femininity, issuing from male literary traditions that define them as eternally other. Poetry presents, they argue, even more problems for women in its genres and conventions than prose fiction.

> The sonnet, beginning with Petrarch's celebration of 'his' Laura, took shape in praise of the poet's mistress. . . . The 'Great Ode' encourages the poet to define himself as a priest-like bard. The satiric epistle is usually written when a writer's manly rage transforms 'his' pen into a figurative sword. And the pastoral elegy . . . traditionally expresses a poet's grief over the death of a brother-poet.[14]

Poetry's roots, in a classical education that women were denied, created greater barriers to a woman's successful entry into a community of educated male authors. The anxiety brought on by such daunting conditions impels women to react against the predominant images created by men in a form of rebellion that involves a 'duplicitous self expression' concealing 'true selves' behind 'socially acceptable façades'. These true selves are frequently identified by Gilbert and Gubar in the images of imprisoned madwomen, who, they argue, are 'usually in some sense the author's double'. The writers need to proceed by 'unlearning not to speak', and their work documents a movement from confining textual conventions to a liberating overthrow of what they are expected to be.

The difficulty with Gilbert and Gubar's mythology of the woman poet, whom, taking a cue from Virginia Woolf, they call Judith Shakespeare, remains that whatever other interpretation is placed on an individual work, any woman poet's main theme can always be narrowed down to a single narrative, the female quest for self-definition. Gilbert and Gubar find a model of feminine poetic creativity in the self-enforced imprisonment of Emily Dickinson who, they suggest, refused 'the danger to be sane' to create a self-contained world of 'romance and revelation'. The victories that Gilbert and Gubar celebrate, in their outline of a female tradition of creativity, appear decidedly Pyrrhic. The overall implications are of a kind of pessimistic psychological essentialism that Juliet Mitchell has identified as accompanying the negation of the realm of language in women's writing. The adoption of binary opposition, she claims, can bring only a reversal of, not an escape from, the dominant order. She uses the supposition of a lost femininity, repressed at the point of the Oedipal stage, which could only find expression by creating for itself an alternative Symbolic order. For:

... if the carnival and the church do not exist independently of each other the pre-Oedipal and the Oedipal are not separate discrete states – if instead the Oedipal with the castration complex is what defines the pre-Oedipal, then the only way you can challenge the church, challenge both its Oedipal and pre-Oedipal is from within an alternative symbolic universe. You cannot choose the imaginary, the semiotic, the carnival as an alternative to the symbolic, as an alternative to the law. It is set up by the law precisely as its own ludic space. . . . So that politically speaking it is only the symbolic, a new symbolism, a new law, that can challenge the dominant law.[15]

Juliet Mitchell is drawing on terms developed from Freud, most notably by Jacques Lacan whose work stresses the importance of language in constituting the subject within a culture, and whose theories have been adapted to serve the needs of French feminism. Lacan distinguishes between two orders of language, which he terms the Imaginary and the Symbolic. The former dominates the pre-Oedipal stage when the infant experiences itself as an illusory whole, undifferentiated from the adult (most often the mother) who satisfies its needs. With the acquisition of language, some aspects of this experience of an omnipotent self are excluded from the new Symbolic order and remain in the Imaginary. The Symbolic is the embodiment of all the abstracted rules governing relationships within a society. Because Western society is patriarchal, this Symbolic is dominated by 'the name of the father', and the 'I' position is the privileged locus of the male subject. The feminine is thereby constituted as a lack, the mere other of a male positive pole, so that the little girl's relationship to the Symbolic is necessarily a negative one.

Julia Kristeva is the literary theorist most frequently invoked by feminist critics as offering a way of escape for the alienated and marginalized subject, whose femininity has suffered censorship by the Symbolic. If the Symbolic realm necessarily displaces what is feminine in pre-Oedipal experience to its outer margins and represses it, a lost feminine identity might be located in what Julia

Kristeva has termed the 'semiotic order'. This is a space she identifies as linked to pre-linguistic oral and anal drives, at the time when the infant remained in dyadic unity with the mother, and which lies inseparably behind the Symbolic order. These drives, drawn together in a chora, are subject to processes of repression through the combined working of the castration complex, and the imposition of a phallic Symbolic order. Kristeva does, however, trace their presence as they erupt into the Symbolic through rhythms, gaps, and interruptions she identifies in the workings of modernist poetic texts.

The 'feminity' so repressed is non-biological, equally repressed in male as well as female writing, and for the greater part of her discussion of modern poetry Kristeva concentrates on readings of men's writing. For Kristeva, this feminine consciousness can disrupt from within the text's overall structure, in its anarchic disturbance of the workings of the surface smoothness of symbol and time. However, she seems disturbingly to return to the same message of a fall into madness when the speaker/poet under discussion is a woman.

In the section 'I Who Want Not To Be' in *About Chinese Women*, she discusses the emergence of this semiotic as the call of the mother:

> For a woman, the call of the mother is not only a call from beyond time, or beyond the socio-political battle . . . this call troubles the word: it generates hallucinations, voices, 'madness'. After the superego the ego founders and sinks. It is a fragile envelope, incapable of staving off the irruption of this conflict, of this love which had bound the little girl to her mother, and which then, like a black lava, had lain in wait for her all along the path of her desperate attempts to identify with the symbolic paternal order. Once the moorings of a word, the ego, the super ego, begin to slip, life itself can't hang on: death quietly moves in.[16]

She characterizes Sylvia Plath as 'one of the women disillusioned with meanings and words', and sees in the rhythms of *Ariel*, for 'those who know how to read her, her silent departure from life'.

The sum total, then, of each of the theoretical moves to establish the particular differences of written style created by gender results in a view of the female artist that assumes that pain, suffering, and imprisonment of hope can only be escaped through madness. For Gilbert and Gubar, women's writing will be blighted by the male precursors who take centre stage and leave them only the margins to inhabit. Women's writing can only be fully understood if interpreted as part of a literary subculture, and their passivity and suffering are identity markers in a writing scene in which they need to struggle for space and endure only by disguise. French feminisms, on the other hand, though formulating subjectivity as a relationship to language rather than life, are still deterministic in the total authority accorded language, to whose Symbolic repression, psychosis or silence appears the only resistance. Both stances reinforce the otherness of gender difference, locating the stories of the female self in negation and imprisonment and reinforcing the negative focus of the critic. In order to unsettle what begins to look like different versions of a biological determinism, what is required is a shift of emphasis from essence to experience.

Cora Kaplan has a useful way out of the cul-de-sac, shifting women's relationship to the Symbolic order from a 'negative' (polar opposite) to a 'difference'. She argues that this difference is not an essential one, but a product of Western societies' exclusion of the girl at puberty from the public realm of discourse. She identifies two stages at which women's disadvantage in language is set:

> The first is at the Oedipal stage, where the child, constructed as a speaking subject, must acknowledge social sex difference and align herself with women and restricted speech – a distinction blurred by the restrictions on children's speech. The second stage, puberty, further distinguishes girls from boys by the appearance of adult sex differences and access to public discourse for men.[17]

It is the shift from locating the exclusion in language itself, to the context of language in use, that allows the alienating effect of the Symbolic on women to be seen as local and contestable, rather than monolithic and deterministic.

In this brief summary of some of the ways in which the work of women poets have been received, I have been concerned to illustrate that the outcome of any reading is as dependent on a framing context and reader expectation, as on those formal properties that can be described as literary competence. Although reading is a rule-governed activity, it is, of course, never innocent, and its final outcome will be as dependent on its context as any appreciation of a revolution in poetic language. In the following readings of three women poets, Emily Dickinson, Sylvia Plath, and

Marianne Moore, the centrality of their relationship to the dominant discourses and cultural practices of their respective contexts will be a central concern. It is my intention to establish this relationship to discourse as the basis for reading their poems, rather than for speculation about personal crises or mystery lovers.

Emily Dickinson (Miss Eccentric Spinster) has been the object of frequent biographical speculation and interpretative strategies that search for the writer in the work, rather than for the textual strategies she deploys. The fact that many of her poems are written in the first person fuels this quest for a hidden life, despite the poet's own disclaimer to her first reader, Higginson, that 'when I state myself as the Representative of the verse – it does not mean – me – but a supposed person'.[18] Despite such warnings, a good deal of time and creative energy has been spent in trying to identify a secret lover whose renunciation, many have assumed, is a central theme of the poetry, and to whose loss can be ascribed Dickinson's withdrawal from the world. Ted Hughes, in his preface to a selection of her poetry, makes just that point:

> the eruption of her imagination and poetry followed when she shifted her passion with the energy of desperation from this lost man to its only possible substitute – the Universe in its divine aspect.[19]

Neither are the lesbian feminists' counter-claims, put forward by Lillian Faderman and Adelaide Morris, which find in her poetry accounts of (suppressed) homosexual desire, and interpret many of the love poems as addressed directly to a woman, radically different. In their determination to read the poetry as a direct reflection of the poet's experience, they substitute references to her female acquaintances for the lawyer and preacher of others' speculations.[20]

The theme of the naive, untutored poet is further fuelled by the way in which previous selections and school-room experiences of Emily Dickinson's poetry have foregrounded the 'little-girl' poems. More recently, feminist critics have begun to re-read Dickinson's writing in more positive ways. Adrienne Rich, looking in her own work for the influence of a woman's tradition, finds in her a powerful fore-mother, and a use of language that is 'more varied, more compressed, more dense with implications, more complex of syntax, than any American poetic language to date'.[21]

Cora Kaplan also locates the importance of Emily Dickinson in the language strategies she adopts to explore psychological, rather than autobiographical, truths. Kaplan argues that Dickinson's 'fragmentary and opaque language' is married to an approach which is 'analytical, intellectual even', where gothic, fantasy and reality, are elided to create dream states, scenes.[22] Kaplan further illustrates how many of the lyrics work through metonymic or synecdochic tropes to create the sense of dislocation and movement between inner and outer experience.

Such lines of enquiry, locating themselves in the language of the text, rather than some guessed at hidden prior cause, do better justice to the power and range of Dickinson's poetry. The critical emphasis is shifted towards perceiving textual difficulties and deliberate ambiguities, which indicate that language is being pushed to the limits of what can be said, rather than used to encode messages of secret unfulfilled loves. It is in her contest with contemporary 'high' language in an attempt to recreate meanings, that Dickinson's importance to feminism lies, rather than in the myth of seclusion, renunciation and loss.

This language, even when it presents itself at its most direct and simplest, becomes, as one reads on, paradoxically more elusive, more evasive. What is striking about the following poem is the disjunction created between the discourse of Romantic love – the lover surrendering self to the desired object ('I gave myself to him') and the mysticism of the implied metaphysical lover – and the intimidatory discourse of economic exchange, centred in a futures market of mutual risk and gain.

> I gave myself to Him
> And took Himself for pay
> The solemn contract of a Life
> Was ratified this way –
>
> The Wealth might disappoint –
> Myself a poorer prove
> Than this great Purchaser suspect
> The Daily Own – of Love
>
> Depreciate the Vision –
> But till the Merchant buy –
> Still Fable – in the Isles of Spice –
> The subtle cargoes – lie –
>
> At least – 'tis Mutual – Risk –
> Some – found it – Mutual Gain –

> Sweet Debt of Life – Each Night to owe –
> Insolvent – every Noon – [23]

The incongruity of a deliberate investment, and the ratification of formal contracts, sits uneasily both with the passionate sense of abandonment projected in the first line and the enigmatic 'Daily Own of Love'.

Dickinson's yoking together of discordant discourses is disconcerting; the poem seems to refuse a totalizing structure that would allow an interpretation that settles for either a transcendental or earthly lover, or even a decision as to which of the pair is the most dissatisfied with the exchange. Does 'the Wealth' refer to her 'gift' (of self), or her 'pay'? It is impossible to decide. Such questioning serves to highlight the paradoxical 'economic' self-interest of both Puritanism and self-sacrificial profane love. This feature is presented more strongly in the straightforward later dismissal of any economic relationship between herself and God.

> Is Heaven an Exchequer?
> They speak of what we owe –
> But that negotiation
> I'm not a Party to – [24]

The latter poem is a more straightforward refusal of the notion of ransom and indebtedness between God and the believer. The former throws into question the possibility of finding adequate language to articulate that relationship, except in terms of 'high' language that can deal only in profit and loss, or formal contracts and obligations, and which obliterates the fantastic and exotic promises of Spice Islands or visions. Once alerted to such voices within the text, the reader notices further evidence of the uneasiness of economic exchange in less obvious contexts, as in this earlier poem:

> If I should die
> And you should live –
> And time should gurgle on –
> And morn should beam –
> And noon should burn –
> As it has always done –
> If Birds should build as early
> And bees as bustling go –
> One might depart at option

> From enterprise below;
> 'Tis sweet to know that stocks will stand
> When we with daisies lie –
> That commerce will continue –
> And trades as briskly fly –
> It makes the parting tranquil
> And keeps the soul serene –
> That gentlemen so sprightly
> Conduct the pleasing scene[25]

This directly follows the poems of daisies, birds and bees, that have contributed to the image of a naive and untutored poet, which was first encouraged by Higginson's prefatory essay to the 1890 volume, 'An Open Portfolio'. Higginson ignores the formal qualities of the verse, which in letters to the poet he had complained of, disliking the irregularities and discordant rhythms, but substituting praise for the originality of her metaphors.[26]

In fact, any reader experiences the same feelings of disjuncture and discord which arises from two contrasting discourses brought together for ironic effect. The language of a simple, child-like observation – 'morn should beam', 'birds should build', 'bees . . . bustling go' – along with 'empty' qualifiers – 'sweet', 'tranquil', 'pleasing' – is counterpointed and intruded on by more formal voices from other discourses – 'depart at option', 'stocks', 'Trade'. This is the point where, reading as a feminist, a discussion of Lacanian theories of the subject as they appear in the adaptations of French feminists, to pinpoint the writer's disadvantage in the structures of the codes that reinforce the 'name of the father' (that is, the Symbolic order), seems a more productive strategy than rehearsing myths of personal loss.

If language is an area in which all identity, whatever the gender, is to be played out as alienation, and in particular one that confirms woman's secondary role, then the struggle to force meaning from language systems that marginalize and ignore her creates the tensions and obliquity that are a central experience of reading Dickinson's poetry. I have chosen to highlight discords between the material and metaphysical in the contradictions of the discourses of commerce and affection, but it is just as possible to concentrate on the juxtaposition of the Biblical and liturgical with profane desire, that creates tension between earthly and heavenly affection, *agape* and *eros*. It is precisely these poems, though, that have fuelled so much biographical speculation about the identity of a lost lover. Women's writing is repeatedly read in such a frame of autobiography, rather than within what Jan Montefiore calls the politico-literary myths that are used to read the male writers.[27] A prime example of a writer whose personal 'experiences' are always granted precedence over her writing process or relationship to literary genre is Sylvia Plath, Jeni Couzyn's archetypal mad girl, whose work is often simply read as an announcement of an intention to commit suicide.

Alvarez, writing in his introduction to *The New Poetry*, praised her 'naked' treatment of experience, and began the process whereby the fact of suicide is read back into the poetry. Her readers are always discovering fresh evidence of a death wish or an account of personal trauma, while discussing her writing as evidence of psychopathological impulses. Her poetry is assumed to be a direct response to the experience of anger, misandry and loss. David Holbrook, for example, draws on the writing of R.D. Laing on schizophrenia to 'explain' the cult of violence he finds in Sylvia Plath, and performs a psychoanalysis of the poet through her poetry. In Holbrook's interpretation, the discourse of the critic has been replaced by that of a psychiatrist, who invites his reader to share his fascinated horror at the spectacle of an unbalanced mind in the process of disclosure. For this critic, the voice of the narrator and that of the poet are essentially one.[28]

In reconsidering Plath's significance in relation to a particular literary scene, a more important feature than the supposition of a fragmented self is the fragmented non-sequential nature of the narrative elements she deploys. In 'Lady Lazarus', for example, a circus strip-tease act, a miraculous raising from the dead that is also a vampire story, and the atrocities of the Nazi death camps, are interwoven as device, rather than the uncontrolled reflection of a disturbed mind. Starting to read from such a narrative frame, what becomes more apparent are the rhetorical correspondences between T.S. Eliot and Sylvia Plath. Interestingly, this 'invisible' poet is himself rarely read in a frame of autobiography: 'objective and pointed' are the qualifiers usually applied to his monologues, although Peter Ackroyd's recent biography has revealed just the kind of aberrant detail that would fuel critics attracted to Emily Dickinson or Sylvia Plath.[29] T.S. Eliot's modernist, conservative intonations about the fragmentation and discontinuities of culture are paralleled in Plath's distortions and fragmentations of the discourse which regulates domestic and family relationships. To simplify the analogy, Plath could be said to be interrogating the political dimensions of sexuality and the family, in the way that Eliot pointedly questions the disintegration of spiritual and conservative cultural values.

One of the most discussed poems, 'Daddy', when shorn of explanatory details which speculate about the writer's relationship with father and husband, becomes a parodic confessional. Here, I am using parody to suggest that the role is adopted to mock dependency. It is a 'masquerade' of femininity in the way Luce Irigaray suggests 'woman' can only be represented as the man's desire situates her.[30] In the poem, the woman enacts the role of dependent victim. The stridency of nursery rhythms set against evocation of the concentration camps, Auschwitz, Belsen, Dachau, strikes the reader as excessive and melodramatic, if intended metaphorically to represent father/daughter, husband/wife, relationships. Such gothic elements form part of the rhetorical disintegration, so that the childish voice which gloats over the death of two men is no more nor less autobiographical than Prufrock lamenting growing old or being ignored by singing mermaids. In each poet, discordant and disjunctive images that spread along metonymic, rather than metaphoric, lines, deliver an ultimately political statement about the positioning of the subject in relation to a dominant discourse.

For Eliot, it is within the high discourse of culture that he, as subject, is placed, and his fragmentation of the discourse of Art and Literature works ultimately to re-unify, and resist change. His writing is, despite the recurrent glimpses it offers of a corrupted present, consistently urbane; images of sordid urban landscapes and aimless human flotsam serve only to increase the value of the art forms of the past, typified by the evocation of Spenser's 'sweet Thames' flowing through a Wasteland strewn with fragments of past cultural wholes. Sylvia Plath's poetry, on the other hand, is disruptive of the accepted patterns of poetry's 'high' discourse, and breaks all the rules of poetic decorum. In her use of metaphor, Sylvia Plath frequently employs a vehicle that breaks away from the tenor, to create a startling range of associations, marking a movement away from the rational and lucid to more surreal fantasies. Poppies are 'little bloody skirts', pregnancy a 'train there's no getting off, a bruise, the sea sucking in a pit of rock'.[31] The effect is to push metaphor away from simple correspondence or contrast, towards metonymic chains of signification, with the emphasis on remoteness, rather than contiguity. There is no propriety in the choice of Nazi atrocities as the vehicle for disrupted family relationships or individual suffering, or of Hiroshima's radiation for a high temperature.[32] The choice of nursery rhymes and insistent child-like rhythms adds to the sense of disharmony by offering compulsive repetition of sound, rather than the closure of serious rhyme. While Eliot's images ultimately work to suggest a nostalgic harmony from which the poem's persona is excluded, Sylvia Plath's fragmented narrative structures are less important than the female subject's position in each narrative thread. Each fragment mirrors an element of the absence or lack that Lacan identifies as the central fact of representation of self in language.

Emily Dickinson and Sylvia Plath, it might be argued, attract a kind of peeping-Tom interest in the life, because they choose to adopt the first person singular for many poems, and create speaking voices which are taken to be representations of self. It is possible to apply the feminist myth of exclusion and silence about each of them. But what of a poet who does not fall quite so readily into Couzyn's perceived stereotypes of eccentric spinster or mad girl? Marianne Moore is a writer whose professional life as a poet and literary editor of *The Dial* has been foregrounded, so that except within the boundaries of professional relationships with other modernist writers such as Ezra Pound and William Carlos Williams, discussion is centred on her writing and her innovations of style. In 1935, T.S. Eliot judged that 'her poems form part of the small body of durable poetry written in our language',[33] and there has been a continuing, though limited, academic acceptance of her importance, though this has often taken the form of including her in lists, while denying her any detailed examination.[34]

In addition, despite a general emphasis on her contribution to the practices of modernism, there is still a patronizing tone in the voices of male critics. Writing for her seventy-seventh birthday, Lowell's suggestion that 'her excellence is a woman's in its worldly concreteness'[35] echoes Pound's ambiguous comments about Moore and Mina Loy in 1918, at the beginning of her career:

> without any pretence and without clamors about nationality, these girls have written a distinctly national product, they have written

something which could not have come out of any other country, and (while I have now seen a deal of rubbish by both of them) they are interesting and readable (by me that is).[36]

The title of Hugh Kenner's essay, 'Supreme in her Abnormality',[37] speaks for itself. Without inviting the limitations of gender by not writing with the 'I', but with the 'eye' (finding 'the exact words for some experience of the eye'), her work is yet read, firstly, as the production of a woman, and secondly, as a contributor to modernist poetics. William Carlos Williams writes without any such condescension about 'poems such as Miss Moore's [with] their cleanliness, lack of cement, clarity, gentleness . . .'[38] but it is usually Williams, rather than Moore, who is cited as the possessor of these qualities. The cases of Emily Dickinson and Marianne More, then, are not as far removed as one might first have supposed, and all three poets depend on the framing readings which establish a pattern for subsequent response.

Their similarity can be located in their relation to the language, particularly their counterpointing of the rhetorical and cultural codes which govern discourse. Henry Gifford suggests that 'their interest in the capacities of the English language both learned and colloquial, in its American variety' allows for a comparison to be made between Emily Dickinson and Marianne Moore. Of the latter, he suggests:

> [her] work harbours a museumful of detail, drawn from her own observation, from her readings in such books as *Strange Animals I Have Known*, from art galleries and from *The Illustrated London News*. She has assembled all these objects and impressions for the imagination to work into a new arrangement. So with language, the specimens of its use for a myriad purposes are presently given their place in a poem.[39]

Gifford describes Emily Dickinson's and Marianne Moore's similarities of language usage, whereby latinate and colloquial phrases are juxtaposed in order to explore the possibilities of words as a set of correspondences. He suggests that because these go beyond accidental similarities of nationality and gender, they can be explained as a shared philologic interest. However, in the light of earlier discussion regarding the placing of the subject in language, I would like to suggest that because gender and language are inseparably bound together, Moore's modernist preoccupation with language, not only in the process of signification, but also through tone, movement, and arrangement on the page, effects the same questioning of dominant cultural discourses as the idiosyncrasies of vocabulary and syntax of Emily Dickinson. In fact, the language of all three poets I am considering carries the cadence and persuasiveness of the conversational. If Plath's language problematizes domestic niceties in:

> Kindness glides about my house
> Dame Kindness, she is so nice[40]

and Emily Dickinson's juxtaposes simple colloquialisms with various power or 'high' discourses:

> I'm ceded – I've stopped being Theirs –
> The name they dropped upon my face
> With water – in the country church
> Is finished using, now[41]

then Marianne Moore's is a collage of the visual artist's language:

> In that Persian miniature of emerald mines
> raw silk – ivory white, snow white,
> oyster white and six others –
> that paddock full of leopards and giraffes –
> long lemon-yellow bodies
> sown with trapezoids of blue

the discourse of 'high' or classical culture:

> That is with Hercules
> in the garden of the Hesperides

and

> the black obsidian Diana
> everyday banalities or cliches:
> a very trivial object indeed

and

> I am yours to command

with phrases that have the weight of proverbial wisdom:

> Everything to do with love is a mystery

and

> the heart rising
> In its estate of peace
> as a boat rises
> with the returning of water

Emily Dickinson's and Sylvia Plath's poems were read earlier as fractured, or disrupted, narratives, where key elements are left indeterminate, like the subject/object relationship in 'I gave myself to him', and the father/lover role in 'Daddy'. It is, however, quite possible for readers to recuperate a time continuum in each of these poems, and string out a narrative line from the given elements. The poem 'Marriage'[42], from which the fragments quoted above have been taken, denies in a much more resolute way the efficacy of such a strategy. Connotation and chains of signification spin off from the title, but there is no closing gesture, no structured machinery or fixed skyline on which to pin a final reading. Marianne Moore's writing exemplifies the way in which texts escape structure, so that what is foregrounded is that

> [each] code is a perspective of quotations, a mirage of structures . . .
> they are so many fragments of something that has always been already read, seen, done, experienced[43]

The horizons which open up to the reader are boundless. The story of the Fall with its determined role for woman:

> See her, see her in this common world
> the central flaw
> in that crystal-fine experiment

is interwoven with what might be the musings of a cautious civil servant on a prepared public statement:

> This institution,
> Perhaps one should say enterprise
> out of respect for which
> one says one need not change one's mind . . .

'Of marriage there is no solution in the poem and no attempt to make marriage beautiful',[44] William Carlos Williams commented in 1925. Today few readers would expect a 'solution' to either a poem or marriage. Instead, they are drawn into a chain of significance that sets 'public promise', 'obligation', 'central flaw', 'dazzled by the apple', 'ritual of marriage', and 'condemned to disaffect', against 'a striking grasp of opposites', 'Liberty and union/now and forever', whatever the latter's irony. The effect of reading is of encountering what appear to be half-remembered quotations that open out onto other discourses, other 'solutions'. For example, this passage, which consists of relative pronouns whose referents are lost:

> the O Thou
> to whom, from whom
> without whom nothing

seems to echo Milton's account in *Paradise Lost*, book IX, of Adam and Eve's dialogue after the Fall, where Adam's declaration of solidarity for Eve soon turns to recrimination. Milton's high-sounded speeches are represented in outlining collocations that are empty of reference, void of meaning. Is 'the uncertain footing of a spear' a reference to Worcester's promise of adventure to Hotspur in *Henry IV Part I*, which the former describes as an 'unsteadfast footing of a spear'? This would encode mock-heroic, false bombast and mistaken promise. Ironically, this is not the source that Marianne Moore cites in her notes, which list 'statements that took my fancy which I tried to arrange plausibly'.[45] She gives the original as Hazlitt's *Essay on Burke's Style*, which hints at the kind of infinite regress to which language is subject, from Moore to Hazlitt to Shakespeare to Holinshed.

The general effect of quotation from sources which are not part of any central literary canon (in contrast with Eliot's practice), is of a fracturing and disintegration of a multiplicity of discourses and voices. These include the statesmanlike, the epic, the political and philosophical, and the journalistic, all of which bear on marriage but none of which is granted precedence or given the power of explication. The effect is of diffusion, rather than a gathering together of the shards and fragments of a fractured culture. The poem's unity depends on the confident tone of an orator, sure of the material under discussion, illustrating ideas with measured aphorisms: 'equally positive in demanding a commotion/and stipulating quiet', 'that striking grasp of opposites/opposed each to the other, not to unity'. The meanings of specific words or units of text are subordinated to the rhetorical rhythms or pulsations of the patterns of language, which create expectations of a serious philosophical statement that are undercut by the veering away from a summative statement. Language, rather than marriage, is the subject of the interrogation, and it is the 'high' language encapsulating a predominantly male perspective that has been invaded and subverted through its being wrenched out of context, and placed into a collage of unresolved contests for meaning. In a discussion of the 'lyric of feeling' which includes a discussion of Emily Dickinson, Cora Kaplan concludes:

> However formal their presentations, they [lyrics] are, by virtue of their fragmentary and opaque language, torn away from a chain of meaning which would secure them to larger interpretation. Their sybilline quality means that they can be inserted into almost any theory about women as subjects, and about high culture as an expression of women's suppressed and distorted subjectivity.[46]

Kaplan warns that because of their undecidability such texts are most frequently appropriated by feminist critics, as well as their male counterparts, to 'buttress interpretations of women's experience drawn from their prose fictions', or to 'substantiate specific psychoanalytical theories of femininity'. What is a far more important consideration, she points out, is the way in which the poets, by interrogating states for which they have no ready explanation, cause the reader to interrogate her own theory and politics.

Although the writing practices of the poets under consideration cannot be said to disrupt discursive practices to the extent that they achieve the new Symbolic that Juliet Mitchell posits as the goal for feminist poets, or a practice of Utopian feminism after the French sense, each poet enacts the difficulty of the engendered subject's entry into the Symbolic realm of public discourse by disrupting the smooth generation of meaning.

I began this chapter by demonstrating how conventional habits of receiving women's writing have provided a very limited and limiting frame of responsive readings. If we accept the importance of making explicit those competencies that are expected of the reader within an academic institution, it is equally important to establish that the process of such a rule-governed activity is never innocent, and that the final outcome of a reading will be as dependent on the framing context and interpretive conventions, as it will on the specificity of formal elements. Wolfgang Iser, cited earlier as representative of one strand of reader-response criticism, does allow for 'the reader's own disposition', including such factors as 'memory, interest, attention, and mental capacity'. These, however, are subjective factors, and cannot account adequately for the kind of cultural reinforcement to which certain modes of interpretation are subjected. It is Barthes's *S/Z*, with its emphasis on the drawing together of cultural codes by the reader (who is 'not innocent'), as the site of the intersection of a plurality of intertextual networks, that provides a better working model for such readings. It is a method that stresses the process of structuration, rather than the structure, and it allows the reader to reassemble the voices of disparate discourse, different codes, so that the female psyche thus engendered can be interrogated as a function of language, rather than mythologized as an absence or silence which cannot be overcome.

5 No Poetry for Ladies: Gertrude Stein, Julia Kristeva and Modernism

Sara Mills

Introduction

This chapter is intended to be a working through, working with, working out, of Julia Kristeva in relation to modernism. With a complex and controversial theorist such as Julia Kristeva it was felt that a straightforward 'application' of her theory to a reading of texts would be a significant reduction of the potential of such a theoretical position and could have the effect of falsely containing French semiotic theory within the comfortable range of New Criticism. Such a move must be resisted, and it is for this reason that the analysis section concerns itself as much with the shortcomings as with the advantages of the theory. Indeed, Kristeva herself states:

> Literature does not exist for semiotics. It does not exist as an utterance like others and even less as an aesthetic object. It is a *particular semiotic practice* which has the advantage of making more accessible than others the problematics of the production of meaning posed by a new semiotics, and consequently it is of interest only to the extent that it is envisaged as irreducible to the level of an object for normative linguistics.[1]

Therefore, Kristeva's critical text can be *read* through the discussion of the literary text, as much as the literary text can be read through Kristeva. In her early work at least, she is very drawn to this idea of semiotics as a self-critical discipline; she says: 'At every moment of its elaboration, semiology thinks its object, its instrument, and their relation, thus thinks itself, and becomes in turning back upon itself the *theory of the science that it is*.'[2] Thus, a discussion of Kristeva's work should be a discussion of its gaps and silences, how it does *not* work, as much as how it does. Therefore, in this chapter, I have felt it necessary to augment Kristeva's theory of text production with a theory of text reception, to enable the analysis to take account of gender, an extremely important factor in much female modernist writing. As Claire Pajaczkowska remarks, Kristeva's work has been generally appropriated by English literature departments to 'buttress the monument of the (literary) masterpiece';[3] this is not the intention of this chapter, since instead of discussing Kristeva's work in relation to male canonical texts, a rather more marginalized figure has been chosen, that of Gertrude Stein. Furthermore, rather than buttressing the canon of male modernist writers, it hopes to question their status through an analysis of the exclusion of such writers as Stein. As Sandra Gilbert and Susan Gubar suggest, modernism is a particularly male domain, as can be seen from Joyce's comment on the publication of Eliot's *The Waste Land* which he felt 'ends [the] idea of poetry for ladies.'[4] It is this 'poetry for [and by] ladies', and perhaps 'poetry unfit for ladies' which will be the focus of attention of this chapter. In this way, Kristeva's model of textual production is supplemented by a model of text reception.

Julia Kristeva
Most Anglo-American feminist criticism concerns itself with the analysis of realist prose, and it is for this reason that Kristeva's work is interesting in that she theorizes modernist writing. Toril Moi notes that Kristeva is not interested in literary texts as such, since her work on modernist poetry

> ... focuses on the signifying process, that is to say, that she is trying to answer the question of exactly *how* language comes to mean [signify], but also the equally important question of what it is that *resists* intelligibility and signification.[5]

I have chosen for this analysis Kristeva's early work *Revolution in Poetic Language*, which was published in 1974 in France, because it is there that she lays out most clearly her position on the revolutionary nature of experimental writing. She has since written against many of her statements in this book, especially their political nature, stating, for example, in a conference at Warwick in 1987 that *Revolution in Poetic Language* was not a political work; however, the reader can choose to read it as a political text or as Kristeva now wishes it to be read. It can also be usefully drawn upon as a position against which to react for the purposes of discussing female modernist poetry. Much of the book is concerned with theoretical discussion and it is this section which has been translated into English; but she also attempts to read modernist writing in the light of this theoretical position and analyses the writing of Mallarmé and Lautréamont.

Kristeva formulates a theory of the child's psychic development in relation to language, and then goes on to describe an analogous process at work in the language of experimental texts. In the following section, I will consider this theorizing on the child's development, and the relation between this and experimental texts, particularly the role of the thetic break and fetishism.

Revolution in Poetic Language is truly interdisciplinary in that it is based on Lacanian psychoanalysis as well as linguistics, semiology, and philosophy; this interaction of subject areas leads to a useful critical position on psychoanalysis. Whilst her psychoanalytic base is Lacan, in terms of the reading of texts her most important difference from him is in her discussion of the *symbolic* and the *semiotic*. For Lacan, the Imaginary is the prelinguistic, undifferentiated sphere within which the child experiences the world. The Symbolic Order is the sphere of language, and for Lacan, with the acquisition of language, the child also becomes aware of the difference between herself and other beings and of herself as a gendered subject. The Symbolic is also the sphere of patriarchal and institutional control, since for Lacan it is characterized as the sphere of the Law of the Father. The child has to take up a subject position within this system – for male children, the position is aligned with the Law of the Father, and for female children, there is only the choice of lack.

Kristeva takes Lacan's model of signification, but redefines it through grafting a Kleinian stress onto the pre-Oedipal period and the role of the mother.[6] Instead of the Symbolic and the Imaginary being two separate spheres, as they are for Lacan, with the Imaginary taking some sort of shadowy role in the background, bubbling up to the surface from time to time, Kristeva emphasizes the active and continuing role of the semiotic, her replacement for the Imaginary, in the process of signification. In the pre-Oedipal stage, the semiotic drives or *pulsions*, as Kristeva prefers to call them, articulate a *chora* which she describes as a 'non-expressive totality formed by the drives and their stases in a motility that is as full of movement as it is regulated.'[7] Thus, the *chora* is an entity that is not spatial and which is traversed by oral and anal impulses; and whilst we can describe it, we can 'never give it axiomatic form' (p. 94).

It is the semiotic which is most important for the understanding of the development of the child in language, and by stressing the importance of this stage, and its continuing presence in all language use, Kristeva finds a way around the problem of the supposed female 'lack' in Lacan. Kristeva understands the symbolic as a patriarchal order and, unlike Lacan, she looks for possible forms of resistance to it.[8] One form of resistance is to build the semiotic more thoroughly into the process of signification; that is, in order to communicate, one draws upon the semiotic as well as the symbolic, although generally the symbolic is dominant. A further way in which Kristeva resists the dominance of the symbolic is to concentrate her attention on the pre-Oedipal stage. As I noted above, the semiotic consists of drives and impulses which traverse the body, oral and anal sensations to which the body responds, by either resisting or submitting. Although Kristeva is never very explicit about this, the semiotic, because in it the pre-Oedipal mother is of utmost importance, seems to be a position which is available most easily for female subjects. The impulses are organized around the figure of the mother, as she says: 'The mother's body . . . becomes the ordering principle of the semiotic *chora*' (p. 95). However, Kristeva should be interpreted as saying that 'feminine' subjects can be seen to have a more closely linked position *vis-à-vis* the semiotic. This seems to be close to falling into the problematic binaries of male-logical, female-illogical, male-plenitude, female-lack, unless we stress that the feminine subject position is available to both male and female subjects. In later work, such as 'Woman can never be defined', she states quite clearly that it is not 'woman' which she is discussing, but feminine positions which may be adopted: 'The belief that "one is a woman" is almost as absurd and obscurantist as the belief that "one is a man".'[9]

In *Revolution in Poetic Language*, Kristeva describes how these processes in the development of the child have some relation to the construction of texts:

> All these various processes and relations, anterior to the sign and syntax, have just been identified from a genetic perspective as previous and necessary to the acquisition of language, but not identical to language. Theory can 'situate' such processes and

relations diachronically within the process of the constitution of the subject precisely because *they function synchronically within the signifying process of the subject himself*, i.e. the subject of the cogitatio. Only in *dream* logic, however, have they attracted attention, and only in certain signifying practices, such as the text, do they dominate the signifying process. (p. 96)

Here, Kristeva seems to be using the word *text* in the way Roland Barthes has used it, to mean a piece of writing where the reader is forced to make an effort to understand, and is involved in the process of meaning.[10] Kristeva also seems to be drawing on Roman Jakobson's notion of the 'poetic' function, whereby in certain texts there is a concentration on the poetic function so that attention to language is foregrounded.[11] Indeed, she goes on to discuss the ' "mysterious" functioning of literature as a rhythm made intelligible by syntax' (p. 97). Thus, in experimental, avant-garde texts, it is the materiality of words which is focused upon. Kristeva is therefore radically departing from the Lacanian model of language by stating that the semiotic is influential in all signification, but also that, in certain types of texts which are experimenting with meaning and language, the semiotic itself is foregrounded.

The semiotic is at play in all signifying practices to a certain degree, and not just in experimental texts. As Ann Rosalind Jones says, 'The semiotic . . . enters into an adversary relationship with the symbolic, persistently pushing against rational discourse but never dissolving it into pure (psychotic) nonsense' (p. 59). It is this mixture of semiotic and symbolic which Kristeva terms *signifiance*, where the energies of the semiotic surface to challenge the symbolic, but are nevertheless represented through the medium of the symbolic.

For Kristeva, the semiotic surfaces, or can be called upon, in poetic writing, in the rhythmic patterns and in elements which seem to resist 'making sense'. She says:

> All poetic 'distortions' of the signifying chain and the structure of signification . . . yield under the 'residues of first symbolizations'. . . . In 'artistic' practices the semiotic – the precondition of the symbolic – is revealed as that which destroys the symbolic. (p. 103)

The semiotic is called upon by 'feminine' subjects who resist the Law of the Father, and 'the unsettled and questionable subject of poetic language (for whom the word is never uniquely sign) maintains itself at the cost of reactivating [the] repressed instinctual maternal element.'[12] Thus, by drawing on this maternal energy in the semiotic, poetic language actively works against 'making sense' in a conventional way, and is seen as an attack on the symbolic, whilst still being expressed within its realms.

Kristeva describes the way in which the semiotic manifests itself in poetic language. She describes the drives in a way which is interesting for the analysis of Stein's poetry, for she says 'the term "drive" denotes waves of attack against stases which are themselves constituted by the repetition of these charges' (p. 95). The drives constitute stases and they also constitute the energies which disrupt those stases; these disruptions mark 'discontinuities in what may be called the various material supports susceptible to semiotization: voice, gesture, colours' (p. 96). Here, Kristeva is concerned with the foregrounding of the semiotic in art forms in general; elements such as rhythm, musicality (the musical sound of the individual syllables and words), the presence of 'voice', and the disruption of syntax, type-face and layout are the traces of the stases and motility of the semiotic in poetic texts.

Kristeva is especially interesting in her analysis of the relation between meaning and this musical quality of language in poetic texts, since for her, a new type of meaning is thereby created:

> . . . musicality is not without signification; indeed it is deployed within it. Logical synthesis and all ideologies are present, but they are pulverised within their own logic before being displaced towards something that is no longer within the realm of the idea, sign, syntax and thus *Logos*, but is instead simply semiotic functioning. (p. 114)

And she goes on to say: 'No text, no matter how "musicalized", is devoid of meaning or signification; on the contrary, musicalization pluralizes meanings.' (p. 116)

A further element of Kristeva's work which is of interest, in the context of Gertrude Stein's poetry, is what Kristeva calls the 'thetic break'. She states that this break occurs in the formulations of propositions, that is in the identification of subject and object which is a necessary condition for all signification: 'All enunciation whether of a word or a sentence is thetic. It requires an identification; in other words the subject must separate from and through his image, from and through his objects.' (p. 98). In this way, the thetic can be seen as a compartmentalizing of the subject and that about which she speaks, which must be submitted to in order to 'make sense'.

It is the thetic which is disrupted by the foregrounding of the semiotic. The semiotic is predominant in texts when we are aware of the musicality of the language, the rhythms and repetitions of words and phrases, and when there is a disruption of syntax:

> . . . when the semiotic *chora* disturbs the thetic position by redistributing the signifying order, we note that the denoted object and the syntactic relation are disturbed as well. (p. 108)

Kristeva herself stresses however that whilst 'some . . . contend that one can find in poetry the unfolding of [the] refusal of the thetic, something like a direct transcription of the genetic code' (p. 104), this is in fact impossible, since all texts require structuration and completion.

> This completion constitutes a synthesis that requires the thesis of language in order to come about, and the semiotic pulverises it only to make it a new device – for us, this is precisely what distinguishes a text as *signifying practice* from the 'drifting-into-non-sense' that characterises neurotic discourse. (p. 104)

However, even though all texts are structured and are effects of this thetic break, it can be seen that in some experimental writing, there is a significant difference in terms of propositionality, and subject and object positions, from that in other texts.

Kristeva goes further than many theorists in her description of the thetic and the semiotic, for she states that not only does modernist poetry disrupt meaning within the text, but also that this disruption of the thetic break and of the symbolic has an effect on signification in general:

> . . . when poetic language – especially modern poetic language – transgresses grammatical rules, the *positing* of the symbolic (which mimesis has always explored) finds itself subverted. . . . In imitating the constitution of the symbolic as meaning, poetic mimesis is led to dissolve not only the denotative function but also the specifically thetic function of *positing* the subject. In this respect modern poetic language . . . attacks not only denotation (the positing of the object) but meaning (the positing of the enunciating subject) as well. (p. 109)

A further element of Kristeva's work which is important in this context is the notion of the fetish.[13] Fetishism, for her, is a temporary stasis in signification, and she suggests that this stasis results in a materiality of the sign which is pleasurable. She even suggests that art itself might be 'the fetish par excellence' (p. 115), since the reader is encouraged to concentrate on the surface of the words, their sound and rhythm, as well as on their meaning. But fetishism does not mean that the object of poetic utterance is an object of materiality in itself without necessarily having any signification; no matter how fetishized the poetic object, it is never completely a fetish, since it produces meaning, however diffuse and difficult to grasp; as she says, 'What distinguishes the poetic function from the fetishist mechanism is that it maintains a *signification.*' (p. 115)

To sum up, there are several elements in Kristeva's work which can be used in the discussion of poetic texts: the semiotic, the thetic and the fetish. And, according to Kristeva, these elements, when drawn upon by writers, can lead not only to a revolution of the rules of signification, but also to a revolution in the reader's position and in social structures. It is this assertion of revolutionary potential which I will now turn to.

The type of writing which privileges the semiotic is that which Kristeva labels revolutionary, because for her it is a writing which destabilizes the subject position of the reader. Colin McCabe comes to this conclusion, in his work on James Joyce, when he says 'Joyce's writing produces a change in the relations between reader and text, a change which has profound revolutionary implications.'[14] He goes on to say: 'Joyce's texts . . . refuse the subject any dominant position from which language could be tallied with experience. *Ulysses* and *Finnegan's Wake* are concerned not with representing experience through language but with experiencing language through a destruction of representation' (p. 4). This is a position which is very close to Kristeva, for she states that, as well as disrupting the reading subject's position,

> The disturbance of sentential completion or syntactic ellipsis leads to an infinitization of logical (syntactical) applications. Terms are linked together, but, as a consequence of non-recoverable deletion, they are linked *ad infinitum*. The sentence is not suppressed, it is infinitized. Similarly, the denoted object does not disappear, it proliferates in mimetic, fictional, connoted objects. (p. 109)

For her, a revolution takes place in signification, and this revolution links to a wider destabilization of social relations.[15] Kriseva does not suggest that this type of writing is always revolutionary:

> Multiple constraints – which are ultimately socio-political – stop the signifying process at one or another of the theses that it traverses; they knot it and lock it into a given surface or structure. . . . Among the capitalist mode of production's numerous signifying practices, only certain literary texts of the avant-garde (Mallarmé, Joyce) manage to cover the infinity of the process, that is reach the semiotic *chora*, which modifies linguistic structures. (p. 122)

Although Kristeva claims that this type of use of language is revolutionary in social terms, and she suggests that it only occurs at certain times of political crisis, she is not very specific as to how this revolution takes place. One is led to believe that it is through the disruption of subject positions in 'feminine writing' and through an infinitization of stable meanings. Within Marxist thinking at the time when Kristeva was writing, it was felt that simply changing economic relations was clearly not enough and patterns of thought and understanding had also to be changed. However, whilst this is evident, it is debatable quite how much experimental writing affects the status quo, since experimental writing is read by very few, and Stein is among the least read of modernists. It is further debatable whether even the subject positions of this restricted group of readers are radically destabilized. As Jones says, 'This is a curiously private revolution' (p. 60). However, that is not to suggest that nothing happens because of experimental writing, but perhaps that the term 'revolutionary' is excessive. Whilst one is aware that political change is useless without a similar change in subject positions, it is doubtful whether the link between these can be discussed in the simple way Kristeva does.

There are several problems with Kristeva's work for the purposes of this chapter and the analysis of poetry in general. Firstly, her approach, although very sensitive to the relation of the subject to the production of text, lacks any treatment of the constraints on textual production which lie outside the subject or the context in which an author's work is judged. It seems unclear whether the author is a Romantic individual freely choosing to call upon the semiotic, or whether s/he is an individual manifesting symptoms of psychological disorder. This problem is apparent when Kristeva describes the poet as an individual who experiences 'marked scopophilia' and 'a resistance to the discovery of castration' (p. 113). It is therefore unclear whether one *chooses* the semiotic, or whether the semiotic is simply a *symptom* of some unresolved psychological disorder.

Secondly, it is uncertain whether Kristeva's work can be used for feminist purposes, since on several occasions she has spoken out strongly against feminism, and she has also not addressed the question of women as writers. The 'feminine' writers whom she analyses are all, surprisingly, men. Women feature not as agents within her writing (except as mothers), but as objects of the gaze, as representations by men. Thus, the specificity of female textual production is lost. This does not mean, however, that her work *cannot* be drawn on for the analysis of women's writing, as I hope to show in the analysis of Gertrude Stein's work.

Finally, one very surprising fact about Kristeva's work is that although the theoretical framework is extremely challenging, the readings of specific poems that she herself produces are rather disappointing and verging on the banal. As Jones states:

> Focusing on sound, repetition and disruptions of grammar, she relates [Mallarmé's] written texts to archaic psychosomatic processes. Mallarmé himself had an elaborate theory of the expressive potential of various letters, 'p' suggests a piling up or holding on to riches, 'r' suggests a pushing away, 't' has a stabilising, stopping effect. Such onomatopoeic essentialism is not surprising in a poet, but it is surprising that a post-Saussurean linguist accepts it, given the structuralist insistence on the arbitrariness of sound/meaning links in language. (p. 59)

However, despite these problems, Kristeva's work is extremely useful in that it equips us with a vocabulary for describing experimentation in writing, and the possible effects this has on the reader. It is not necessary to agree with Kristeva that experimental texts instigate the destabilization of the social order, but it is clear that experimental texts affect readers in a different way from realist texts. And what needs to be added to this model is the factor of gender difference.

Female Modernism and Gertrude Stein

Conventional writing on modernism tends to try to characterize this literary trend according to various parameters: firstly, critics such as Malcolm Bradbury and James MacFarlane define modernism as a literary movement which occurs within the period 1890–1930, and as a simple reaction to real world events, such as industrialism, the First World War and changes in social structure. In their attempts to synthesize modernism, they produce a homogenizing account which papers over the cracks in an extremely diverse literary movement.[16] A second trend in the analysis of modernism is that which concentrates on linguistic innovation, on modernism as a style, without considering the social context in which modernist writing was produced.[17]

Many of the critics on modernism ignore the diversity of modernist poetry, ranging from such writers as Ezra Pound and T.S. Eliot to H.D. and Mina Loy; moreover, these critics rarely include women's work within the modernist canon. When they do, they include women's writing on the same terms as male modernist work, as if the conditions of production were essentially similar. Kristeva is part of this tradition, in that she does not analyse female modernist writing at all. This is perhaps so that her category of the 'feminine' position will not be confused with 'female', but her remarks on women writers in general suggest that this is not the only reason, and that for her, female writing is too obsessed with women's themes to be interesting. Her discussion of modernist women's writing in *On Chinese Women* is in fact, as Jones notes, rather disturbing in that she suggests that the experimental writing of certain female writers, such as Sylvia Plath, was a contributing factor to their suicide.[18]

When female modernism is discussed as a separate category, usually by feminists, it is invariably in relation to biographical details. Although the histories of female modernists are fascinating, the relevance of the details of, for example, their sexual preference to a discussion of writing is debatable. Gillian Hanscombe and Virginia Smyers have attempted to produce an overview of the British and American women writers, such as Djuna Barnes, H.D., Dorothy Richardson, and Mina Loy, who have been largely ignored in conventional modernist criticism.[19] They have tried to show that this body of writing is significantly different, but they have done so by positing an unproblematized link between the writers' life styles and the way they wrote. As they say,

> Most of these writers were women; and most of their partnerships were not conventional marriages. Was there perhaps a connection? Might this group – what they did, thought and wrote – have something

other than literary experiment to tell us now? Was it for them . . .
evident that a woman artist might not only be original in her art but
must also (to achieve that art) be original in her lifestyle? . . . the
lesbian alternative chosen by many of them is seen to have direct
bearing either on their conditions of work, or on the contents of what
they wrote or both. (xiv/v)

Carolyn Burke also considers that the lives of female modernists and the texts they produced are intricately linked. She suggests that the collage and the splice are the two most important elements of Gertrude Stein's work, in that she juxtaposes elements which are then merged by contiguity; this splicing, she states, 'evokes psychosexual joining',[20] suggesting that there is a similarity here between Stein's writing and her lesbian relationships. She also suggests that we can see reverberations from the term 'collage' (which in French means a couple living together) in Stein's experiments in poetic collage.

Whilst it is necessary to be aware of the specificity of female modernism and its difference from canonical male modernism, lapsing into essentialism is not theoretically useful. Even so, it is impossible to ignore such questions, since Stein, like other lesbians, was forced to develop a form of self-censorship to write about lesbian sexuality, using male characters instead of females and coded words such as 'cow' and 'marriage' to refer to orgasms and love-making. Lilian Faderman states:

> She invents a secret sexual language which can be decoded only
> through familiarity with the body of her work; she includes incidents
> from daily life with Alice which, on the surface, are irrelevant to the
> focus of the work; and she uses repetition and frequent deletion of
> crucial subject or verb, which serves to obfuscate the subject matter.[21]

It is clear that for a lesbian poet like Stein social convention impinges very closely on the production of texts. However, it is simplistic to imagine that texts are produced by life style alone, given the radical questioning of the autonomous creative genius of authors by post-structuralist critics such as Michel Foucault and Roland Barthes.[22] As McCabe says,

> If we are to use psycho-analytic concepts in the analysis of literature
> then it will not be to study the work as a product of the life, for this
> would presume a divorce between symptom and conflict which we
> have seen to be impossible. Psycho-analysis denies to a life that

independence which could allow it to function as origin for the work. What we can attempt to study is how the work relates to the forms in which it is written and how those forms can be understood in relation to the fantasy – to the figuration of desire and sexuality. One will also, inevitably, study a life but it will be in the process of analysing the movement across narrative, plot, character, language. For it is that movement, that interweaving of forms, which constitutes the writer as it constitutes the text. (p. 12)

It is, therefore, not as a consequence of discussing textual difference that life histories or sexual preferences need to be detailed, and the following analysis is an attempt to discuss the difference of female modernism without problematic biographical anecdotes.

Sandra Gilbert and Susan Gubar have also attempted to analyse the specificity of modernist women's writing (if we can call their descriptions and plot summaries analyses). One of the interesting points in their book *No Man's Land* is their discussion of what they term the 'female affiliation complex'; for them, women writers have a complex decision to take as to which writing tradition they are affiliating to, the male or the female. Female modernist writers are obviously a case in point, since the affiliation to the male tradition for them, although not impossible, was more difficult. The male modernist tradition tends to draw more on past literary work and on parody, pastiche or inclusion of elements of past styles – 'logopoeia' as Pound terms it. As Carolyn Burke states, 'In such poetry, this kind of self-referential irony "the citadel of the intelligent" revealed a new poetic sensibility that was at once highly literate and critical' (p. 99); thus, the modernist male writers were at one and the same time destabilising the literary canon and asserting their reverence and indebtedness to it. Such a position was not open to women writers in this period to the same extent. There are few women writers who indulge in literary reference and parody (with the possible exception of H.D.), since their relation to the poetic tradition is a problematic one.[23] However, instead of thinking of female modernism as a lack, Burke suggests that 'we think about the female modernists as involved in a revisionary project that critiques the (perhaps unconsciously) phallogocentric principles implicit in male modernisms'. (p. 116)

It is a matter of much speculation how much female modernism is, in essence, different to male modernism and how much it has been *judged* to be different. Gilbert and Gubar describe the problematic literary representations of writing women at this time, and see this as a symptom of the fear engendered in male writers by the proliferation of women writers. The reception of female modernist texts can be seen as a product of this 'nervous[ness] about female literary power' (p. 143) on the part of the male critic.

The question with female modernist texts is whether the text is different in itself or whether it is the reception which has made the difference. By joining Kristeva to a more materialist approach we are able to historicize the production and reception of the text, without losing sight of the constraints on the author as a gendered subject.

Gertrude Stein has generally been received in a rather negative way by the critical tradition; she was attacked by Tristan Tzara for 'falsifying essential Modernist principles and for her underlying simplicity'.[24] She is also termed a 'prose-poet' by Bradbury and MacFarlane, rather than a poet, which is similar to the attempt to label women's poetry 'verse'.[25] Some conventional critics have already tried to assimilate Stein to a psychoanalytic reading; for example, David Lodge states: 'it seems that Gertrude Stein was at this time deliberately and programmatically cultivating a kind of writing corresponding to the Similarity Disorder or Selection Deficiency type of aphasia of which Jakobson speaks',[26] and he goes on to show that her later writing resembles 'the speech of aphasics suffering from Jakobson's second disorder, Contiguity Disorder or Contextual Deficiency' (p. 488). This quotation illustrates the problems of a crude psychoanalytic reading, in that women's writing, or experimental writing in general, can be read as a type of disorder or lack. Many critics do not read Stein, and in fact a great many of them assert that all of her writing is the same: Lodge gives an extract from *The Making of Americans* (1906–8), after which he says, 'And so on' (p. 487). Thus, just as in her lifetime when she was forced to publish her work herself, Stein's work is not taken seriously by critics.

For many critics, reading Stein and writing critical essays on her is a question of gaining control over her, of being able to capture the meaning of Stein, to produce one reading. Lodge, for example, says:

> What she was after was to make 'a whole present of something that it had taken a great deal of time to find out' – that is, to capture the

living quality of a character or experience she had long observed or brooded over without giving the impression of *remembering* it. It was a technique of repetition, though she denied that it was repetition, and compared her method to the (metonymic) art of film, because 'each time the emphasis is different just as the cinema has each time a slightly different thing to make it all be moving'. (p. 487/8)

Lodge here is willing to abandon his usual belief in intentionality and ignore statements which do not fit in with his Jakobsonian system of analysis.

We should thus be aware that not only is a text's meaning and status a result of pressures and constraints upon the producer of the text, but also of similar pressures and constraints on those who interpret and circulate the text.

Gertrude Stein experimented with a wide variety of styles and subject matters. This wide stylistic range is often ignored by critics, who tend to concentrate on one particular style which has become recognizable as Steinian. A further factor which many critics ignore when approaching her work is what Burke terms her 'gender-consciousness' (p. 100). It is almost as if the only way that her work can be discussed is in respect of how similar to male modernists it is, and thus the foregrounding of gender is not mentioned. Stein said that 'literature – creative literature – unconnected with sex is inconceivable'.[27] Her views of textual production are surprisingly similar to Kristeva's in that she has the notion of the 'composition', an amalgam of cultural structures which are reflected in textual productions.

I have chosen two sections of a long poem by Stein called 'Patriarchal Poetry'. The poem is composed of many different styles of writing and various subject matters loosely connected to the notion of patriarchy. The first section is perhaps most stereotypically Stein and it is the type of work by which most critics characterize her.

Let her be to be to be to be let her be to be be let her to be let her to be let her be to be when is it that they are shy.
Very well to try.
Let her be that is to be let her be that is to be let her be let her try.
Let her be let her be let her be to be to be shy let her be to be let her be to be let her try.
Let her try

Let her be let her be let her be let her be to be to be let her be let her try.
To be shy.
Let her be.
Let her try²⁸

    The best way to approach Stein's work is to read it out loud; in this way the reader gets a sense of the rhythmic quality of the words and their positioning, and as she reads, the musicality of the repeated phrases begins to take on a life of its own. By repeating certain phrases, one becomes aware of the rhythmic patterns or pulsions of the phrases, so that a highly complex but ordered rhythm of phrases is emitted. In this way, the reader becomes aware of the way rhythm is present in every communicative act; the rhythm of words is a part of the communicative process, but we are not generally aware of the rhythmic quality of our speech – we tend to concentrate more on the content. This rhythmic quality seems to correspond quite closely to the semiotic, where rhythmic qualities and musicality are the most important features. The reader begins to get a sense not of the meaning of the words, although that is not totally lost, but of the effect these words have when they are repeated. It is very like the effect of repeating a mantra, in that the reader begins to lose sight of the communicative value of the word. In a mantra one loses the sense of the communicative value and the materiality of the word, since it is a vehicle for the achievement of a state of higher consciousness. But in Stein's work, it is the very *materiality* of the word which is the focus of attention. Words begin to be seen, not as parts of communicative acts, but as sounds which add up to a rhythmic pattern. It is, as Allon White says, 'a refusal to conceal or repress the signifier, the material operation of language itself'.²⁹

    In this section of 'Patriarchal Poetry', the reader is aware that the functioning of the semiotic cannot be made manifest, except through the symbolic. However, although the words and phrases are part of the symbolic, they are disrupted by the semiotic pulsations, broken up by the base line of 'be'. It is this interdependence of the semiotic and the symbolic which is evident even in the most experimental writing.

    In this style, Stein seems to be closest to Cubist painting, as Bradbury says:

> Her methods are synchronic, a-logical, dependent on repetition and accumulating verbal motif; lexical simplicity generates complexity by

patterned reformation, a mode clearest in character in some of her verbal portraits, which have direct Cubist analogies. (p. 636)

By juxtaposing elements of the subject matter and splicing these elements together, as in Cubism, a new meaning for the subject matter is achieved. Cubism was less concerned with repetitions of elements than with the rearrangements of elements to expose the two-dimensionality of painting, and to expose illusionism. In a similar way, through her use of repetition, Stein achieves a similar exposure of illusionism in language, the illusion of reference. Words themselves become fetishes – they reveal themselves as barriers to communication – rather than windows onto the world, and they impede the movement from word to world.

In a strange way, the reader understands all of the words and yet does not understand them in combination. All of the phrases, 'Let her be', 'Let her try' and 'let her be shy' make sense in isolation, but once spliced together like this, their meaning begins to be transformed. In this example particularly, the words are 'infinitized', in that through their repetition a complete, stable meaning is never bestowed upon them but always deferred. That is not to say that each repetition of a phrase is the same. Most critics when discussing Stein's phrase 'A rose is a rose is a rose . . .' usually gloss this as referring to the endlessness of tautological statements; however, it can be read to state that the first 'rose' in the phrase is in fact completely different to the second and succeeding 'roses'. Thus in this section, as the reader reads through the poem, the phrase 'let her be' changes in meaning and tone, because of its appearance in a variety of contexts and because of the very fact of having been repeated. Stein said:

> A noun is the name of anything, why after a thing is named write about it? A name is adequate or it is not. If it is adequate then why go on calling it, if it is not the calling it by its name does no good.[30]

Thus, Stein is not concerned with simply 'communicating', that is, with the reference of the words, but she is interested in experimenting with the meanings which are generated by the juxtapositions of words and phrases. In many ways this is the 'revolution of the word' referred to by McCabe;[31] in this type of writing 'the word is never uniquely sign'. The word is no longer a simple vehicle which transmits an idea or a message but its materiality is focused upon; we are forced to take notice of the word as word.

The reader is called upon to make an effort to make sense of the words, and if she knows something of Stein's work, she will probably realize that she will not be gratified in 'making sense' of, or finding the key to it all. Because the poem does not follow the conventions for punctuation, with the phrase 'let her be', the reader is not sure if it is 'meant' in the sense of 'leave her alone' or whether it is a false start for 'let her be shy', or whether it means 'let her exist'. In a sense, the phrase 'means' all of these possibilities and words are thus infinitized. Stein's work has the possibility of multiple interpretations, because it is not 'anchored' in the way that other texts are; the elements which normally limit a text's meanings are omitted. It is a different type of reading to that of reading a novel or non-experimental poetry, and a certain effort is demanded of the reader. Here the reader knows that she probably will not be able to gloss the words with a phrase like 'Stein is trying to say this or this'. Thus, a very different subject position is mapped out for the reader – one where making sense is not guaranteed at the end of the reading. For most readers this is not a particularly comfortable reading position, and this is part of the reason why Stein is so little read.

Many readers, assuming as Lodge does that Stein's work is the same all the way through – simple endless repetitions of the same meaningless or minimally meaningful phrases – read only shortened versions of the texts, or choose to read the more self-contained of her works, such as 'Tender Buttons', 'Study Nature' and 'Dates', where there seems to be a clear subject to the work, around which a meaning can be constructed. In the poem called 'Dates', for example, the reader begins to piece together (with some difficulty) some sort of narrative through the association of certain words in the poem, 'Dates – worry – pies and pies – Wednesday – add send dishes', since the poem has the style of a hastily written shopping list or *aide memoire*.[32] (It is still possible for the triple meaning of dates, that is, appointments, chronological points, and food, to hold simultaneously within the text.)

Thus, it is possible to construct a cohesive meaning for some of the poems. However, that is not to say that Stein's more experimental work is meaningless; it obviously does have meaning, since she is using words which are recognizably words in the English language, and she has joined them into small phrases which are also recognizable as phrases. What is innovatory in her work is that she has put phrases together which could possibly co-occur, but she has repeated this process so that meaning is deferred. There is a fetishistic unwillingness to complete the sentence, a desire to hold back and to hold on to the word itself. The meaning of her poems is thus of a very different nature to that of other poetry, since, with most poetry, the reader assumes that with sufficient work, and knowledge of other poets, a point will be reached where a determinate meaning will be achieved. With Stein, this meaning process is not the same, since a different model of communication is involved. Repetition of words normally leads to breakdown of communication, but Stein is experimenting with what repetition can mean, if we give up a model of language based on the notion of perfect communication.[33] It is surprising how much it is possible to understand even with poems which seem potentially impossible to interpret, and one begins to 'sense' meanings that the poem has or might have, whilst not being able to state that the poem means *one* particular thing. The 'meaning' of the poem seems to be concerned with the play of meaning itself.[34]

The reader is no longer entirely constrained by linear reading, since it is possible to jump about in such a text and search for meaning to appear later on in the text; there is no reason why this text should be read consecutively. As Kristeva says,

> ... the truth signified by the text is no longer single but plural and uncertain; the object being represented is called into question. The speaking subject risks losing its identity . . . [while] the topic of the text becomes its own semiotic functioning. (p. 61)

The position of the reader is made more complex, because it is not clear where this stream of words is emanating from; we no longer have a clear idea of an author who intends certain effects and certain meanings, and who is guiding her words towards a particular purpose. The words appear almost orphaned, and seem to take on a disturbingly machine-like quality, so that we cannot relate them back to a friendly author-figure whose presence will explain them to us. It is this absence of authoring which also leads to the position of the reader being de-stabilized. As Burke says,

> Stein learned to let the 'I' become just one element among many in a text by submitting her conscious mind to the rhythms of the external world in order to re-create those rhythms on the page. (p. 116)

and she notes that certain contemporary writers have been

influenced by this attempt to permit a 'backing off of the performing ego to allow the mysteries of language to come forward and resonate more fully'.[35] This is clearly resonant of Kristeva's notion of the *sujet-en-proces* – the subject on trial, or in process, where a fixed subject position is impossible.

Analysing the first extract from 'Patriarchal Poetry', using a Kristevan framework, enables us to describe a range of effects in the language which conventional literary terminology does not permit us to do. Although Kristeva is concerned primarily with the production of texts, it is possible to use her theoretical framework for understanding the effects such language use might have on the reading subject.

The second section of 'Patriarchal Poetry' is the following:

> Patriarchal she said what is it I know what it is it is I know I know so that I know what it is so I know so I know what it is. Very slowly. I know what it is it is on the one side a to be her to be his to be their to be in an and to be I know what it is it is he who was an known not known was he was at first it was the grandfather then it was not that in that the father not of that grandfather and then she to be sure to be sure to be sure to be I know to be sure to be I know to be sure to be not as good as that. To be sure not to be sure to be sure correctly saying to be sure to be that. It was that. She was right. It was that.
> Patriarchal Poetry

> A SONNET
> To the wife of my bosom
> All happiness from everything
> And her husband.
> May he be good and considerate
> Gay and cheerful and restful.
> And make her the best wife
> In the world
> The happiest and the most content
> With reason.
> To the wife of my bosom
> Whose transcendent virtues
> Are those to be most admired
> Loved and adored and indeed
> Her virtues are all inclusive
> Her virtues her beauty and her beauties
> Her charms her qualities her joyous nature
> All of it makes of her husband
> A proud and happy man

Patriarchal poetry makes no mistake in estimating the value to be placed upon the best and most arranged of considerations of this in as apt to be not only to be partially and as cautiously considered as in allowance which is one at a time. At a chance at a chance encounter it can be very well as appointed as appointed not only considerately but as it as use.
Patriarchal poetry to be sure to be sure to be sure candidly[36]

This is a quite different style from the earlier example but seems to be offering a similarly subversive reading practice, in two ways. Firstly, the 'semiotic' type of writing undermines the seemingly 'symbolic' type of writing (that is, the 'sonnet') and within the 'symbolic' section we become aware of the 'semiotic' at work. There are elements of similarity in the two sections which enclose the sonnet, which I will call 'the frame'. As in the earlier example, there is much repetition of phrases and words to foreground rhythmic patterns. These framing sections, because they are more varied in the selection of words, seem to be making more sense than in the first example. The reader gets a sense of the problems of articulating the meaning of the concept 'patriarchal', despite the fact that 'I know what it is'. 'Patriarchal' seems to be associated with lineage through the father and the grandfather, possession ('to be her to be his to be their'), and with quality, ('not as good as that'). Thus, although it is difficult to describe 'patriarchal' in a straightforward fashion, Stein attempts to associate words and ideas, and ends, 'She was right. It was that'.

However, what marks this style of poetry off from the previous example is the inset part which is entitled 'a sonnet' (but which is not formally a sonnet, that is, in terms of rhyme, metre, length of line and so on). This 'sonnet' parodies the ideology of romantic love by exaggerating certain sentiments which are normally expressed in the sonnet form. It should be noted that although it is entitled 'A SONNET', it is also framed within another title, 'Patriarchal Poetry', as if the sonnet is being given as an example of this type of poetry. In this way the poetry has to be read as a mediation between these two titles. The very placing of this sonnet between sections of more Steinian experimentation is enough to subvert the type of sonnet on which it is based. The naturalized banalities of romantic love become apparent. Therefore, although the sonnet might be read ironically even if it were not surrounded by experimental writing (since a sonnet addressed from a woman to a woman is fairly subversive), the fact of its positioning makes the reading strategy clear. Even though the symbolic is foregrounded in this section, the proximity of the semiotic disrupts the surface of the normally stable language. The similarity to Cubist collage techniques is evident; the placing of objects existing in the real world within a frame problematizes their position and makes us question their 'naturalness'; here Stein has turned the sonnet into an equally problematic form, by placing it within the parentheses of her 'own' writing.

There is a further way in which the sonnet's singular meaning is subverted, since there are elements in the sonnet which begin to seem very like the frame, for example, there are repetitions of structure and splicings: 'may he be good and considerate/gay and cheerful and restful/the happiest and the most content/loved and adored/her charms her qualities her joyous nature/a proud and happy man'. In this way, within the supposedly straightforward 'symbolic' representation, the reader becomes aware of the presence of the semiotic bubbling up to the surface. It is the simple proximity of Stein's framing style which draws the reader's attention to the rhythms within the sonnet. The reader begins to recognize the elements of the semiotic which are present in the most apparently symbolic of language forms.

Conclusions
With poetry such as Stein's, it is clearly not sufficient to read it as a form of code for her sexual preferences. Although there are passages which refer explicitly to lesbianism, it is not *only* about lesbianism. It can be read as a radical redefinition of the way meaning takes place, not only in poetry but in all discourse. In reading Stein, our models of meaning are dislocated, and we are unsure of what is 'meant'. However, we might ask ourselves whether this destabilized 'I' position for both author and reader amounts to revolution. Ann Rosalind Jones suggests that 'We need to go on asserting the truth of a political "we" as well as a semiotically agitated "I".' (p. 70). And Allon White echoes this view when he says:

> For myself Kristeva's project is a brilliant essay in psychoanarchic aesthetics, but which replaces a repressive, phallocentric logos by something far worse, a 'new' subject, drifting, dispersed, and as politically impotent as it is ever possible to be. (p. 17)

Thus, whilst the destabilizing which goes on in experimental texts is important, a more truly political writing is that which impels action or which changes consciousness, as some of Stein's work does, because of her discussion of patriarchy or sexuality. We might also ask ourselves whether stylistic features can ever be necessarily revolutionary. For example, Kathy Acker's style is similar in many ways to Stein's. In the following example from Acker's *Blood and Guts in High School*[37] the reader notices that there are a great many repetitions, and there is a conscious experimentation with typeface size and positioning.

> I don't even adore my emotions anymore. Whatever the fuck they are.
> Living locked-up in a slave trader's room is easy. I mean you have the same emotions over and over again, the same thoughts, the same body, and after a while you see it's all in your mind: you're stuck to your mind.
> SLAVESLAVESLAVE.
> The only thing I want is freedom. Let me tell you: I don't have any idea what that means. Depending on someone/something who's stable makes me happy. I don't find the external world stable unlike Francis Ponge. To base myself (?) on who/that which is stable and to have no regard for anything else makes me happy.)
> DEFIES WHAT IS: NOT LIFE, BUT OBLIVION
> DEFIES DEFIES DEFIES
> NOT THOUGHT, BUT DEFIES
> every howl of pain is a howl of defiance
> every howl of pain is a howl of romance

Acker's is most definitely not a 'poetry for ladies', since she specializes in the description of sexual encounters and gory details of violence; nor does she constitute a poetry for feminists, because her poetry seems, unlike Stein's, to present without mediation or challenge a range of opinions and actions which reinforce patriarchal power, as in the above example, where a sado-masochistic relationship is portrayed in a neutral or favourable light. It is this difference which a Kristevan analysis is unable to account for – a difference between poetry which attempts in a conscious way to undermine assumptions about power relations and signification, and poetry which ends up uncritically reinforcing them. Only by reintroducing at this point, not a simple idea of intentionality, but an awareness of particular contexts in which the text is produced and received, can we ensure a fully historical and political, rather than a formalist, approach.

6 Difficult subjects: Black British Women's Poetry

Patrick Williams

> How many people today live in a language that is not their own? Or no longer, or not yet, even know their own and know poorly the major language that they are forced to serve? This is the problem of immigrants, and especially of their children, the problem of minorities, the problem of a minor literature, but also a problem for all of us: how to tear a minor literature away from its own language, allowing it to challenge the language and making it follow a sober revolutionary path? How to become a nomad and an immigrant and a gypsy in relation to one's own language?[1]

With this statement, Gilles Deleuze and Felix Guattari set out a two-part problem: the complex relation to a dominant form of language of people who are in some way distanced from it or disadvantaged by it, and, perhaps no less importantly, the simultaneous desirability and difficulty of a particular strategy of language use by 'native' speakers of that language. Although the distinction is a rather difficult one to draw, this essay will concentrate more on the former aspect. The implications and effects of this situation extend far beyond the realm of culture, but Deleuze and Guattari confine their analysis to literature, especially what they term – as in the quotation above – minor literature. As they say:

> There has been much discussion of the questions 'What is a marginal literature?' and 'What is a popular literature, a proletarian literature?' The criteria are obviously difficult to establish if one does not start with a more objective concept – that of minor literature. Only the possibility of setting up a minor practice of major language from within allows one to define popular literature, marginal literature, and so on.[2]

The final point is also emphasized elsewhere, where they say: 'A minor literature does not come from a minor language; it is rather that which a minority constructs within a major language'.³

The latter is a useful clarification, since it helps to break down what, on the surface at least, is a curious opposition created in the first quotation above, between, on the one hand, immigrants and others whose condition is seen as something unavoidable, something which in addition is passively accepted, and on the other hand, native speakers who are actively opposing or subverting particular linguistic practices. Just what sort of literature is being constructed by Black writers, especially Black women poets, working in England and within the constraints of the English language is the central question which this essay addresses.

It is, of course, a particularly sensitive area: questions of how it should be approached, or whether indeed it should be approached at all, are much in evidence. There are those who would deny 'literary' status to Black writing. There is still the school of thought which says that contemporary literature is not a proper subject for academic study.⁴ There is also the feeling that although Black British writing is valuable, the time may not yet be right for critical analysis of it. As Lauretta Ngcobo says in her introduction to *Let it be told*, 'The time for an extensive critical study of Blackwomen's writing in Britain may not yet have come'.⁵ One of the major problems facing Black writing, however, is precisely the fact that to some people the time never has seemed right, and that in the past serious attention and the notions of value which academic study confers on the object of its examination have constantly been withheld from Black writing. There would seem to be no grounds for doing so any longer.

Questions of who is to write and how to write are no less vexed. The appropriateness of non-Black critics analysing Black writing is open to question in the same way that the participation of men in feminism has recently been scrutinized. Elaine Showalter's strictures on what she calls 'critical cross-dressing'⁶ by men are relevant here, and the urge to something like cultural transvestism needs to be treated with suspicion.⁷ The idea that there is no problem involved in whites analysing Black literature is a legacy of the time when literature (if it was truly literature) was considered 'universal', automatically speaking to all Mankind (I use the term advisedly), and therefore fully comprehensible by all, while the assumed transparency of the properly literary text would present no obstacle to interpretation. Although presented under the guise of neutral academic wisdom, such ideas are an assertion of racial or cultural superiority. White academics have consistently arrogated to themselves the 'natural' ability to elucidate Black literature in a way which would not be held to apply should the situation be reversed. At the same time, Black writers have been encouraged to purge their work of 'parochial' concerns (such as colonialism) and aim for the universal truths embodied in white literature.[8] Nevertheless, in spite of such uninspiring precedents, even for the more theoretically radical or politically committed of Black writers, for instance Gayatri Spivak or Paul Gilroy, there is no *a priori* reason why white critics should not write about Black culture, though the caveats remain numerous.

Just as the activities of white critics need to be regarded with due suspicion, so the literary and cultural theories they use have to be examined for Eurocentric bias. The relevance of Western theory to non-Western culture has been increasingly challenged, and Henry Louis Gates, for example, has argued the urgent need for Black writers and critics to develop their own theories for the analysis of their own cultural products. In the meantime, however, both Black and white critics need to work with existing theories – but which? Of the few theoretical approaches which take any account of the specificity of Black writing, by far the most promising would seem to be the study of colonial discourse, partly because it derives from the work of a non-Western critic (Edward Said) opposed to vested power interests and unexamined assumptions, and partly because of the useful synthesis which Said produces of the work of Foucault and Gramsci. There are, however, a number of problems: the very legitimacy of the synthesis of Post-Structuralism and Marxism which Said makes has been challenged[9]; also, many of the books and articles on colonial discourse which have appeared have worked within the terms laid down by Said. This means that although a number of important critiques have appeared of the way in which, historically, the West has textually and discursively constructed the Orient or Black people as its Other, and of the forms of economic and political domination which these constructs have authorized, nevertheless, non-Western cultures tend to be included in such analyses only as the objects which are produced by Western discourses on them. So although the analyses do not simply repeat the Eurocentric bias of the original discourse of Orientalism (since that is precisely the object of their critique), we are still not much nearer a proper study of non-Western cultural production.

A further problem arises over the extent to which the categories developed for the analysis of colonial discourse are simply transferable to the study of writing produced in the post-colonial period; this is particularly relevant to our purposes, since Black British writing is in the main a post-colonial phenomenon. The problem is especially complex, since although the age of colonialism has (very nearly – the Falklands notwithstanding) ended, the evils of neo-colonialism and economic imperialism are still very much part of the world we inhabit. The complexity is further compounded by the fact that there has been a certain fragmentation (or perhaps productive proliferation) among the critics who come after Said, with some, like Homi Bhabha, being resolutely Post-Structuralist, others, like Abdul JanMohamed, emphasizing the materialist side of colonial discourse theory, and still others producing impressive, sometimes daunting combinations, like Gayatri Spivak, with her articulation of Deconstruction, Marxism and Feminism.

One theoretical approach which has at least the advantage of simplicity, which lacks the problems of periodicity which bedevil the division into colonial and post-colonial, and which, most importantly, addresses Black writing, is the concept of minor literature as developed by Deleuze and Guattari, and it is for these reasons that it is proposed to use it here.

Having, as we saw earlier, stated their belief in the priority of minor literature, Deleuze and Guattari go on to set out in more detail its principal characteristics: firstly, that language in it is, as they say, affected with a high degree of deterritorialization; secondly, that everything in minor literature is political; and thirdly, that everything in it takes on collective value. Although Deleuze and Guattari stress the linguistic side of deterritorialization, its geographical manifestations are, as the opening quotation makes clear, highly likely to be part of the experience of the producers of minor literature. This is very much the case with Black British women writers. Even those who were born in Britain still face the dilemmas of belonging attendant on being part of the Black diaspora. Although most obviously and immediately applicable to those of African descent scattered by slavery and its aftermath, the diaspora also comprises Indians, Chinese and others, enormous numbers of whom were shifted around the globe as sources of cheap labour for the British Empire. The geographical and linguistic displacement did not come to an end with the end of the Empire, however. The power relations which had moved subject peoples and kept them in their place no longer functioned to the same extent, and formerly colonized groups were able to come to Britain in increasing numbers. The fact that many, especially from the West Indies, specifically regarded Britain as the Mother Country only increased the impact of the latest form of deterritorialization which followed the rejection and racist treatment they encountered there.

> The breakdown of the empire increases the crisis, accentuates everywhere movements of deterritorialisation, and invites all sorts of complex reterritorialisations – archaic, mythic, or symbolist.[10]

Deleuze and Guattari are talking here about the end of the Hapsburg Empire, but this is no less true of the situation in the British Empire after 1947. The experience of geographical, linguistic, or psychic displacement, and the attempt to re-establish continuities or certainties (though not necessarily in archaic or mythic terms) is at the heart of much of the poetry produced by Black women in Britain. Geographical deterritorialization is present in very uncompromising form in the work of Meiling Jin, in poems such as 'Strangers in a Hostile Landscape' and 'The Knock'. The hostile landscape is the face Britain presents to the Black immigrant, and the knock, fearfully anticipated, that of the police come to announce arbitrary deportation; 'I have been/right round the globe', says Meiling Jin, 'Not a traveller by choice,/But one who has been dispossessed'.[11] The plight of the dispossessed is compounded by the way in which government legislation turns a country which had previously been – in a legal sense, if no other – home, into another hostile landscape from which they face expulsion in the shape of 'A one-way ticket/To an unknown place/Called Homelands'.[12] Something of the same disquiet is visible in Grace Nichols's poem 'Fear', where seeming incompatibilities of culture mask social injustice, the second-class treatment of Black youth, urban violence . . . a climate of fear for which the speaker feels her daughter is too gentle, suggestive of another displacement, another departure to come.

For those who remain, there are the inevitable absences which follow displacement. The 'island man' in Grace Nichols's poem of that name compensates through dreams, where he summons up

> . . . the sound of blue surf
> in his head
> the steady breaking and wombing

> wild seabirds
> and fishermen pushing out to sea
> the sun surfacing defiantly

From this, however, he

> Comes back to sands
> of a grey metallic soar
> to surge of wheels
> to dull North Circular roar.[13]

In 'Like a Beacon', it is the food of the Caribbean – plantains, saltfish, sweet potatoes – which is a substitute for what has been lost, and which acts as an antidote to the British cold.

Although staying in Britain is a problem, return – temporary or otherwise – to 'the unknown place called Homelands' may be no less so. Many of the poems in Amryl Johnson's collection, whose very title *Long Road to Nowhere* suggests the protracted difficulties of displacement, deal with a return to the Caribbean. Several question explicitly the speaker's relation to her surroundings and her cultural past. A trip in a crowded tourist boat from Trinidad to Tobago ('The New Cargo Ship') evokes memories of the slave ship which first brought the people there, and the suffering this entailed. The speaker suffers, too, from unsureness of place, of relation to these events: 'Where was I in all this?' is asked repeatedly, amidst the fear that then as now she might have been in some ways detached, apart, observer rather than participant. In 'Qu'est-ce qu'elle dit?', the local Keskidee bird seems to interrogate the speaker in images of uncertain journeying: where are you going?, how will you get there?, what will you find there? – questions which the speaker realizes may never be properly answered.

One reason for the lack of straightforward answers may be the element of ambivalence in the experience of return. Although the sequence of poems centring on the pre-Lenten carnival of J'Ouvert is powerfully celebratory, it opens with a rather sombre example ('Far Cry') which, though it chronicles a form of journey from slavery to independence, is nevertheless full of images of suffering and awareness of the ineradicable effect of the violent past on the present. There is a kind of ambivalence, too, in the suggestion that only one person (the speaker?) can unite the disparate strands of the people's experience, but that she will end, silenced, as the carnival ends in the silence of Ash Wednesday. In the same way, after the celebration the sequence ends with three poems ('River', 'And sea', 'River and Sea') which seem characterized by a growing ambivalence towards the island, apparently as a result of the people's acceptance of the negative aspects of their existence, which culminates in a rejection, or at least a determination not to be part of it:

> There was a time when I would sit
> for hours and watch
> the people of the River
> lying easy in the sea
> ecstatic in their pollution
> And then one day
> I said
> no more[14]

The problem may be that same easy materialism whose general acceptance troubles the speaker in 'Far Cry'. Material benefits 'leave small space for doubt/and much room for indulgence', and mask the unequal nature of their distribution; at the same time, they cut people off from those '. . . few with a particular brand/of awareness [who] came to show their people/another road which found them/coming towards the fire'.[15] And the suggestion is that the speaker opts for the refining fire of political commitment rather than the sea of physical comfort.

The journey to the Caribbean in *Long Road to Nowhere* is followed by the return to Britain and the experience which produces the title poem. The realization which is at its centre recalls Eliot in the *Four Quartets*, not so much the idea that 'Home is where one starts from', since the recurrent problem is precisely whether there is a home at all, but rather 'And the end of all our exploring/Will be to arrive where we started/And know the place for the first time',[16] the signal difference being the utterly un-Eliot-like emotion which is engendered. The realization is, among other things, that this has indeed been a long road to nowhere, both in the sense of having in the end come back to the emptiness which characterizes London, and also in the sense of having made no personal progress, of not having 'got anywhere'. Nevertheless, this painful recognition does jolt the speaker into an act of affirmation – to which we shall return later.

If Amryl Johnson's book represents a long meditation on the problem of geographical and psychological displacement, then the second – linguistic – aspect of deterritorialization is embodied and enacted in her poems and those of others, rather than being reflected upon. This is most obviously so in the relation between standard English and dialect, Creole or Nation language in the works of these writers. Regarding the analogous situation of Kafka and other Jews in Prague, Deleuze and Guattari talk of

> the impasse that bars access to writing . . . and turns their literature into something impossible – the impossibility of writing, the impossibility of writing in German, the impossibility of writing otherwise.[17]

The restricted access of Black people in Britain to adequate education, and, even more so, to the rarified sphere of high culture is a shameful fact which gives rise to the first of the 'impossibilities', that of not writing. What Deleuze and Guattari mean by this is that in minority groups the pressure on those who can produce literature to do so is so great as to make the idea of not writing an impossibility, and this group pressure is something to which we will return in terms of collectivity. The impossibility of writing otherwise comprises several different factors: there is the (variable) distance of the writer from the original culture, which results, for example, in some Black writers having only standard English available as a medium of expression; there is also the dominance of standard linguistic and literary forms which can make any thought of deviance seem an impossibility. In her introduction to *Gifts from my Grandmother*, Meiling Jin talks of her struggle with Wordsworthian forms and sentiments which continued, against her will, to structure her poetry, and of her present truce with them, and the English language in general.

For poets of Caribbean descent, there is usually the possibility of an alternative means of expression in Creole, but here there is still the oppressive weight of the dominant forms to be removed or come to terms with. For them, the use of Creole is a deliberate attempt at reterritorialization, and some of them, like Valerie Bloom in 'Yuh Hear 'Bout?', make forceful use of it:

> Yuh hear bout di people dem arres
> Fi bun dung di Asian people dem house?
> Yuh hear bout di policemen dem lock up
> Fi beat up di black bwoy widout a cause?
> Yuh hear bout di MP dem sack because im refuse fi help

im coloured constituents in a dem fight gainst deportation?
Yuh no hear bout dem?
Me neida.[18]

This use of Creole is apparently so uncompromising that it is deemed necessary (even in a book on Black women writers) to provide a 'translation' alongside it! Grace Nichols, on the other hand, uses Creole in a way which is more restrained and contrastive, combining it with standard English in the same poem. Thus, for example, in the sequence 'The Fat Black Woman's Poems', descriptions in standard English are interspersed with sections in Creole which represent the Fat Black Woman's thoughts and utterances. This produces humorous effects, yet at the same time serves to highlight the Fat Black Woman's separation from the white, standard English speaking, world around her. Amryl Johnson's eponymous granny in 'Granny in de Market Place' is a self-possessed individual like the Fat Black Woman, and her hilarious encounters with the market stall-holders are conducted entirely in Creole.

The persistent but ill-informed idea that use of Creole represents a form of linguistic impoverishment or deprivation on the part of the speaker is satirised in Merle Collins's 'No Dialects Please', as are the hypocrisy and ignorance which accompany such ideas, and the efforts of the dominant culture to impose a unified model of language:

> Is not only dat ah tink
> of de dialect of de Normans and de Saxons
> dat combine and reformulate to create a language elect
> is not only dat ah tink
> how dis British education must really be narrow
> if it leave dem wid no knowledge
> of what dey own history is about
> . . . To tink how still dey so dunce
> an so frighten o we power
> dat dey have to hide behind a language
> that we could wrap around we little finger
> in addition to we own!
> Heavens o mercy!
> Dat is dunceness oui!
> Ah wonder where is de bright British?[19]

The felt need to print 'translations' of poems written in Creole also raises questions of whom the poems and the books address – performance audience and reading public – and the implied difference between them, a point to which we shall return in the section on orality. The use of translation does, however, reinforce preconceptions about Black English as alien and/or defective; no one suggests providing translations of the arguably much more impenetrable Glaswegian dialect of Tom Leonard, for example.

The second of Deleuze and Guattari's characteristics of minor literature is that everything in it is political, or, as they say elsewhere, that the individual is connected to a political immediacy. In major literatures, individual concerns somehow manage to remain individual. (Although Deleuze and Guattari do not mention it, a classic materialist retort might point out that such atomistic individualism is an – almost? – inescapable function of bourgeois society under capitalism. Kakfa and others do effect a form of escape through minor literature, though whether this is a willed escape or has more to do with the writer's position as a producer of minor literature is difficult to specify). In minor literature, however, there is not the space to allow individual affairs the leisure of remaining individual: a variety of pressures make apparent their links to numerous larger concerns – economic, bureaucratic, legal, etc. The same point is made in greater detail by Fredric Jameson in a recent article:

> ... although we may retain for convenience and for analysis such categories as the subjective and the public or political, the relations between them are wholly different in third-world culture. Third world texts, even those which are seemingly private and invested with a properly libidinal dynamic, necessarily project a political dimension in the form of national allegory: *the story of the private individual destiny is always an allegory of the embattled situation of the public third world culture and society.* Need I add that it is precisely this very different ratio of the political to the personal which makes such texts alien to us at first approach, and, consequently, resistant to our conventional Western habits of reading?[20]

The political implications of their personal actions are not lost on Black writers. As Maud Sulter acknowledges in her prize-winning poem 'As a Black Woman', 'As a Black woman/the personal is political/holds no empty rhetoric'.[21] At the same time, even writers who appear strongly and self-consciously political can be surprised at just how political other people find their work. In her essay in *Let it be Told*, Amryl Johnson recounts her surprise at a journalist's suggestion that all her work is political. (The reader may be even more surprised when Amryl Johnson then goes on to say that she does not intend to be overtly political in her work.) Her poem on the New Cross massacre of July 1981, 'Circle of Thorns', is perhaps only marginally less political, because more determinedly 'poetical' and allusive, than Brenda Agard's poem on the same subject which is printed alongside it in *Watchers and Seekers*. Whereas Amryl Johnson mourns the deaths of two of her friends in language which echoes John Donne and the Bible, Brenda Agard's poem is an angry shout of protest which fits the protest march she describes. 'Thirteen dead/Nothing said' – the chanted slogan condemns not only official indifference, but also, implicitly, a kind of professional failure, for who among white writers found the deaths of thirteen people in a racist arson attack a fit subject for his/her poetry? In the same way, both Amryl Johnson and Grace Nichols have written poems on the arrogant American intervention in Grenada, yet another subject which failed to inspire white British poets. The range of political subjects tackled is wide (once again, not least by comparison with white poets). Exploitation, both past – in the form of slavery – and present – in the form of international capitalism – recur in a number of works, the former notably in those of Amryl Johnson and Grace Nichols's impressive sequence 'i is a long memoried woman', the latter in poems by Valerie Bloom, Marsha Prescod and Meiling Jin, among others, while the experience of racism forms a kind of backdrop, not always clearly perceived, but none the less present for that. The politics in these poems are radical but non-aligned, pre-eminently of the sort which Immanuel Wallerstein has called 'anti-systemic'.

The dividing line between the political and the collective (the third of Deleuze and Guattari's principal features of minor literature) is a fine one; indeed for some there may be no discernible difference. In the article already referred to, Fredric Jameson says:

> This placeless individuality, this structural idealism . . . offers a welcome escape from the 'nightmare of history' but at the same time it condemns our culture to psychologism and the 'projections' of private subjectivity. All of this is denied to third world culture, which must be situational and materialist despite itself. And it is this, finally, which must account for the allegorical nature of third world culture, where the telling of the individual story and the individual experience

cannot but ultimately involve the whole laborious telling of the collective itself.[22]

Within Jameson's Marxist framework, this collectivity is an inescapably political formation. The idea of a 'collective telling' is also something which Deleuze and Guattari stress. For them, one of the significant aspects of minor literature is a diminishing importance of the individual speaking in her own right, and its replacement by 'collective enunciation'. This, though they are at pains to separate the collective and the political, comes about through the 'contaminating' influence of politics. Speaking collectively is also very much how many Black writers see their role. As Lauretta Ngcobo says:

> Few of our writings are strictly personal in the subjective sense of encompassing individual exploits. Rather, they reflect a collective subject, the common experience of Blackwomen.[23]

Another aspect of collectivity which recurs frequently in Black writing is its connection with the personal in terms of identity. The loss or fragmentation of coherent individual identity which is the result of deterritorialization (or capitalism, which, according to Freud and Lacan, was never there to begin with) can, it is felt, be compensated for through an emphasis on communal identity. In Amryl Johnson's poems, for example, the sort of relentless questioning of individual identity, role and responsibility already mentioned gives way, especially in the carnival sequence, to a feeling of joyful merging with the collective body. Life-enhancing though it may be, such an unreflective assumption of collective identity has its problems:

> Nor can I feel that the concept of cultural 'identity' or even national 'identity' is adequate. One cannot acknowledge the justice of the general post-structuralist assault on the so-called 'centred subject', the old unified ego of bourgeois individualism, and then resuscitate this same ideological mirage of psychic unification on the collective level in the form of a doctrine of collective identity.[24]

This is, I feel, correct. There are, however, a number of possible responses to this situation. One would be to admit the inadmissible, to acknowledge the unacceptable ideological nature of a belief in identity, but to argue for its provisional political importance, even necessity. Given the history of Black people and their present circumstances, there is a clear need to oppose the way they have been described, the way in which they have been conditioned to think of themselves, the way in which it has seemed possible for them to live – and the potential for mobilization which resides in the notion of collective identity is one of the most powerful means available for achieving this. Only if such identity were reified, accepted as the 'truth' about Black people, rather than a way to achieve greater justice, for example, would it truly be a problem. This is equivalent to what, in the context of feminism, Gayatri Spivak has called taking 'the risk of essence'.

Another, more radical response would be to reject entirely notions of identity, and work with different concepts. One which offers itself is that of community based on shared or similar history, experience and traditions, and Paul Gilroy argues that this has displaced the languages of both class and 'race' in the political activity of Black Britain. Here too, there is an obvious danger of slipping into a belief in the community as possessing a unique and unified essence. Such a slippage is not inevitable, however, as Paul Gilroy goes on to suggest:

> This definition of community [as a mental construct] depends on the distinction between symbols and meanings. The former are flexible vehicles for a variety of potentially contradictory readings which may be held by a movement's adherents. . . . The strength of symbols is in their multi-accentuality and malleability. Sharing a common body of symbols created around notions of 'race', ethnicity or locality, common history or identity, does not dictate the sharing of the plural meanings which may become attached to those symbols and cluster round them.[25]

This vital distinction shows the way in which the nature of community has changed as a result of deterritorialization in its most radical form as the Black diaspora. This is typical of what Edward Said has called the movement from filiation to affiliation,[26] in other words from instinctive, biological, or inherited forms of loyalty and collectivity, to consciously chosen alliances. In the same way, even the concept of the political has altered, with the replacement of 'natural' unified class politics by the more random, antisystemic type of 'movement' politics which Gilroy discusses.

The replacement of an unreflective, organic, filiative sense of collective belonging by a conscious decision of affiliative solidarity is perhaps the major insight achieved in Amryl Johnson's *Long Road to Nowhere*. As mentioned earlier, the speaker's feeling of identity engendered by the visit to the Caribbean is shattered in the powerful title poem by the experience of seeing on return to London a crippled Black man. Grossly physically handicapped, perhaps by thalidomide, he obsessively crosses and recrosses the road. The initial reaction is a mixture of shock, physical revulsion and denial of similarity. However, in the face of derogatory remarks and scarcely disguised smirks from the (presumably) white passers-by, the speaker comes to affirm complete solidarity with the crippled man, to the point of anticipated violent confrontation with the society which she feels cages him:

> and now he shares
> my brain
> I want to move aside
> and give him space
> This stranger
> mutilated
> monstrous
> helpless
> I carry him on
> my back
> His eyes
> touch mine
> trapped
> on a zebra crossing
> Two decades
> of being caged
> but
> this gun
> looking at them
> will serve
> us
> both.[27]

Many of the questions of enunciation, collectivity and mobilization which we have been discussing so far cluster round the issue of orality in Black poetry. It is notable how many Black women poets – Valerie Bloom, Merle Collins, Marsha Prescod, Fyna Dowe, Sista Roots, among others – style themselves performance poets, while even those who do not, nevertheless recognize the importance of their poetry being performed rather than silently consumed. Valerie Bloom, for example, notes the importance to Black audiences in Britain of the fact that her poetry embodies elements of oral traditions reaching back to Africa. At the same time, however, she and others recognize that works written for performance run the risk of not matching up to existing presuppositions about how poetry should look or read on the page. Lauretta Ngcobo argues for performed poetry as an automatically inclusive form, as against printed literature which risks being exclusive, since it presupposes literacy, a certain level of education. Also, the fact of being performed makes it far more of a shared and hence inclusive experience than if it were being read in solitude. Emphasis on performance is part of the way in which poetry, especially radical poetry, has changed since the 1970s, particularly in its desire to overturn norms and conventions governing both the form of the work (radical and performance poetry making great use of experimental and fragmentary forms, and, especially in the Black context, incorporating rhythms and other elements from reggae and rock), and its consumption (making a deliberate and energetic attempt to involve the audience).

The ability to speak to and engage with the greatest number of people, and to achieve the minimum separation between poetry and everyday life, between poetry and politics, is an important shared aim for these writers. It is a position which finds support among cultural theorists and sociologists. Gilroy for example recognizes the importance of orality and African traditions in Black expressive culture, and in addition says:

> ... the European distinction between politics and culture cannot be easily and straightforwardly introduced into analysis of distinctly non-European traditions of radicalism.[28]

Black poetry's appeals to oral tradition have been attacked in certain quarters[29] as yet another example of that phonocentrism whose 'metaphysical' privileging of speech over writing in Western culture has been vigorously criticized by Derrida. There are, however, a number of problems with such attacks. Firstly, Derrida's critique, justified though it may be, was directed at Western culture; there is no claim (at least by Derrida) to universal applicability, while problems of transfer of Western concepts to non-Western culture have just been mentioned. Secondly, the oral and the written clearly exist in a culturally unequal relation to one another, but it is by no means clear that their meanings are fixed in the sort of 'violent hierarchy' which Derrida discusses. The fact that 'oral' can signify both better (more direct) *and* worse (more 'primitive') than written would seem to take it out of the stasis of the Derridean type of binary opposition and into that space where meanings are the site of struggle, as analysed by discourse theorists such as Pecheux, Voloshinov and Foucault. Thirdly – forsaking theory for naive empiricism – Black poetry has, historically, incontrovertibly, been oral, through necessity: the option of a written form was simply not available in many cultures. To say this is not to claim that Black poetry is 'naturally' oral, or that it is intrinsically superior because of its oral heritage, but to deny the oral elements in its history and current forms would seem to be, at the very least, wilful. Finally, even if a stress on orality *were* essentializing and de-historicizing (which I do not believe it is), there are still good political grounds for Black people 'taking the risk of essence', in view of the undeniable gains to be made in terms of mobilization and cultural solidarity.

One important factor in the constituting of a minor literature which Deleuze and Guattari do not discuss, and which has yet to be addressed overtly in this essay, though it is inevitably present throughout, is that of gender. Given the ubiquity of women's oppression, women's writing is perhaps the only guaranteed universal form of minor literature (and as such represents a remarkable omission on the part of Deleuze and Guattari). Gender has its own specific relation to the categories of minor literature. In terms of deterritorialization, for example, womanhood is experienced as exile: 'I must be true/to the dark sign/of my woman's nature/to the wildness of my/solitude and exile',[30] or as a double dispossession: as both black and woman, the Fat Black Woman in Grace Nichols's poem struggles repeatedly to claim what is rightfully hers in the face of white male opposition.

Patriarchal oppression and sexism, which are the particular gendered forms of deterritorialization, are not experienced as uniquely white. Though Lauretta Ngcobo says that for reasons of solidarity Black men are treated leniently in Black women's writing, there are still quite a number of poems which with varying degrees of emphasis point out failings on the part of men. These range from Grace Nichols's gently ironic equating of the phallic male with sugar cane in the poem of that name, both unable to survive without the nurturing care of women, to the sarcasm and dislike of unthinking male physicality in Carole Stewart's 'Jerry Perm Poem', to the exposure of sexism so blatant it requires no comment in Rita Anyiam-St John's 'One Man to Another'.

Linguistic deterritorialization is present, too, as the titles of numerous poems attest: 'Nothing Said', 'Nothing to Say', 'No Say', 'No Dialects Please', 'Silence is Nearer to Truth', 'Qu'est-ce qu'elle dit?', while other titles point to an attempt to overcome it: 'Women Talking', 'Woman Talk', 'Girl Talk' – and the very existence of the poems is a kind of triumph over it. Indeed, the fact of speaking to other women, specifically other Black women, speaking out for those who cannot, as is demanded of the silent interlocutor in 'Nothing to Say', or simply for oneself, as the 'Sisterwoman' in 'Woman Talk' is enjoined to do, is perhaps the single most important aim, either implicit or explicit, of the poems. As such, it is clearly linked to the phenomenon of collective enunciation, the desire to escape from racist/sexist stereotyping, and the production of better representations of black womanhood. At the same time the political intent and implications of this writing are clearly felt. Centuries of oppression need not only to be acknowledged but to be brought more into the open, since this is precisely the type of history which, like that of women in general, official versions find it most convenient to gloss over or forget. Paul Gilroy argues for the importance of an awareness of history:

> The final theme which binds together the different Black expressive cultures is the premium they place on history itself. . . . A grounding in history is seen as an essential precondition for the realisation of both individual and collective freedom. . . . The recovery of historical knowledge is felt to be particularly important for Blacks because the nature of their oppression is such that they have been denied any historical being.[31]

It is this particular form of official cultural and historical amnesia which Grace Nichols and Amryl Johnson in particular set out to reverse. While Amryl Johnson's poems interweave past and present, each capable of illuminating the other, in their exploration of the condition of Black people, Grace Nichols's *i is a long memoried woman* traces the experience of female servitude through space and time, from Africa to the Caribbean, from the historyless (unwritten, in some ways undifferentiated, but not unremembered) past to the Haitian revolution and beyond. This localizing helps to offset an idealizing tendency within the poems, the feeling that an essential Black femininity which persists regardless of circumstance is being posited. In addition, although the poems examine the continued servitude of women there is emphatically no acceptance of the idea that Black women are natural victims; on the contrary they are cunningly subversive in poems like 'Love Act', 'Skinteeth', and 'I am Coming Back', while in others such as 'Wind a Change' and 'This Kingdom' they prophesy destruction and the end of white domination. Rejection of the notion of Black women as victims, and of an essential Black womanhood is contained in another of Grace Nichols's poems, 'Of course when they ask for poems about the "Realities" of Black women', where 'their' desire for Black women as 'specimen' and 'abused stereotype' is challenged by the recognition that 'there are Black women/and Black women/like a contrasting sky/of rainbow spectrum' while what the speaker most wants to see is women 'crushing out/with each dancing step/the twisted self-negating/history/we've inherited'.[32]

Denial of essentialist notions of gender and female nature reposes the question of affiliation, this time in an even more complex form. Should Black women form alliances only with other Black women, or with white women as well, making common cause against patriarchy? Or should their first allegiance be to Black men, regardless of the problems of sexism, in order to present a united front against racism and social injustice? Or, finally, should they take their place in the class struggle against the global reach of multi-national capitalism? The poems offer no simple answer (it is scarcely possible to conceive of one), though in quantitative terms their response is women first. To that extent they are clearly opting for the type of social or urban 'movement' politics which Paul Gilroy sees as characteristic of Black activism, and of the way in which contemporary politics in general is changing. In their declaration of 'womanist' (to use Alice Walker's term) allegiance, the texts mark another significant form of affiliation. In their recent book on women writers in the twentieth century,[33] Gilbert and Gubar discuss what they call the 'female affiliation complex', the difficult choice facing women authors over which literary tradition to align themselves with: the patrilineal – dominant, valued, but historically uncongenial to women; or the matrilineal – ignored, undervalued, but where they 'naturally' belong. Black women writers, it would seem, plump unhesitatingly for the matrilineal. The choice announces itself at all levels: at the level of form – the rejection of conventional poetic norms, the fragmented, experimental air of the poems; at the level of content – the choice of 'difficult' subjects (political, sexual); at the level of expression – the willingness to adopt an 'unpoetic' tone, the equivalent of a raised voice (Amryl Johnson's early poems were praised by a publisher but described as a 'scream of rage'), risking categorization as that 'shrill' woman, stock-in-trade of sexist stereotyping. In this, Black women writers register yet another significant achievement in Deleuze and Guattari's terms. The latter talk of the way in which literary movements or genres all seem to strive for a position of mastery and dominance, and they retort: 'Create the opposite dream: know how to create a becoming-minor'.[34] In their affiliative choices in the sphere of gender and politics, Black British women poets would certainly seem to be working in the realm of the 'becoming-minor', opposed, for good historical reasons, to dreams of dominance, capable of leading their minor literature on its 'sober revolutionary path'.

7 Blake in Birdland: Displacement and Metamorphosis in the Poetics of Ishmael Reed

Shamoon Zamir

In 'Al Capone in Alaska', Ishmael Reed compares 'hoodoo ecology' with the 'Judeo-Christian tendency to *let em* have it!'[1] Where the 'American and Canadian Christians/submachine gun the whales/.../as if the Pacific/were a Chicago garage on/St. Valentine's day',

> The Eskimo hunts
> the whale and each year
> the whale flowers for the
> Eskimo.
> *This must be love baby!*
> One receiving with respect
> from a Giver who has
> plenty.
> There is no hatred here.
> There is One Big Happy
> Family here

This 'hoodoo ecology' is an economy of gift exchange or symbolic exchange found in many so-called 'primitive' or 'archaic' societies.[2] The Eskimos make gifts to the whales to ensure their return each year, as the Pueblo Indians of North America sprinkle blue corn meal on the eyes of the dead deer and perform ceremonial dances for the same reasons. In each case, the animals are believed to give themselves to the hunters so that the people will have enough food.

The circulation of the gift, whether between people and the natural environment or within the human community itself, involves the incurring of debt on the part of the receiver. This intertwining of giving and owing, of circulation and return, constitutes a structure of reciprocity which must be understood in terms of both *response* and *responsibility*: this is the meaning of the 'erotic life of property'. This structure of reciprocity, I wish to suggest, is one of the governing principles of Reed's poetics (or 'neo-hoodoo aesthetic'), where poetics is understood as the intersection of 'form' and 'content', which is the point where, following Jean Baudrillard, politics must also be located. Baudrillard, in positing a structural and ideological homology (based on the logic of abstract equivalence) for the operation of use value and exchange value in political economy, and of the signifier and the signified in Saussurian linguistics, suggests the need for developing 'a critique of the political economy of the sign', and argues that symbolic exchange transgresses the logic of political economy. In symbolic exchange there is

> accurately speaking . . . no symbolic 'value', there is only symbolic 'exchange', which defines itself precisely as something distinct from, and beyond value and code. All forms of value (object, commodity or sign) must be negated in order to inaugurate symbolic exchange. This is the radical rupture of the field of value[3]

In contrast to symbolic exchange, the sign transacts a 'directive and reductive rationalization' which occurs not in relation to an exterior, immanent

> concrete reality that signs would supposedly recapture abstractly in order to express, but in relation to all that which overflows the schema of equivalence and signification; and which the sign reduces, represses and annihilates in the very operation that constitutes it (the sudden crystalization of the Signifier and a Signified). *The rationality of the sign is rooted in its exclusion and annihilation of all symbolic ambivalence on behalf of a fixed and equational structure*[4] [my emphasis]

Symbolic exchange transgresses political economy since it is governed not by the logic of abstract equivalence, but by the creation of *ambivalence* in the interaction of response and responsibility, and responsibility must be understood as 'not a psychological or a moral responsibility, but a personal, mutual correlation in exchange' (p. 169). Extending the insights of anthropology to the fields of language and literature, Baudrillard argues that linguistic ambivalence is that which resists 'legibility, the false transparency of the sign' and which 'questions the evidence of the use value of the sign (rational decoding) and its exchange value (the discourse of communication). *It brings the political economy of the sign to a standstill*' (p. 169). Similarly, reciprocity questions the unidirectional structure of communication (transmitter-message-receiver) which Baudrillard sees as inscribed at the heart of contemporary mass media. The unidirectional relation of the transmitter to the receiver is founded on the logic of equivalence or legibility, and constitutes a relationship of power. As Baudrillard reminds us, in 'primitive' societies 'power belongs to one who can give and *cannot be repaid*' (p. 120). The institution of response disrupts this power monopoly.

Baudrillard sees poetic language as one instance of the institution of response. In Saussurian linguistic theory the structure of the sign separates the signifier from the signified, and the sign exists in 'arbitrary isolation', communicating with other signs 'through a code called language'; and here 'a scientific injunction is invoked against the immanent possibility of the terms exchanging amongst each other symbolically, beyond the signifier-signified direction'. By contrast, in poetic language

> as in symbolic exchange, the terms *respond* to each other beyond the code. It is this response that [is] ultimately deconstructive of all codes, of all control and power, which always base themselves on the separation of terms and their abstract circulation (pp. 179–80)

In the following discussion I take Baudrillard's distinction between symbolic ambivalence in poetic language, and the fixed equational structure of the sign as an entrance into the poetry of Reed and its break from the Black Aesthetic.

'The Jackal-Headed Cowboy' – the second poem in *Conjure* (1972), Reed's first book of poetry – culminates in an over-blown rhetoric of violence which parodies the cruder aspects of Black Power language from the 1960s:

> And fast draw Anubis with his crank letters from Ra
> will Gallop Gallop Gallop
> our mummified trail boss
> as our swashbuckling storm fucking mob rides shot
> gun for the moon and the whole sieged stage coach
> of the world will heave and rock as we
> bang stomp shuffle stampede cartweel and cakewalk our
> way into Limbo[5]

Here we end, it seems, not with revolution or effective transgression, but with a walk into 'Limbo'. While limbo suggests a dead-end state of inaction, it is also indicative of a state of transition and transformation. *Conjure* presents a selection of poems written between 1963 and 1970, and is organized to trace the movement away from the Black Aesthetic and the concomitant political programme of the 1960s towards Reed's multi-cultural 'neo-hoodoo aesthetic' and 'epistemology'. The book is dominated by explorations of this neo-hoodoo aesthetic as a means of negotiating a passage out of limbo, until in the final poem, 'introducing a new loa', the 'swinging HooDoo cloud' ('doing a dance they call/"The Our Turn" ') is proclaimed as 'the invisible train for which this Work has been but a modest schedule' (p. 83).

Reed has argued that the Black Aesthetic was 'racist and limited'.[6] For Reed, the Black Aesthetic made literature subservient to political programmes; at the same time, its strategies of self-legitimation were often founded on the assumption of 'blackness' as a transcendent essence which guaranteed the validity of the extreme dichotomies concerning 'black' and 'white' culture. This justified claims for the authenticity of the former against the inauthenticity of the latter, played out in another version as the 'oral' bases of the former's literature against the logocentrism of the latter's.

'I am a cowboy in the boat of Ra' is a key text not only within the context of *Conjure*, but within Reed's work as a whole, since it highlights many of the concerns central to his writing. In it, Reed eschews a language that models itself on the immediacy and transparency of communication often assumed to be inherent in oral communication (be it speech or music). Reed creates, instead, a wilfully dense and ludic language marked by a vertiginous proliferation of puns, allusions and linguistic registers. There is no transcendent referent called 'blackness' *outside* the text to be communicated *through* it. This is not to say that Reed merely reverses the oral–written dichotomy by privileging the written over the oral. Such dichotomies are ultimately of little use in the reading of the poem, since they impose a critical perspective, determined by a previous historical context, which blinds us both to the full breadth of Reed's play on 'blackness', identity and history, and to the complexity and richness of folk and oral materials. The poem demands an act of response, and a responsible reading precisely in the sense in which Baudrillard defines these terms.

The *Rituale Romanum* and Cardinal Spellman, cited in the

epigraph to the poem, represent one of Reed's recurring targets:[7] the (un-)holy alliance of the 'Judaeo-Christian' tradition and *logos*, the transformation of the Word into Law, rather than creative process:

> The devil must be forced to reveal any such physical evil (potions, charms, fetishes, etc.) still outside the body and these must be burned.
> [*Rituale Romanum*, published 1947, endorsed by the coat-of-arms and introductory letter from Francis Cardinal Spellman]

The authority of the *Rituale Romanum*, one of the official liturgical books of the Roman rite used by priests for the administration of sacraments and blessings and for the conducting of processions and exorcisms, depends, in part, on its formulae being followed with minimal variation.[8] John Wesley Hardin, in Reed's novel *Yellow Back Radio Broke-Down*, understands the relation of logos to authority. 'I got so strung out behind the Bible', he tells Drag Gibson, the cattle baron, 'that I went on to study law. Got my degree in jail. I've always been on the side of the Word, killing only those who were the devil incarnate – you know – black fellows'. But even Drag Gibson has understood that 'nigger words . . . move up and down the line like hard magic beads out riffing all the language in the syntax'.[9] While Hardin and his kind try and construct an objectified 'other' (a devil 'incarnate' with 'physical' evil 'outside' the body) from the security of their belief in the mimetic ability of the Word, the poetic personae and fictional protagonists of Reed's work appear as elusive shape-changers, refusing to have their identities pinned down in either physical or linguistic terms. Reed's writing challenges distinctions between language, appearance and reality. When 40s, the militant slave in *Flight to Canada*, tells Raven Quickskill 'you take the words, give me the rifle', Quickskill replies that 'words built the world and words can destroy the world'. Quickskill learns that a flight to Canada is a false promise of freedom; for him 'freedom was his writing. His writing was his HooDoo'.[10] The black writer undermines the authority of the Word through a mastery of language itself.

'I am a cowboy . . .' takes up the challenge of the *Rituale Romanum* and traces the immanent return of all that would be exorcized or repressed. Around the governing motif of the myth of the return of Horus 'vamoosed from the temple', and his war against Set, are organized a multiplicity of histories excluded from the singular version of History installed by the 'Egyptologists who do not know their trips', and the 'School marms with halitosis'. In Egyptian mythology, Set murdered Osiris and usurped his throne. Osiris is a black fertility god and a culture hero who, according to Plutarch, civilized Egypt through the power of his songs, introducing agriculture, the observation of laws, and the honouring of gods.[11] Horus, the son of Osiris, was protected from Set until he came to maturity; he then returned to challenge the unlawful reign of Set, the god of chaos and the forces of darkness (pp. 87-9). Although Horus is never named in the poem, he is clearly the figure fighting for 'the come back of/Osiris'. Even when Horus was under the protection of Isis, Set managed to have him 'bitten by savage beasts and stung by scorpions',[12] and this is what is alluded to in the first strophe of the poem:

> I am a cowboy in the boat of Ra,
> sidewinders in the saloons of fools
> bit my forehead   like   O
> the untrustworthiness of Egyptologists
> who do not know their trips. Who was that
> dog-faced man? they asked, the day I rode
> from town

His presence in the boat of Ra also identifies the cowboy as Horus: Horus fought the battle against Set from the boat of Ra, having obtained the magical power to transform himself into a winged disc from Thoth.[13] However, the persona of the poem is not exclusively identified with Horus: as one who 'bedded/down with Isis' he is also Osiris; Anubis as the 'dog faced man'; he appears later as 'Loup Garou', a Voodoo loa of the fierce Petro cult of Haiti; and he is also 'cowboy', a Voodoo priest calling for his 'bones of JuJu snake', and a gangster calling his 'moll' ('C/mere a minute willya doll?').

The return of Horus enacts a union and unification and marks the return of the excluded, often through images of violence. Union and violence, not as mutually exclusive but as *inseparable halves of the same movement*, also characterize the linguistic strategy of yoking together a diversity of cultural material which dominates the poem. The union of Isis and Osiris in the third strophe is echoed later in the mating of Pisces and Aquarius (strophe 7), promising the coming of a new age (the age of Aquarius), as well as the union of the female (Pisces) and the male (Aquarius). Through a sexual pun reminiscent of the sexual punning found in blues songs, Reed leaps from Eygptian mythology to nineteenth-century America:

> I am a cowboy in the boat of Ra. I bedded
> down with Isis, Lady of the Boogaloo, dove
> down deep into her horny, stuck up her Wells-Far-ago
> in daring midday getaway. 'Start grabbing the
> blue', I said from top of my double crown

The 'Wells-far-ago' of Isis recall not only Langston Hughes' 'The Negro Speaks of Rivers', but are also a distortion of the name of the Wells *Fargo* company, founded in 1852. The company carried mail, silver and gold bullion, and provided banking services. 'In less than ten years', Alvin F. Harlow tells us, the company had 'either bought out or eliminated nearly all competitors and become the most powerful company in the Far West'.[14] The economic monopolization represented by the Wells Fargo Company parallels the monotheism of Judaism and Christianity which have banished not only the other gods (Osiris, the Voodoo loa), but have also suppressed their own traditions of unorthodoxy. One such tradition is present in the figure of Pope Joan:

> I am a cowboy in the boat of Ra. Pope Joan of the
> Ptah Ra. C/mere a minute willya doll?
> Be good girl and
> bring me my Buffalo horn of black powder
> bring me my headdress of black feathers
> bring me my bones of Ju-Ju snake
> go get my eyelids of red paint.
> Hand me my shadow

Pope Joan was fabled to have been a woman who, disguised as a man, became Pope between the ninth and eleventh centuries, and who was discovered only when she gave birth during a procession between the Colosseum and St Clement's in Rome.[15] Pope Joan is also a card game in which one of the cards, the nine of diamonds, is removed from play.[16] The outlaw cowboy's cry 'start grabbing the/ blue' refers to 'blueback', an archaic term (and a deliberately *literary* use of 'vernacular') for a paper note of Confederate money, so called for the contrast of blue ink on its back to the green ink used on the back of the Northern 'greenback'. With Horus speaking from the 'top of [his] double crown' in the next line, the blueback carried by the Wells Fargo Company can be taken as symbol of the division between North and South in the 'United' States. The double crown is the symbol of a unified Eygpt in Egyptian iconography, and one of the manifestations of Horus was 'Har-mau', or 'Horus the uniter', upholder of the unification of northern and southern Egypt (Hart, p. 89).

The experience of Reed's poem is akin to the experience of surrealist collage which collapses together different times, different places, and different 'orders' of objects, and which 'delights in cultural impurities and disturbing syncretisms'.[17] The effect is one of defamiliarization. The intertwined movements of unification and disruption which are found in 'I am a cowboy . . .' can be restated as *translation* and *displacement*. The two are, of course, the same in as much as displacement, the movement from one place to another, is the meaning which lies at the etymological roots of the verb 'to translate'. As James Boon writes, 'passing from one culture to another does not *directly* facilitate moving on to a third', just as the ability to translate another language into one's own might make it easier to translate a third, 'but not because [the translators] have become any "closer" to language Y through language X, much less located a more abstract deep structure connecting the two. Rather, having once managed to *dislodge* themselves from their own language, they have perhaps decreased their resistance to doing so again'.[18] As Jerome Rothenberg points out, the process of translation always involves a process of 'mutual completion'.[19]

'I am a cowboy . . .' dislodges mono-polized versions of history (monotheism, or the 'West' as the centre of global history), and replaces them with histor*ies*. Reed is critical of the neglect in academia not only of 'ethnic' literature, but also of genres such as the detective novel and western fiction, and of white authors like William Burroughs.[20] Not surprisingly, then, the return of Horus is narrated as a showdown in a western novel. It is not simply a matter of the return of what has been displaced, but also of the wilful displacement of the reader through these various histories as the familiar is made unfamiliar in the confluence of various myths, times, and linguistic registers into one *place*. Elsewhere, Reed is more explicit about the displacement of the reader which his writing attempts to enact. In 'beware: do not read this poem', he warns the reader that 'the hunger of this poem is legendary/it has taken in many victims/back off from this poem'. But, as we read the poem it is already too late. The 'greedy mirror' of the poem swallows the reader who is transformed from the second-person pronoun into the third-person pronoun: 'relax now & go w/this poem/. . ./this poem has yr eyes/this poem has his head/. . ./this poem is the reader & the/reader this poem' (pp. 48–9). Here 'the poem itself becomes the visible resonance of the text-reader relationship'.[21] Baudrillard quotes Roland Barthes' criticism of non-reciprocity in 'our literature' in support of his own argument for the need for linguistic ambivalence. For Barthes, there is a divorce between the author/producer of the text and the reader/user which reduces the latter to passivity, and makes him or her 'intransitive' (p. 171). 'I am a cowboy . . .' is both less obvious and more radical in its challenge to the passivity of the reader than 'beware: do not read this poem'. Here, Reed employs what we may call a strategic use of deferral to pull the reader out of the immediate text and involve him or her in an act of investigation and writing, which allows a re-entry into the poem through a different door. The case of Horus illustrates what I mean: despite the fact that the myth of the return of Horus is the central governing motif behind the 'narrative' of the poem, Horus is never named. He is displaced from the text as he is displaced from the monopolized version of History, and must be discovered *outside* if one governing thread of the text is to be located. What is important here is that, despite his exclusion, Horus continues to exert a powerful influence on the shaping of the text; similarly, Reed seems to suggest, 'other' histories do not become impotent by their mere exclusion or suppression.

Discussing 'I am a cowboy . . .', Chester J. Fontenot writes that 'one might suspect that the town the cowboy is run out of is history itself', and adds that the 'battle over the ontological status of history threatens to entrap the Black Artist in a double consciousness'.[22] Fontenot is referring to the well-known passage in *The Souls of Black Folk* where Du Bois writes that the Afro-American 'inhabits a world which yields him no true self-consciousness, but only lets him see himself through the revelation of the other world'. It is this 'sense of always looking at one's self through the eyes of others' which yields a double consciousness, a split between being both 'American' and 'Black'.[23] Reed no longer accepts the utility of this notion of an Afro-American identity, as if there were only an either/or choice involved, and parodies the notion in his poem called 'Dualism in ralph ellison's invisible man' (p. 59):

> i am outside of
> history. i wish
> i had some peanuts, it
> looks hungry there in
> its cage
>
> i am inside of
> history, its
> hungrier than i
> thot

The choice for Reed is not simply being 'in' or 'out' of History, deciding whether one is 'American' or 'Black'. Given the range of materials in his writing and his emphasis on shifting individual and cultural identities, these terms are increasingly placed in doubt in the same way that Reed's writing challenges the Black Aesthetic dichotomies. Turning to myth provides Reed with an alternative to the rigidity of double consciousness, which is not to say (as Fontenot does) that he writes *mythically*; rather, Reed writes *mythologically*. Through an exploration of myth (as history excluded, rather than an escape from history), Reed attempts to develop a 'grammar' for the movement across and between cultures that negates the structure of fate called double consciousness which consigns the Afro-American to a perpetual impasse. A closer look at the second strophe of 'I am a cowboy . . .' allows us to elaborate on Reed's exploration of history and myth by identifying more clearly how this exploration is governed by the strategies of deferral and displacement:

> School marms with halitosis cannot see
> the Nefertiti fake chipped on the run by slick
> germans, the hawk behind Sonny Rollins' head or
> the ritual beard of his axe; a longhorn winding
> its bells thru the Field of Reeds

Who is the 'hawk' behind the head of jazz saxophonist, Sonny Rollins, in the second stophe of the poem, invisible to the school marms? Certain jazz figures immediately suggest themselves: Coleman *Hawk*ins; Charlie '*Bird*' Parker. Horus also appears as a Hawk, and the supreme deity of Egypt, Ra, the Sun God, is often depicted as a falcon. The name of Sonny Rollins also echoes that of Ra (*Sun*-ny *Ra*-llins, American pronunciation). Perhaps an even more obvious allusion is to the innovative jazzman, Sun Ra and his jazz *Ark*estra. If the boat of Ra holds the promise for the future, like

Noah's Ark, and is the place in the poem where all the materials come together, then we should also recall that Sun Ra and his Arkestra (variously known as the 'Solar Arkestra', the 'Space Arkestra' and the 'Intergalactic Myth-Science Arkestra')[24] have been leading proponents of 'experimental jazz', introducing into the music a wide range of cross-cultural *and* inter-media materials. In an interview published in 1968, the same year that 'I am a cowboy . . .' was first published, Reed sees his work as attempting an exploration of myth '[j]ust like Cecil Taylor's trying to do it, just like Bill Dixon's trying to do it, just like Sun Ra's trying to do it'.[25] Sun Ra's work is, for Reed, part of a truly international imagination which he sees developing within the modern technological environment. In the same interview he says that

> [w]ith a televised technology tribalism and separatism are impossible. Given what McLuhan and Buckminster Fuller have shown us, you *can't* be a separatist. . . . Once you become an international mind-miner it's all over. That's where the Afro-American artist is today: John Coltrane going to Ali Akbar Khan, Afro-American ragas, Bill Dixon doing science-fiction music, Sun Ra into Gustav Holst.

Reed's use of Sun Ra suggests not the attempt to trace an aural effect of music in his poetry, but to develop a way of knowing, what he has called his 'hoodoo epistemology'.[26] Sun Ra's multi-media and performance emphasis also suggests the need to redefine the meaning of oral today, to include what Lorenzo Thomas, in his discussion of the Umbra Poetry Workshop, has called 'the oral tradition of radio and T.V.'. If this proposition seems unacceptable to some, then we can only say, along with Thomas, that 'one hopes that we've chosen the right end of the body electric'.[27] Reed himself was part of the Umbra Workshop in the early sixties, and has acknowledged the influence of Umbra and of Thomas on his early writing.[28]

However, the sound structure of jazz is at least as much a part of the grammar of Reed's hoodoo epistemology. Mark Shadle, in an excellent study of Reed's *Mumbo Jumbo*, has already pointed out that the many sub-plots and inter-texts of Reed's novel suggest the polyrhythmic structure of African music in their lack of resolution and/or multiple resolutions. He adds that 'this is an "additive" rather than "divisive" principle (and also applies to Eygptian mythology)'.[29] Given the African and 'New World' emphasis of 'I am a cowboy . . .' one can find an obvious structural analogy between the synchronic historicism of the poem and the cross-rhythmic or horizontal emphasis found in African music. However, the presence of Charlie Parker as another deferred figure behind the head of Sonny Rollins, suggests a more precise analogy with the 'poetics' of jazz within the poem. Parker, who is also a key representative of the neo-hoodoo spirit of 'Jes Grew' in *Mumbo Jumbo* and related there to the bird-headed Egyptian god of writing, Thoth, was the leading innovator of 'bebop' jazz in the 1940s (and gave his name to the celebrated New York jazz club 'Birdland'). As Joachim Berendt tells us, one distinguishing characteristic of bop is (in the words of a bop musician) that *'everything that is obvious is excluded'*. Berendt adds that bop 'is a kind of musical shorthand, and one must listen as one would read a stenographic transcript, *'establishing ordered relationships from a few hasty signs'*.[30] Berendt also points out that, prior to free jazz, no style in jazz was closer rhythmically to African music than bebop (p. 168). In drawing an analogy between jazz and Reed's poem, I wish to suggest that the sound structure of the poem is rhythmically organized in a way that is reminiscent more of the improvised rhythmic strategies of bebop, and jazz in general, than of any regular metrical prosody, and that this organization relates to the broader issues of history and poetics raised by the poem.

Despite the visual layout of the poem, which seems to suggest a possibly regular stanzaic pattern that is then dislocated towards the end, no such pattern exists in the poem. The number of lines per strophe varies. Nor does the poem employ a regular meter; no one foot dominates, and the number of feet per line varies from one to seven, and that of syllables from two to fifteen. One can point to a tendency in the poem, after the first strophe and up to line 40, to employ a line of six feet (with some of seven, five, and a few shorter ones), with the number of syllables varying from between ten and fifteen (again with a few shorter exceptions). Keeping exceptions in mind (as with the feet and syllables), one can also say that the number of stresses tends to hover between five and seven in this section of the poem. Accentualism provides the real key to the sounding of Reed's poem, and offers us a way of understanding its essential lack of formal regularity being superimposed on the barest skeleton of a regular measure, hinting at some hidden, but severely disrupted, 'normative' structure. The final incantatory section of the poem, building up to the cowboy's going after Set, refers us to William Blake; the 'bring me my Buffalo horn' section quoted above echoes Blake's 'Bring me my Bow of Burning Gold' from the 'Preface' to his *Milton*.[31]

Milton is one of Blake's 'prophetic' works, and helps us place 'I am a cowboy . . .' as a prophecy of the coming of the 'new loa' in the final poem of *Conjure*. What is important for the present discussion is Blake's insistence on the inseparability of his own formal innovations and his radical politics, of the emancipation of the poetic line, and the visionary emancipation of the poet Milton (and of Blake himself). Blake writes in the prefatory remarks to 'Jerusalem', another prophetic poem written in the same year (1804) and in the same meter (fourteeners) as 'Milton', that he first considered writing in 'a Monotonous Cadence like that used by Milton and Shakespeare and all writers of English Blank Verse', but that he 'soon found that in the mouth of a true Orator such monotony was not only awkward, but as much a bondage as rhyme itself. *I therefore have produced a variety in every line, both of cadence and number of syllables*'. He adds, 'poetry Fetter'd, Fetters the Human Race!' (p. 146). While Blake's charges against his predecessors, as well as his claims for his own poetry, may be overstated, it is fruitful for a reading of Reed's poem to look more closely at just where the innovative aspects of Blake's formalism lie. It is true, as John Hollander has pointed out, that in these works by Blake the fourteener is never very far away, and that Blake 'never completely surrenders to the Whitmanesque program of claiming that rhythm is its own meter', despite the apparent claims of his preface to *Jerusalem*.

> What [Blake] in fact does in *Jerusalem* is to extend the loosening of
> the fourteener in several directions, from regular to loose, from
> syllabic fourteeners with only five or six major stresses to cluttered
> ones of eight[32]

In his 'Foreword' to *Conjure*, Reed acknowledges the influence of Blake, along with that of Yeats and Pound, on his early poetry, though he half-mockingly adds 'excuse me. I know that it's white culture. I was a dupe, I confess' (p. viii). In an interview given four years later (in 1976), he is less tentative when talking of his experiences at University: 'I admired Blake and Yeats, people who created their own systems, or revived their own national cultures', says Reed. 'So that's what I wanted to do. When these guys call me avant-garde, I'm really only using models I learned about in English departments. I wanted to create a mythology closer to me . . . that's why I got into Egyptology and Voodoo. My experience of these things comes right out of Blake and Yeats' (*Shrovetide*, 283). If Reed seems to go to the other extreme in his appreciation here, we should remember the context of his remarks: he gave the interview in reply to questions arising out of his being denied tenure at the University of California, Berkeley. It was hinted, apparently, that one reason for the denial, was that his writing was too 'avant-garde'. I do not think it would be distorting the truth to locate it somewhere between the respective pragmatic exigencies of the 'Foreword' and the interview.

As a way of sounding 'I am a cowboy . . .' and of foregrounding the historicism of its formal strategies, I wish to suggest that the poem can be read as a further loosening of meter, initiated by Blake by means of a more emphatic accentualism, created by the splicing together of Blake and a rhythmic sense derived from jazz. If Hollander, in qualifying Blake's claims for a radical prosody, is correct in suggesting that the practice of enjambment in *Jerusalem* allows 'a mono- or di-syllabic word at the line break to count for a strong stress, even though the principle of [Blake's] free accentualism throughout his work has been to let speech stress, in its syntactic and rhetorical context, govern the metrical role of syllables' (p. 209), then it is significant that it is precisely through creating a rhythm in opposition to normative speech stress that Reed finds the music of his own free accentualism; he finds, as it were, a field of possibility within Blake's contradictions. Reed does not write in fourteeners, but the disordered skeleton of his six foot line not only echoes Blake's challenge to the dominance of the iambic pentameter in English verse, but suggests a further unfettering of verse by logically following through the literary disruptions of Blake himself.

If we read 'I am a cowboy . . .' following normative speech stress, the sound falls flat. Reading the first strophe in this way, the stress would fall something like this: line 1, on the first syllable of 'cowboy', on 'boat' and 'Ra'; line 2, on the first syllable of 'sidewinders', the second of 'saloons' and on 'fools'; line 3, on the first syllable of 'forehead' and on 'O'; line 4, on the second syllable of 'untrustworthiness', and on the first and third syllables of 'egyptologists'; line 5, on 'do', 'know', 'trips', and the second 'who';

line 6, on 'dog', 'asked', and 'rode'; and on 'town' in line 7. I would suggest a different accentuation with a greater number of stresses and half-stresses: line 1 would then have additional stresses on 'I' and the second syllable of 'cowboy'; line 2 could possibly have a greater emphasis on the second syllable of 'sidewinders'; line 3 would have additional stress on 'bit' and 'like', again with a possibly stronger emphasis on the second syllable of 'forehead'; in line 5 on the first 'who' (so playing on 'hoodoo') and 'not'; and in line 6 on 'faced', 'man', and 'day'. Line 4 and line 7 would remain unaltered (and it is appropriate that the line with the 'untrustworthy Egyptologists' should be marked by polysyllabic words and the flattest rhythm, having as it does only three stresses). This heavy rhythmic emphasis is found throughout the poem, and is supplemented by Reed's equally marked use of assonance and alliteration which help both to underline the rhythmic emphasis, and to draw attention to syllables otherwise unstressed. An example of the former would be the 'o's of line 5 or the 'd's of line 6, and of the latter the 's's of line 2 where the alliteration gives the first syllable of 'saloons' greater prominence than the other unstressed syllables of the line. The effect of the combination of alliteration and assonance with the stress pattern, is to create a tension between vertical and horizontal elements in the poem: the heavy accentualism counteracts the horizontal flow of the line, while the alliteration and assonance tend toward a *fuller sounding* of all the elements of each word, and so create a flow of sound in each line at the very moment that they supplement the vertical tendency to stress a greater number of words. The same vertical-horizontal pull can be seen in the poem's enjambment: the run-on lines pull us forward, but Reed's frequent stressing of usually monosyllabic words at the end of the line, or at the very start of the next, has a halting effect.

The sound structure I am trying to describe in Reed's poem, finds a counterpart in bebop and in jazz in general. As LeRoi Jones points out:

> [i]n bop melodies there seemed to be an endless changing of direction, stops and starts, variations of impetus, a jaggedness that reached out of the rhythmic *bases* of the music. The boppers seemed to have a constant need for a deliberate and agitated rhythmical contrast[33]

Gunther Schuller's elaboration of his point that the 'democratization' of rhythmic values is a major source of the uniqueness of jazz rhythm, provides us with a more precise analogy with Reed's formal strategies, and suggests also their political implications:

> By the 'democratization' of rhythmic values, I mean very simply that in jazz so-called weak beats (or weak parts of rhythmic units) are *not* underplayed as in 'classical' music. Instead they are brought up to the level of strong beats, and very often even emphasized *beyond* the strong beat. The jazz musician does this not only by maintaining an equality of dynamics among 'weak' and 'strong' elements, but also by *preserving the full sonority of notes, even though they may happen to fall on weak parts of a measure*. (The only exception to this is the so-called ghost note, *which is more implied than actually played*). This consciousness of attack and sonority makes the 'horn' player [i.e. all wind players] tongue *almost all notes*, even in the fastest runs, though the effect may be that of slurring. *A pure 'legato' is foreign to him* because he cannot then control as well the attack impulse or the sonority[34] [the first two emphases are Schuller's]

Schuller further points out, that it is 'no mere accident that when jazz musicians imitate their playing by singing, they use syllables which have fairly strong, bouncy consonant beginnings' (p. 8). Schuller's discussion of syncopation, the Afro-American musician's adaptation of African 'polymetric and polyrhythmic points of emphasis into the monometric and monorhythmic structure of European music' (p. 15), provides us with one final analogy to Reed's intersection of Blake and jazz suggested above, with his variation of weak and strong stresses, and his creation of a vertical-horizontal tension. Schuller defines syncopation as a 'temporary shifting or displacement of a regular metrical accent; the emphasis on a weak or unaccented note, so as to displace the regular meter' (p. 382), and states that '[s]yncopation is the most direct way a musician has of emphasizing weak beats, other than outright accentuation' (p. 16).

The parallels between all the points emphasized in the above quotations from Schuller, and my preceding discussion of Reed's prosody, should by now be obvious enough not to need restating. We can add that the strophic structure of the poem, with the repetition of the title line at the head of almost every section, acts as a series of improvisations where a phrase or a theme is stated, and then dismantled in the process of improvisation. What I would like to underline is that I do not wish only to trace Reed's reproduction of an aural effect derived from music; such a mimesis can, at best, be only approximated in the medium of language. Nor do I wish to 'authenticate' Reed's writing by my emphasis on a specifically Afro-American 'oral' register, or to suggest that it is qualitatively different from any other writing which is indebted to the oral (Jack Kerouac's 'bop prosody', for instance). What emerges from an examination of Reed's prosodic strategies, as well as from his use of Blake and his mythological and historical materials, is a broader sense of his *poetics*, or poetic grammar. Considering all the elements that have been discussed so far, *displacement* can be taken as a key function of this grammar or 'epistemology': exclusion, suppression and deferral (whether of particular histories or of beats in poetry and music, and here the implied 'ghost note' is another figure of deferral) on the one hand, and the return of the excluded and the repressed (Horus or Pope Joan, or the 'democratization' of the beat, and here Blake's mythic system and prosody are both parallels) on the other, are both movements of displacement. As I will argue in more detail later, displacement marks the possibility of both resistance to cultural authoritarianism and (as 'translation') of mutual completion and transformation in both ethnically specific and more general cultural contexts.

In Reed's work, the avatar of his 'hoodoo epistemology' is consistently the shape-changing trickster (the cowboy, Loup Garou, Papa Labas, 'Jes Grew', Raven Quickskill), and his language of satire and comedy, always on the move, criss-crossing the landscape of the texts, weaving them into being. Railroad Bill, the Conjure Man, is one such trickster:

> Railroad Bill, a conjure man
> Could change hisself to a tree
> He could change hisself to a
> Lake, a ram, he could be
> What he wanted to be (p. 9)

When Railroad Bill is murdered, the whites rejoice at having disposed of him, but the blacks know that *physical* death is not the end of the matter:

> Wasn't so the old folks claimed
> From their shacks in the Wabeek
> Wood. That ain't our Bill in that
> Old Coffin, that ain't our man
> You killed. Our Bill is in the

> Dogwood flower and in the grain
> We eat
> See that livestock graizing there
> That Bull is Railroad Bill
> That mean one over there near the
> Fence, that one is Railroad Bill (p. 13)

As the title of a poem appearing later in *Chattanooga* states, 'Loup Garou Means Change Into' (p. 49). This, according to Reed, is why he often alludes to Osiris:

> where once man animals
> plants and stars freely
> roamed through each other's
> rooms, ikhnaton came up
> with the door . . .
> I'll take osiris any
> time . . .
> he'd rather dance than rule (p. 43)

The terms here respond to and exchange amongst each other, moving from one place to another until blocked by Akhnaten's authoritarian institution of monotheism. The trickster and his language oppose the separation that Baudrillard finds in the structure of the sign. Response, the movement 'beyond the signifier-signified direction', distinguishes metamorphosis from metaphor. Metaphor only replaces one sign with another, and the second continues to represent the first. Gilles Deleuze and Felix Guattari, in their study of Kafka, suggest that metamorphosis is the contrary of metaphor. Their comments offer useful insights into why the trickster appears at the centre of the matrix of translation and recriprocity in Reed's work. In metamorphosis, write Deleuze and Guattari:

> there is no longer any true meaning or figurative sense, but a distribution of states in the word's fan. . . . It is not a matter of resemblance between the behaviour of an animal and that of a human, even less a play of words. Now there is neither human nor animal. . . . It involves a matter of becoming which instead includes the maximum difference as difference of intensity, the crossing of a threshold . . . a circuit of states which form a *mutual becoming* – within an arrangement that is necessarily multiple or collective[35]

As the editor of Deleuze and Guattari points out '*becoming-animal*' is not to be confused with *'becoming an animal'*. Gregor, in *The Metamorphosis*, does not become an insect, but remains a man who is becoming an insect (p. 32).

The transformations of a Railroad Bill defy the fixed relationality of metaphor imposed on the Afro-American, whether by racist whites who see the black person as the 'devil incarnate', or by blacks themselves who try to reverse racist dichotomies by privileging one term over the other. The latter, strictly speaking, is also a racist strategy. In metamorphosis, as in the sphere of the symbolic, there is no 'value' as such, only exchange and process, and it is here that Reed's writing imagines an escape from the schizophrenic split of double consciousness. The transcendent black subject is transformed into one who is perpetually becoming at the confluence of translation and metamorphosis, displacement and transformation. The alignment of metamorphosis and the symbolic is further reinforced by the fact that Baudrillard, as well as Deleuze and Guattari, locate these processes within a radically disruptive use of language. Deleuze and Guattari's idea of 'minor' use of a major language, echoes Baudrillard's emphasis on the non-mimetic or non-communicative; they write that:

> a minor literature is not a literature of a minor language, but the literature a minority makes in a major language. But the primary characteristic of a minor literature involves all the ways in which language is effected by a strong co-efficient of deterritorialization. (p. 16)

For Deleuze and Guattari, 'what Blacks today can do with the American tongue' is a prime example of a minor usage, and reinforces their argument that minor usage is always political (p. 16). Where the 'ordinary use of language could be called extensive or representative' ('the reterritorializing function of language'), in minor usage 'language ceases to be representative in order to stretch toward its extremes or its limits' (p. 32). In the words of their editor, the terms 'territorialization', 'deterritorialization', and 'reterritorialization' 'may be defined as the creation and perpetuation of a cultural space, the dissolution of the space, [and] its recreation'. While codification, decodification, and recodification may serve as rough synonyms, by stressing cultural space, 'Deleuze and Guattari can formulate as alternatives to coded behaviour, a dissolution of cultural boundaries and the movement of a nomad through territory'. If these formulations 'seem particularly appropriate to the mobile and metamorphic geographies which Kafka presents in his narratives' (p. 28), they also provide an entrance into Reed's versions of the nomadic and metamorphic, namely, his recurrent formal and 'narrative' concerns with displacement and transformation.

In using the work of Deleuze and Guattari in my reading of Reed, I do not wish to suggest that their concept of 'minor' literature, or the relation of 'minor' to 'ethnic', are completely unproblematic. What is useful in their work on literature is the shift of emphasis beyond the sociologically descriptive terminology of 'ethnicity' to a more acute politicization of language. Such a refocusing allows us to place a writer like Reed, who is simultaneously 'ethnic' and 'avant-garde', more accurately by questioning the status of ethnicity and the avant-garde as (self-contained) cultural spaces. If Reed's work has as much in common with white, 'non-ethnic' writers such as Nathanael West, Thomas Pynchon and William Burroughs, as with Charles Chestnutt, Ralph Ellison and Charles Wright, then the territorial spaces of ethnicity and the avant-garde must be opened up beyond the usually sociological demarcations of the first, and the literary ones of the latter. In this dissolution is implied a whole cultural politics and praxis which goes beyond both the historically necessitated, but ultimately self-defeating, attempt to mark identity and difference exemplified by the Black Aesthetic, and the blatantly racist suppression of minority cultures within the dominant culture and its academic institutions.

Although Reed's antagonism towards certain aspects of Western culture may appear to be deeply dichotomizing, exaggeration in his writing works in both directions. The satire on the academy and the church is not counterposed to a heroic black voice, but to an equally parodic and exaggerated use of Afro-American vernacular, and a comic vision of the return of the 'baaaaad' trickster, which owes as much to the western tradition of tall-tale and boasting humour found in dime novels[36] and to comic books and television, as to Afro-American folklore's rich resources. 'I've never seen Europe as a monolith', says Reed, 'that's why I don't get involved in "Black Power" confrontations' (*Shrovetide*, 230). 'Every culture appears, vis-a-vis every other, exaggerated (just like every language)', writes Boon, 'hence the exhilaration of the imperfectable effort we call translation' (p. 26). Berndt Ostendorf's work on nineteenth-century American minstrelsy supports Boon's argument that exaggeration and translation are intertwined. Without underplaying the racism of minstrelsy, Ostendorf points out that 'minstrelsy anticipated on stage what many Americans deeply feared: the blackening of America'. It created

> a symbolic language and a comic iconography for 'intermingling' culturally with the African Caliban while at the same time, 'isolating' him socially. . . . Yet, however caricatured this vision of blackness may have been, it began the translation of black music, black song, and black dance into the mainstream of American popular culture[37]

Furthermore, black minstrelsy subverted the white racial stereotypes through greater exaggeration or 'artistic hyperbole . . . so grotesque and absurd that the performance entered the realm of surrealism (a tradition which has gone right into the making of Ishmael Reed)' (pp. 83–4).

Discussing cultural contact, James Clifford asks 'should our ideas of rationality be drawn from the metaphors of conversation, hospitality, and exchange, as humanists like Massignon, Levi, and Mauss have urged? Or must we prefer the figures of military maneuver proposed by Foucault. . . ?'[38] I wish to suggest that we need not conceive of these two options as being, of necessity, always incompatible. 'Antagonistic reciprocity' (the 'fighting' with property, the incurring of debt) can be an important part of symbolic exchange's function of creating response and social cohesion. The violence of exaggeration, as well as the violence of antagonism and critique, do not lead to a closure of dialogue in Reed's work, but establish new terms for exchange. To read his work only as 'getting to whitey' is to impose a reductive reading on his use and adaptation of satire.

In the work of Reed, the exploration of the function of the poet goes hand-in-hand with the consideration of the trickster and of clowning and carnival, and it is through satire and disruptive laughter that the trickster and the sacred clowns function in 'primitive' societies in their respective spheres of myth and ceremony. Robert D. Pelton has described this sense of comedy as a 'metaphysics of delight', something Reed finds lacking in the orthodoxies of both Judaism and Christianity, not to mention what he refers to (rather simply) as 'Marxism' and 'existentialism':

> In this metaphysics the trickster is neither first cause nor last end. He

is an exemplar of wit in action, the most practical joke of all as he pulls the chair out from under the system to keep it moving, as he bounces back from beyond every beyond with a gleeful shout that there is really here'[39]

In the conclusion of his study, Pelton argues that we can name the 'mysterious power' which shapes the trickster

> with the word grown ever more oxymoronic over the centuries, too ambivalent for even Freud to use, too ironic for Marx, and say that this love to contradict, this passion to rise and make love, which finds in the trickster an image of transforming joy as he weaves his web of purpose and dances of delight, is nothing less simple and more complex than love. (p. 284)

As Jake the Barker tells the children in *Yellow Back Radio Broke-Down*, 'shucks, I've always been a fool, eros appeals more to me than logos' (p. 25). Or, as Reed says of the Eskimos and the whale, 'This must be love baby!'

Reed's adoption of an essentially anarchist stance must be placed in the context of the political disillusionment which marked the close of the 1960s for many Americans. Along with the experience of the collapse of the Civil Rights Movement and the impact of the Vietnam war, Reed shares with many Americans a profound distrust of the Left. The works which follow *Mumbo Jumbo* in the reactionary decades of the 1970s and 1980s, are witness to the diminishing of Reed's optimism. Pessimism and bitterness become more prominent, and as one attempts to assess Reed's political strategies in his fictions, one is increasingly made aware of the fact that if the trickster is a god of ambivalence and mutual transformation, the Hermes-god is also the god of the market place, of merchants and of bankers.

8 Image, Text and Performance: Inter-artistic Relationships in Contemporary Poetry

Hazel Smith

The greater awareness which critical theory has produced of the connections between language and other systems has made inter-artistic relationships the focus of a renewed interest in the study of poetry. Similarly many contemporary poets have used language in ways which accentuate its relationship to painting or music or have engaged in inter-media work. In this chapter I hope to show how an appreciation of some of the theoretical considerations involved in the relationship between poetry, painting and music can help us to appreciate contemporary poetry and also how some contemporary poems enact the central issues of critical theory. Frank O'Hara's poem 'Why I am not a Painter'[1] will be used to demonstrate the relationship of poetry to painting, and Jackson Mac Low's inter-media piece 'A Notated Vocabulary for Eve Rosenthal'[2] that of words to music. In both cases a discussion of relevant issues in critical theory will precede their application to the poems.

The traditional comparison between poetry and painting, based on the issue of representation, argued that, since visual images could resemble objects while words could only point or refer to them, there was a more natural link between visual images and the world and a more artificial link between words and world. Furthermore because a poem had to be read from beginning to end, while images in a painting could be viewed simultaneously, poetry was considered to be a temporal and painting a spatial art. While not denying that a poem is different in certain respects from a painting, modern theory has undermined these oppositions by emphasizing the man-made, cultural and artificial in painting as well as in poetry and by showing that both poetry and painting are temporal-spatial constructs. Modern theory, then, can be said to have *deconstructed* the opposition between poetry and painting, since deconstruction is the critical strategy whereby two things where are thought to be opposed are shown to have a common factor which destabilizes any argument based on clear-cut oppositions or categories. The relationship between poetry and painting has been well discussed by W.J.T. Mitchell and Wendy Steiner but these writers differ in their approach and range of reference.[3] The following is a synthesis of these accounts but also provides my own perspective; it develops the argument by applying the concepts of representation and abstraction to modern poetry.

Poetry and painting: Text and image
A fundamental factor in the comparison of poetry and painting is the nature of the system on which each is based. A poem is a text made from language, itself composed of discrete units, words, whose aural and visual forms are signifiers. In a poem a network of signifiers produces signifieds with which the signifiers have only an arbitrary connection. This means that however much a poem may appear to refer to objects and events, it is always disjunct from them.[4] A painting on the other hand is a complex of visual images whose elements are *not* discrete units like words. So in a picture it is difficult to know what the basic element (or signifier) is – for example whether it is a single brushstroke – and how to identify each instance of that element. In addition there is a less arbitrary connection between signifier and signified, image and object; for example a picture of a chair is experienced as closer to an actual chair than the word 'chair'. Painting is therefore, in one sense, felt to be more natural, or to use the critical theory term, more 'motivated', than its verbal counter-part.

This led traditional theorists to maintain that painting had a more natural link with the world than poetry but modern theory has emphasized that any picture, however natural it may appear to be, is still always a sign. As such it is man-made and artificial and involves artistic conventions and artistic structuring, that is, manipulation of its sign-system. A representation of a chair, for example, however similar it may be to an actual chair, involves some artistic structuring, so that a difference from the original always emerges. Furthermore abstract painting (that is painting which concentrates on internal formal relationships rather than representing objects) relies on structural arrangement rather than similarity.

On the other hand a poem can appear much more natural or motivated than the structure of language might seem to allow: that is, it can seem to have a non-arbitrary connection with what it signifies. The grammatical and syntactical structures of language may be used to describe a chair in such a concentrated and vivid manner that the process of signification becomes largely invisible and we feel that we are directly experiencing the object, rather than a linguistic concept of it (in prose this would be known as realism). Conversely, grammatical and syntactical structures can be broken up so much that the connection between signifiers and signified becomes progressively ruptured, for example in the construction 'chair reach chain'. When this occurs a new arrangement of signifiers arises whose signified breaks free from the impression of reference which language normally creates and is analogous to the signified in an abstract painting.

Poems and paintings then are alike in that they are signs but conceal their sign-functions so that an appearance of naturalness occurs. But the preceding argument also suggests that there is no such thing as absolute 'representation' or 'abstraction'; every painting and poem oscillates between depicting the world and structural arrangement of its own elements, manipulation of its sign-system. Our argument culminates therefore in a deconstruction of the terms abstraction and representation, which are interdependent. All 'representations' (whether verbal or visual) depart from similarity and involve an element of structural arrangement which, because it does not seem to point to anything outside itself, is seem as 'abstraction'. Conversely all 'abstractions' (i.e. verbal or visual non-representations) are not entirely structural arrangements but have elements which point to objects and events outside the poem or painting.[5]

The other opposition that modern theory has deconstructed is that of poetry as temporal and painting as spatial. Traditionally the reading of poetry, because it took place in time, was thought to involve successive perception while painting, because it involved spatial relationships, was thought to require instantaneous perception.[6] Modern theory has, however, deconstructed this opposition by showing us that the scanning of the surface of a picture takes place through a succession of moments in time, while the act of reading a text requires simultaneous perception of various elements which are removed in time. Moreover the necessity for simultaneous perception of disparate and heterogenous elements once the work of art has been successively perceived is common to both arts. Time and space, successivity and simultaneity cannot be separated from each other and interact in both poems and paintings.

To sum up, the comparison between poetry and painting shows that their similarity arises from the differences *within* poetry and painting which they share.[7] This is because all paintings and poems oscillate between the abstract and representational, the temporal and spatial. However it is also important to emphasize that this argument has wider implications: artistic structures do not exist in isolation but in a complex relationship to the social formation and if this is more apparent in poems because they use language, it is still pervasive in painting. Therefore the terms abstraction and representation, spatial and temporal are not value-free and do not only encompass artistic concepts. Mitchell has pointed out that the traditional poetry–painting opposition was often used to prioritize one art form over the other, for example, by suggesting that painting was superior to poetry because it formed a more 'natural' link with the world. This has been undermined by critical theory whose deconstructions put the two art forms on an equal basis.[8]

'Why I am not a Painter'
When we first read Frank O'Hara's 'Why I am not a Painter' we are likely to be captivated by its lively conversational manner, its humorous minute-by-minute account of the ups and downs of the artistic process, the way it allows us to eavesdrop on a social and artistic encounter where drinks are mixed freely with creative endeavour. We find ourselves participating in its exuberance and wit which keeps us in perpetual motion. Yet however many times we read the poem it never really gives its meaning up. Is it about the differences between poetry and painting or the similarities? What does it tell us about painting or poetry? The title of 'Why I am not a Painter', which uses the negative rather then the positive (why I am a poet), seems to start an elusive chain of argument which rivets our attention but never fully stays on course: this instability of meaning is part of the fascination of the poem. In fact 'Why I am not a Painter' is not about either the difference or similarity of poetry and painting but *both*, for in the poem similarity is constantly turning into difference and difference into similarity. As such the poem

enacts humorously and engages us in the deconstruction of the poetry-painting comparison I have outlined above.

On the one hand the poem is about the differences between poetry and painting: a painter is not a poet, the painter works with images and the poet with words. The painter begins with an object, sardines, while the poet begins with a concept, the colour orange. The painter can represent sardines while the poet can only begin by talking *about* orange. The painter feels that his canvas is overcrowded, 'it was too much' and empties it out while the poet feels he has not put enough into the poem:

> There should be
> so much more, not of orange, of
> words, of how terrible orange is
> and life.

The poet then expands the poem into pages of prose. They both produce different objects, one a painting called Sardines associated with a canned food, the other a poem called Oranges associated with a natural food.

On the other hand the poem is about similarities between the poem and painting. Both seem to involve words and images; SARDINES, for example, could be word or image or both and the most satisfactory image turns out to come from 'just letters'. Both poet and painter, who seem to have the vaguest of artistic intentions, find what they want in the process of working. Both keep putting things in and taking things out and change the way they depict the object of their original attention; Sardines becomes 'just letters', that is becomes less of an image, while orange becomes Oranges, changing from the conceptual to the concrete, from colour to fruit. Sardines and Oranges are both foods but also commodities and both poem and painting have their respective titles within them. SARDINES and ORANGES could each either be abstraction or representation.

In fact both poet and painter are oscillating between the possibilities of their media. They want to create the impression of direct expression, of apparent 'naturalness' which can, however, only be achieved by artistic juggling, that is by manipulation of the sign-system. Poet and painter approach the medium in different ways but both must work with it to achieve the most direct and forceful effect. As we have already seen this can be achieved through 'representational' or 'abstract' modes which, because they are interdependent, are indissolubly linked: in the poem representation and abstraction become interchangeable. When the painter is asked about his representation of SARDINES he responds in terms of formal arrangement, structure: 'it needed something there', while the poet, however much he relies on the grammatical and syntactical structures of language: 'It is even in prose', must concentrate on the formal arrangement of the words, not their meanings, to convey 'how terrible orange is and life'. Both poet and painter, therefore, move backwards and forwards between depicting an object and the structural arrangement of their material. In addition the poet oscillates between the temporal and spatial possibilities of his medium; his fluctuation between the poem as pages of words and the poem as lines, implies that simultaneity is as important to its conception as ordered succession. Both poet and painter are involved in the differences *within* poetry and painting which they share.

'Why I am not a Painter' is not merely *about* the difference and similarity of painting; it *demonstrates* it. It conveys a sense of its difference from painting through its use of the grammatical and syntactical structures of language to make certain distinctions, 'I am not a painter, I am a poet', to convey the passage of time, 'I go by and the days go by/and I drop in again' and to convey snippets of conversation. At the same time it demonstrates its similarity to painting by employing the poetic equivalent of representational and abstract modes which are shown to be interdependent. It uses real names, characters and events (Michael Goldberg is a painter, was a friend of O'Hara's and did paint a picture called Sardines) and represents the incident through social conversation and colloquialisms in such a way that, in some respects, language seems transparent, the processes of signification are concealed and we feel as if we are witnessing it directly. At the same time the poem fails to close off its meaning, which is constantly deferred. For example, the initial statement, 'I am not a painter, I am a poet', which seems to be quite definite, is immediately modified by a statement which neither completely follows on from the first nor completely negates it, 'Why? I think I would rather be/a painter, but I am not'. In an abstract painting objects and events and their perceived relationships are broken down and structural relationships between colours and shapes predominate. Likewise, in 'Why I am not a Painter' logical and narrative discontinuity encourage our active participation in the structural arrangement of the poem whose 'push and pull' moves us in and out of difference and similarity.[9]

The poem also undermines its temporal dimension through simultaneity. Though it involves the passage of time its argument is circular rather than linear: its only conclusion is to send us back to the beginning again. The second and third stanzas could in fact be laid out opposite each other on the page since the effect of the poem will be to move us backwards and forwards between them, to make us view them simultaneously, rather than to progress through them.

Overall the poem behaves like a painting in the dynamic interaction it displays between structural relationships and depiction of the world. It does not, however, enact the poetry-painting comparison in isolation: it points to a variety of artistic and social implications and ramifications for that comparison. Written in 1956 during the Cold War, when Abstract Expressionist painting in American was being promoted as the supreme expression of human values, it demonstrates humorously that poetry can do anything painting can do. Alluding to Pop Art (characterized by representation of objects such as sardines and oranges) and Abstract Expressionism (characterized by gestural images and structural relationships) it suggests also that art, whether verbal or visual, should not be separated into movements. Apparently opposed artistic tendencies can be combined, as they sometimes were in the works of the New York School of painters such as Michael Goldberg and in O'Hara's own work. And the use of consumer goods, sardines and oranges, as images to be manipulated, demonstrates how both poems and paintings are inescapably involved in a complex relationship between artistic endeavour and political and social formation.[10]

'A Notated Vocabulary for Eve Rosenthal'

'A Notated Vocabulary for Eve Rosenthal', written in 1978, is an inter-media piece which involves both words and music. Before looking at the ways in which critical theory can help us to approach it we should consider some of the problems the piece raises. Most obviously, containing both words and musical notation, it questions the boundaries between poetry and music. It takes the form of a *score* with instructions (see Appendix, pp. 211–213), with considerable freedom for the performers who are responsible for many of

A Notated Vocabulary for Eve Rosenthal–22–25/5/78.
Copyright © 1978 by Jackson Mac Low. All Rights Reserved

Image, Text and Performance   157

the details. The piece will therefore differ from performance to performance and this makes the role of the critic, who must decide whether he should deal with it at the level of score or actual erformance, highly problematic, since the score is not the blueprint of a particular performance but only the scheme within which it takes place. The piece also postulates creativity as joint activity; the performers work in co-operation with each other (they are told to 'listen and relate') as well as interacting with the rules produced by the poet-composer. Since the work is completed in performance, the composer-poet cannot be regarded as expressive agent of the poem, instead he sets the limits within which a particular performance can take place. The words and notes are all derived from a name which is used as structural basis rather than because it carries any information about the author's attitude to the person concerned. Words and notegroups are written out in a discontinuous style which, spread out on a single page, emphasizes the simultaneous availability of the different elements of the score rather than their ordered succession. Since the individual units can be combined in any order, meanings derived from such a score will inevitably be multiple and variable. This raises the question of what kind of meaning the piece has, whether it has any overall continuous meaning, and whether the search for a meaning is itself a meaningful pursuit.

So the piece presents three areas of difficulty: questions of genre raised by the relationship of words and music, of how we relate performance to structure and of how we construe its meaning/ signification. Before returning to the piece in more detail let us see how critical theory addresses these problematic areas. To do this it will be necessary to refer to a wide body of critical theory including musical analysis. In fact the influence of literary and musical theory has been symbiotic: musical analysis has been very strongly influenced by linguistics, semiotics and structuralism while literary theory, in its greater emphasis on structural analysis, has moved closer to procedures which have always been fundamental to musical analysis.[11]

Genre: words and music
Critical theory has repeatedly undermined the boundaries between different types of texts and between verbal texts and other types of discourse. As you are reading this you are probably feeling doubtful about whether the inclusion of a piece with some musical notation in

a book about poetry is appropriate and this response has mainly been generated by your having certain assumptions about what a poem is, assumptions which critical theory has repeatedly challenged. For example in his essay 'From Work to Text' Roland Barthes says 'the Text does not stop at (good) Literature; it cannot be contained in a hierarchy, even in a single division of genres. What constitutes the Text is, on the contrary (or precisely) its subversive force in respect of the old classifications.'[12] More specifically, critical theory has also made us more aware of the qualities in literature which are like music and the qualities in music which relate to literature. Roman Jakobson, for example, has demonstrated how the sounds of the words (signifiers) interact with their sense in poetry so that 'words similar in sound are drawn together in meaning'.[13] Jakobson has also demonstrated how word-patterning is crucial to the effect of a poem; this word-patterning is in fact very similar to the patterning of pitch and rhythm we find in music and interacts with the meanings of the words, themselves highly unstable. On the other hand some musical sociologists have argued that music has a connection with the world outside it and is not just a self-enclosed set of structural relationships. For example, sometimes musical codes may relate to the beliefs and attitudes of the culture in which they arise or are perceived.[14] Both poems and pieces of music (like paintings) involve, to different degrees, internal formal relationships and a stance towards the world: again the separation between two different art forms, music and poetry, is at least partially deconstructed.

Performance
Performance has always been essential to music for realizing the written score as aural event, but its role has been enormously expanded in certain areas of contemporary music where the music is either completely or partially decided by the performers. Poetry on the other hand, though it was originally part of an oral-aural tradition, gradually developed into a genre which was written down and designed to be read, but the oral-aural aspect has been revived in contemporary 'text-sound' which concentrates on the sound aspect of poetry and presents the text as score.[15] Since performance has up till now seemed more central to music, the problems of analyzing performances and the relationship of performance to

score have been confronted more in musical analysis than in literary analysis and are summarized by Ian Bent in *Analysis*: 'Music is not tangible and measurable as is a liquid or a solid for chemical analysis. The subject of a musical analysis has to be determined; whether it is the score itself, or at least the sound-image that the score projects; or the sound-image in the composer's mind at the moment of composition; or an interpretive performance; or the listener's temporal experience of a performance. All these categories are possible subjects for analysis. There is no agreement among analysts that one is more "correct" than others – only that the score (when available) provides a reference point from which the analyst reaches out towards one sound-image or another, a "neutral level" (to use the language of semiotics) which furnishes links between the creative activity and aesthetic experience.'[16] (Bent does not, however, mention improvisation here, the most complete instance of the closing of the composer-performer gap). If literary theory has confronted the matter of performance less directly, many of the insights of literary theory can be seen to be applicable to the concepts of performance as composition. For literary theory has emphasized the activity of the reader and played down the importance of the role of the author: in other words the reader becomes a co-composer producing the text. For example in 'Musica Practica' Barthes says the reading of a modern text consists 'not in receiving, in knowing or feeling that text but in writing it anew. . . .'[17] In 'From Work to Text' he also draws an analogy between the performer in contemporary music and the reader of a contemporary text: 'We know that today post-serial music has radically altered the role of the "interpreter" who is called on to be in some sort the co-author of the score, completing it rather than giving it "expression". The text is very much a score of this kind: it asks of the reader a practical collaboration.'[18] The idea of an author as a producer of the text, Barthes tells us in 'From Work to Text', is something of an illusion and a limitation: 'To give a Text an Author is to impose a limit on that text, to furnish it with a final signified, to close the writing'.[19] In fact critical theory has very much undermined the idea of the work of art as the expression of a unified self and has emphasized that a poem or novel arises from a multiplicity of forces which are set into play by the author, rather than generated by him. The meaning of a poem results from the joint participation of author and reader. Consequently critical theory makes way for the idea of the work of art as collaboration between several different people and also for the idea that a work of art may be better seen as a mobile construction, partly determined by the reader's or listener's interaction with it, than as a fixed and finished product of authorial intent.

Meaning/Signification
Theory has helped us to appreciate that in verbal texts signification is not single but multiple; 'The Text is not a co-existence of meanings but a passage, an over-crossing; thus it answers not to an interpretation, even a liberal one, but to an explosion, a dissemination'.[20] In music, however, the questions of what the signifier is or what is being signified are difficult, perhaps unanswerable. In musical compositions pitch, rhythm or dynamic are not discrete units but interact continuously and modify each other; furthermore they do not usually systematically point to objects and events outside themselves. Theory however helps us to appreciate that meaning results from the interaction of signs within a particular system so that words mean within poems while sounds 'mean' within a piece of music. Any text which involves the cross-over of two systems combines different types of meaning and therefore alerts us to a wider concept of meaning within art.

The performance nature of 'A Notated Vocabulary for Eve Rosenthal' will inevitably make any transformation of critical theory into an approach to it problematic. The score and instructions must form the basis for an analysis but imagined instances of the score (where the reader or critic constructs or performs the work for himself) and actual performances of the score should also play a part. In my analysis I will therefore, from time to time, refer to a live performance of a piece I took part in and which was recorded.[21] Nevertheless my purpose is to suggest approaches to the piece rather than attempting a full analysis of a particular performance. The main areas of discussion again will be the relationship of words and music, structure in performance and meaning/signification.

Words and music
In 'A Notated Vocabulary for Eve Rosenthal' the words and music are co-equal, the words do not in any way serve as a vehicle for the music, instead the piece demonstrates their interdependence. The

musical aspect of language, or the importance of sound in language is emphasized because the words are taken from a single name, causing considerable overlap of their sounds. Consequently groupings of the words, e.g. 'rove rote trove nose' or 'servant resent leaven' will tend to produce assonance, alliteration and rhyme, etc., drawing as much attention to the sounds of the words, and their connection through sound, as to their meanings. The delivery of the words will also be strongly affected by musical considerations such as dynamics, attack and rhythm. On the other hands the words can add an illustrative aspect to the music. For example in the live taped performance the words 'then tear' which open the piece are followed by forceful chords on the piano, while later on the words 'then leave' are followed by a short silence in all the parts.

Performer/structure
There are in 'A Notated Vocabulary for Eve Rosenthal' two levels of structure: an intrinsic level and a performing level. Both levels of structure are inextricably tied up with the performer-composer-listener relationship but the intrinsic level involves the score and instructions and their potential, while the performing level involves the structure as it arises in performance, the piece as it *sounds*. The performing level is always dependent on the intrinsic level.

The fundamental features of the intrinsic level, then, are the score and the instructions. Whereas a traditional score is written on linear staves and requires successive reading, this is presented in the form of a discontinous design. The fragments, placed at a variety of different angles, are dispersed in a swirling arrangement round the score, allowing disparate elements to be viewed simultaneously; though whichever way up the score is, some of the fragments will always appear upside down. The fragments can be read or played in any order and even the actual position of the score is not fixed, so the performer can choose to have the page in any one of four different positions or can change the position of the page during the performance. This makes the score much more flexible than a traditional one and maximizes the possibility that any element, whatever its position on the page, can follow any other. The words and notes are all taken from a single common source (the name Eve Rosenthal) chosen by the writer/composer, so in this sense the piece is tightly structured and carefully controlled by the writer/composer and is minimalist in conception. The choice of notes depends on the letters, however in performance the notes played will cover a wider range than is apparent from the score, since the performer can choose which musical clef he puts in front of them and can play them in any octave. This means that almost any note could sound in the finished performance while the range of words appearing will be more restricted, since only words on the score, words from the name Eve Rosenthal (or the few extra words which are permitted to make phrases or sentences) will be heard.

Since the score is mobilized by them, the instructions are as important to an understanding of the intrinsic structure as the score itself. The instructions maintain a subtle balance between freedom and control, between being 'closed' and 'open'. For example, the performer's range of words is restricted but he/she is free to move between and combine the words in any way. So the words can be permuted in many different combinations such as 'hearse art love' or 'ear nose enter'. Likewise the sequence of notes has to be followed but consecutive notes can be played simultaneously, or as a chord or tone cluster, and notes can be played in any octave. Many of the instructions are themselves open to interpretation. For example, 'Words must be clearly audible, but seldom if ever so loud as to seem to reflect violent feelings' will be interpreted by performers in different ways, since what characterizes a violent feeling and how it is reflected in speech are matters of opinion.

Because the score and instructions impose certain limits as well as encouraging certain freedoms every performance will have some structural features in common. They will all involve patterns of words and notes, overlaying, superimposition, repetition and falls in the amount of activity when individual silences take over. However the performance structure of the piece will always be different and any analysis of that performing structure will involve study of the patterning of the words and music and also how they interact with each other in that particular performance. For example, at one point in the live performance on tape, against a musical backcloth, two voices enter an overlapping dialogue, which begins as follows:

```
voice one: enter ever heaven
voice two:              enter rove lean
voice one: enter ever revel rat
voice two:              enter rove lean
voice one:              halt strove enter ever oar steer sheen
```

Here assonance and alliteration abound in each line, but the voices form verbal patterns through repetition of the word 'enter' and the conjunction 'enter ever'; through the placing of the word 'enter' to the third word in the string after three repetitions of it as first word and through the rhyming of strove and rove. In addition this dialogue was both preceded and followed by several uses of the phrase 'enter ever' and previous use of the phrase 'enter ever heaven', making it part of a broader pattern within the performing structure of the whole piece.

An analysis of the performing structure of the piece would also have to document those aspects left open by the score and instructions, such as attack, speed, dynamics and timbre, which contribute very substantially to its overall affect. For example, in the live performance of this piece, to which I have been referring, there are considerable fluctuations in the density; at certain points the voices and instruments all crescendo together and overlap producing a 'quarrelling' effect, so that individual words cannot always be heard, but instead form clusters of words rather like musical tone clusters. In another passage, in the same performance, a single voice spaciously delineates the words 'resent halt resent enter save' to a quiet piano and glockenspiel accompaniment. In fact enunciation has always played a significant part in the reading of poetry, both when it is read out loud and when it is read silently, for the emphasis a reader gives, or the speed at which he reads, can substantially influence his conception of the poem. The importance of this in the appreciation of poetry has been generally underestimated but such factors are central to text-sound poetry whose verbal scores often contain markings which indicate speed, emphasis or dynamics for delivery of the poems. Such markings are also to be found in other poems by Jackson Mac Low.[22] Analysis of these features, which may include transcription of them, probably needs to become a more prominent feature of poetic analysis, which has not fully addressed itself to them and which could borrow from musical notation for this purpose. This would be a new way that poetic practice could feed back into poetic theory and analysis just as it has done in the past.

It is in a discussion of the performing structure of the piece that the inadequacy of merely looking at the score breaks down, we need to hear how it *sounds*. However this does not necessarily just mean listening to it but also performing it. Anyone with an interest in poetry can perform at least the words and anyone with a rudimentary knowledge of musical notation could attempt to realize the notes; he/she would then be collaborating in the making of the text. This does not necessarily mean that the resulting performance would be the same as when the piece was performed by people with an advanced musical technique and a great deal of experience of performing such scores. But the experience of performing the piece, thereby collapsing the distance between the performer and listener, is an important aspect of its appreciation, since one of the purposes of composing or writing a piece in this way is to transform radically the composer/writer–performer–listener relationship. In fact, to peruse this score at all is to begin to see combinations of words, to begin to perform it.[23] Active participation through performance may also be useful in enhancing understanding of certain aspects of critical theory, since it makes more immediate the kind of interpretive operations which critical theory claims are present in the reading of all texts.

Meaning/Signification

The question remains of what potentiality for meaning the score has, what it signifies: most obviously the score carries the meanings of the words on the page. Words and combinations of words might seem to suggest quite specific types of content, e.g. the words servant or slave have political overtones; Lares, Thor and Lethe have mythological ones; heaven and roseate suggest religion; throes, heart, love etc. emotional states. The word-strings, phrases and clauses which any performer generates and their interaction with those generated by other performers can set into motion a whole range of complementary and conflicting meanings. For example, the sequence 'servant resent loathe' could suggest a servant resenting and loathing his position as a servant, or conversely that servants are resented and loathed by the people who employ them. Or the sequence 'enter hearse art' could suggest that artistic creativity is a kind of death or that the experience of death is itself creative. It is evident from the dual nature of my interpretations here that no one meaning will come through clearly: many of the words have several meanings, and most combinations of the words will contain words with fairly disparate meanings. The difficulty of combining specific words into syntactic sentences during a performance will probably mean that a performer will not form many such sentences. However even where a performer, using the extra words that Mac Low permits, orientates his performance towards more syntactic sentences such as 'he ran to the event there' he is unlikely to sustain a particular direction of meaning for very long. In addition the meanings of any performer will constantly be mingling with the meanings generated by other performers and with his own and their musical phrases. This means that the piece continually hovers on the edge of semantic breakdown and that no one meaning will ever be logically followed through. Meaning in the piece then is of two types: the first type is that generated by individual words and combinations of words which provide flashes of meaning and connected meanings. The second type arises from its musical and linguistic structural relationships.

'Why I am not a painter' and 'A Notated Vocabulary for Eve Rosenthal' are only two examples of how contemporary poetry intersects with painting or music. Other instances in contemporary culture abound such as concrete poetry, the 'happenings' of the sixties, collaborative work which draws together artists from different disciplines and the large body of contemporary poetry which is not so overtly connected with music or painting.[24] In addition the inter-artistic comparison can be relevant in helping us to see how in more traditional poems representation and abstraction, temporal and spatial relationships, sound and sense, the aural and the written interact. For the proximity of music and painting, neither of which use language, makes us more aware of how the meanings of the words in poems contend with structural arrangement and senuous appeal to create new and more complex meanings. It emphasizes the fluid, dynamic relationship between signifier and signifier, signifiers and signified, and makes us more aware of the differences within language itself which poetry exploits and celebrates.

9 On Misreading Mallarmé: The Resistance to Modernity

Bernard McGuirk

> If one recalls Mallarmé's repeated insistence on poetry's abolition of simple referentiality . . . one begins to suspect that the traditional reading of Mallarmé's nonreferentiality is inadequate[1]
>
> BARBARA JOHNSON

Barbara Johnson claims, in *The Critical Difference*, that 'what is revolutionary in Mallarmé's poetics is less the elimination of the "object" than [the] construction of a systematic set of self-emptying, non intuitive meanings'. She also insists, however, that ' "leaving the initiative to words" is not as simple as it sounds'.[2] Taking her analysis further and accepting the invitation to see how later *poets* have read Mallarmé, I wish to concentrate on the word 'traditional'. Firstly, I shall discuss a poem by the Nicaraguan writer Rubén Darío (1867–1916), generally regarded by literary historians as the founder of *modernismo*, and shall question his capacity to absorb fully the implications of Mallarmé's break with traditional epistemology. Secondly, I shall try to show how another Latin American poet, the Peruvian César Vallejo (1892–1938), responding to Mallarmé *through* Darío, challengingly reads the latter's misreading. In this chapter, the whole question of poetic influence will be examined and, as the reference to misreading in my title suggests, I shall be using and assessing the theories of the North American critic Harold Bloom.

Following Bloom's tenets that poems lie primarily against three adversaries – 1. themselves 2. other poems 3. time[3] – I shall echo this trio with the three critical approaches of 1. textual criticism 2. intertextuality 3. influence study. While my aim will be to operate all three together, the more general implications of Bloomian analysis can also be drawn out.

First, Bloom's claim that the 'dialectic of influences . . . reveals that literature itself is founded upon rivalry, misinterpretation, repression, even plain theft and savage misprision'[4] can be viewed in the broader context of a North American reaction against *merely textual criticism* – both the New Critical 'Verbal Icon' variety of Bloom's own early conditioning (Brooks, Wimsatt, Trilling *et al.*), and later, structuralist equivalents. The technical and formal nature of my concerns in juxtaposing a Darío sonnet with one by Mallarmé should by no means exclude speculation on intentionality, indeed, might serve to remind us, as Frank Lentricchia has it, that 'the human writes, the human thinks, and is always following after and defending against another human'.[5] Equally, a Bloomian analysis might provide an antidote to that 'anti-humanistic plain dreariness of all those developments in European criticism that have yet to demonstrate that they can help in reading any one poet whatsoever'.[6]

This brings me to the second question, that of Bloom's use of intertextuality. There can be no doubt that Bloomian analysis *is* Post-Structuralist in its conforming to certain basic propositions concerning the nature of literary language. Firstly, such analysis conforms to the commonplace of *le déjà écrit*, for instance, in the formulation of Tzvetan Todorov: 'No statement exists without the intertextual dimension. Whatever the object of the word, that object, in one way or another, has always already been said; and one cannot avoid encountering discourses held upon that object'.[7] Moreover, Bloomian analysis performs according to Antoine Compagnon's recent theories of citation: 'To write, since it is always to rewrite, is no different from citing. Citation, thanks to the metonymic confusion over which it presides, is reading and writing; to read or to write is to perform an act of citation'.[8] It is even possible to set Bloomian analysis within a Derridean context since, again, it performs according to the claim that 'we can pronounce not a single destructive proposition which has not already had to slip into the form, the logic, and the implicit postulations of precisely what it seeks to contest'.[9] Thus, in my Mallarmé-Darío example, the potential Freudian dimension of the 'son'-inheritor-ephebe's proposed 'destruction' of the 'father'-precursor-master would be but another, inevitable, failure of the attempt to construct a metaphysics of presence, of self-presence. The fact that, as I hope to show in the juxtaposition of the two poems, poetic meaning is always dialectical, poetic expression always an 'anxiety' for originality in a non-unique discourse, merely confirms, conforms with, repeats with a difference, the differentiality of Derrida's deconstruction of Western metaphysics in general.[10]

My third category is influence study itself. What kind of text is that of Harold Bloom, what kind of text is my own 'influence study' of Mallarmé and Darío? For Bloom, the answer is clear, if habitually 'strong' (and most *un*-modest): poetry criticism always parallels poetry in its antithetical dialectical relationship with previous criticism *and* with poetry. For Bloom, 'all criticism is prose poetry'.[11] As such, criticism cannot escape a dialectical reciprocity which constantly defers its own status or 'presence'. What I am writing at this present moment differs from, but is deferred towards, both precursor critics *and* poets.

> I do not believe that poetic influence is simply something that happens, that it is just the process by which ideas and images are transmitted from earlier to later poets. On that view, whether or not influence causes anxiety in the later poet is a matter of temperament and circumstance. Poetic influence thus reduces to source-study.
> HAROLD BLOOM[11]

Time and again an influence may be traced or asserted; yet influence study generally proves inconclusive to the extent that it remains at the level of established *fact*. Far more interesting is the question of *how* influence works and why. In this respect, the recent work of Bloom, particularly in *The Anxiety of Influence* (1973) and *A Map of Misreading* (1975),[12] has both revitalized and rendered more systematic the 'influence' approach. My intention here is to apply in detail Bloom's so-called 'revisionary ratios' to 'Yo persigo una forma' and to argue that Darío's poem constitutes a creative 'misreading' of Mallarmé's 'Mes bouquins refermés sur le nom de Paphos', I will begin by quoting what may be considered as Bloom's most succinct statement of his methodology:

> The first principle of the proper study of influence, as I conceive it, is that no strong poem has sources and no strong poem merely alludes to another poem. The meaning of a strong poem *is* another strong poem, a precursor's poem which is being misinterpreted, revised, corrected, evaded, twisted askew, made to suffer an inclination or bias which is the property of the later and not the earlier poet. Poetic influence, in this sense, is actually poetic misprision, a poet's taking or doing amiss of a parent-poem that keeps *finding* him, to use a Coleridgean

turn-of-phrase. Yet even this misprision is only the first step that a new poet takes when he advances from the early phase where his precursor floods him, to a more Promethean phase where he quests for his own fire, which nevertheless must be stolen from his precursor. I count some half-dozen steps in the life-cycle of the strong poet, as he attempts to convert his inheritance into what will aid him without inhibiting him by the anxiety of a failure in priority, a failure to have begotten himself. These steps are revisionary ratios.[13]

The six ratios, by now classical or notorious according to one's attitude to Bloom, are *Clinamen, Tessera, Kenosis, Daemonization, Askesis* and *Apophrades*. I shall give Bloom's definition of each in the course of my application and would only add that I have chosen to apply them in an order slightly different from the above. This is not a random choice but one dictated by the development of Darío's sonnet. Thus, I have arranged my discussion of the Bloom ratios according to their occurrence in a *linear* reading of 'Yo persigo una forma' in juxtaposition with Mallarmé's 'Mes bouquins refermés sur le nom de Paphos'.

> Mes bouquins refermés sur le nom de Paphos,
> Il m'amuse d'élire avec le seul génie
> Une ruine, par mille écumes bénie
> Sous l'hyacinthe, au loin, de ses jours triomphaux.
>
> Coure le froid avec ses silences de faux,
> Je n'y hululerai pas de vide nénie
> Si ce très blanc ébat au ras du sol dénie
> A tout site l'honneur du paysage faux.
>
> Ma faim qui d'aucuns fruits ici ne se régale
> Trouve en leur docte manque une saveur égale:
> Qu'un éclate de chair humain et parfumant!
>
> Le pied sur quelque guivre où notre amour trisonne,
> Je pense plus longtemps peut-être éperdument
> A l'autre, au sein brûlé d'une antique amazone.

(My books shut on the name of Paphos, it amuses me to choose with my spirit alone a ruin blessed by a thousand foams, far off, beneath the hyacinth of its triumphant days.
  Let the cold run with its sickle silences, I shall not lament an empty refusal if this most white revel on the earth's surface deny to any site the false landscape's honour.
  My hunger that is satisfied with no fruits here finds in their learned lack an equal savour: let one burst with flesh human and odorous!

My foot on some serpentine andiron where our love stirs the fire, I
think longer – perhaps with desperation – of the other, of the burnt
breast of an ancient Amazon.)[14]

> Yo persigo una forma que no encuentra mi estilo,
> botón de pensamiento que busca ser la rosa;
> se anuncia con un beso que en mis labios se posa
> al abrazo imposible de la Venus de Milo.
>
> Adornan verdes palmas el blanco peristilo;
> los astros me han predicho la visión de la Diosa;
> y en mi alma reposa la luz como reposa
> el ave de la luna sobre un lago tranquilo.
>
> Y no hallo sino la palabra que huye,
> la iniciación melódica que de la flauta fluye
> y la barca del sueño que en el espacio boga;
>
> y bajo la ventana de mi Bella-Durmiente,
> el sollozo continuo del chorro de la fuente
> y el cuello del gran cisne blanco que me interroga.

(I pursue a form not found by my style, pansy [thought] bud which
seeks to be the rose; with a kiss placed on my lips it announces itself
to the impossible embrace of the Venus de Milo.
  Green palms adorn the white peristyle; the stars have foretold to
me the vision of the Goddess; and in my soul the light rests as does
the bird of the moon on a tranquil lake.
  And I find only the word which flees, the melodic initiation which
flows from the flute and the boat of dream [sleep] which floats in
space;
  And below the window of my Sleeping Beauty, the continual
sobbing of the fountain's flow and the neck of the great white swan
which interrogates me.)[15]

The two sonnets, both final poems in their respective volumes,
embody as 'events', a moment of 'bouquins refermés' ('books
re-closed'). Mallarmé's poem echoes the closure of his collection in
the abrupt finality of its opening line. The dismissively low register
of 'bouquins' (*cf* 'livres'), furthermore, only serves to underline the
relative unimportance of *Poésies*, as of any book read at the fire-
side, when compared to Mallarmé's dreamed-of project of 'The
Book, spiritual instrument'.[16]
  Mallarmé's dissatisfaction with traditional literature – the mere
'bouquins' reminiscent of Verlaine's dismissive 'And all the rest is
literature'[17] – nonetheless permitted him to envisage what it might

achieve: 'I believe that literature . . . will furnish us with a Theatre, whose representations will be the true modern cult; a Book, explanation of man sufficient for our most beautiful dreams'.[18] I wish to argue that the perceived gap between Mallarmé's own *style*, in *Poésies*, and the *form* of his 'dream-project' allows for one of Darío's major strategic revisions of Mallarmé in 'Yo persigo una forma'. I shall therefore consider briefly Mallarmé's pursuit of an adequate form of expression.

The 'difficulty' of reading Mallarmé ought to be stressed from the outset, since any claims regarding Darío's 'misprisions' must be seen in the context of the notorious, cultivated discontinuities of thought and expression which constitute Mallarmé's style. A recent critic, Malcolm Bowie, best summarizes the challenge involved:

> The double effect required to allow Mallarmé's gaps their full disjunctive and destructive power, yet at the same time remain attentive to the multitude of invisible currents which pass back and forth between the separated segments, will strike many readers as inexcusably arduous and unrewarding . . . such moments are of the essence in Mallarmé . . . the type of modern artist . . . intent on breaking up ready-made *Gestalten* and smooth surface textures in order to compel his audience to look elsewhere for artistic coherence, to venture beneath the surface into the difficult, undifferentiated world of unconscious process, to interrupt the easy flow of horizontal perception with strenuous excursions into multi-level, all at once 'verticality'[19]

If the Symbolist aesthetic may best be summarized in Mallarmé's formulation 'to paint not the thing but the effect which it produces',[20] then the closing of literature on the 'nom de Paphos', in this instance, provides a telling example of the form that aesthetic implies: '*To name* an object, is to suppress three quarters of the enjoyment of the poem, which consists of guessing little by little: to suggest it, there is the dream. It is the perfect use of this mystery which constitutes the symbol'.[21] Thus, to cease reading on the very *name* of Paphos takes attention away from historical fact or mythical association. Far from pondering or re-working the *ideas* prompted by a mention of the shrine of Aphrodite on Cyprus, founded by the Amazons, the sonnet struggles against that 'easy flow of horizontal perception', as Bowie suggests, indulging in its quatrains precisely those 'strenuous excursions' of a fanciful proposition posed only to be negated, a conditionally evoked vision of past glory revealed as a sham by the intrusive cold draught of the present fireside setting. While the quatrains proceed, disjunctively, by means of negations, to *le faux* (= 'the false': *cf* 'la faux' = the sickle'), underlining the impossibility of even imaginative access to a historically irrecuperable 'paysage', the tercets construct that 'multi-level, all-at-once verticality' of Mallarmé's most explicit savouring, *in a poem*, of an aesthetic of convoked absence. But to this I shall proceed, in detail, as I follow Darío's swerve away from the Mallarméan model. Meanwhile, suffice to recall the celebrated parallel, *in prose*, of Mallarmé's aesthetic of absence:

> I say: a flower! and, out of the forgetfulness where my voice banishes any contour, inasmuch as it is something other than known calyxes, musically arises, an idea itself and fragrant, the one absent from all bouquets.[22]

For it is against an aesthetic of the precedence of the *word* over the idea, of convoked absence over physical or, indeed, metaphysical presence, that we can see Darío reacting, in performing the first of Bloom's revisionary ratios.

> *Clinamen*, which is poetic misprision proper. The later poet swerves away from the precursor, by so reading the parent-poem as to execute a *clinamen* in relation to it. This appears as the corrective movement of his own poem, which implies that the precursor poem went accurately up to a certain point, but then should have swerved, precisely in the direction that the new poem moves.

Darío's sonnet follows that of Mallarmé in closing a 'bouquin' (*Prosas profanas*) on a note of insufficiency. However, it does so with a corrective desire to modify, or swerve away from, the Symbolist aesthetic. Whereas Mallarmé plays with the traditional content/form distinction whereby the latter first abolishes the former before itself being superseded by the abstraction 'absence', Darío introduces a third element, namely 'style', into the existing dichotomy. Whereas the very objective of Mallarmé's poem is the ironic destruction of the notion that poetic form can express content as *presence*, Darío's sonnet, in its first line, re-establishes form as the object of a quest rendered constantly vain, frustrated by the inadequacies of a personal style. *Absence*, therefore, is by no means a necessary condition, let alone the objective in itself, for Darío's sonnet implies already, from the opening line, a pursuit of transcendence which time and again, in his later poetry, will take the form of a desperate logocentrism, if not a full-blown ethical teleology. For the moment, however, 'Yo persigo una forma' swerves away from the Mallarméan notion that 'it is not with ideas that one makes sonnets . . . but with words'[23] by effectively reopening his own book on a *thought*: the thought that the putative marriage of 'style' and 'form' might indeed bear the fruit of an as yet unattained artistic ideal. In this respect, of course, he is very much the inheritor of an earlier generation of Romantics and Parnassians and, perhaps most of all, of the Wagnerian ideal of *Gesamtkunstwerk* as, indeed, subsequent elements of Darío's sonnet will suggest. In short, and in Bloomian terms, Mallarmé has absorbed such a heritage 'accurately up to a certain point, but then should have swerved precisely in the direction that the new poem takes.' It would appear then, initially, that Darío is unable to accept the non-theological trajectory and implications of Mallarméan aesthetics, perhaps detecting, even at so short a distance, what Malcolm Bowie argues three quarters of a century later:

> Mallarmé occupies a special place in the modern tradition. Among French poets of the nineteenth century he was the most adventurously and the most trenchantly agnostic: his powers of doubt played not only upon the time-honoured theologies and theodicies of Europe, but upon those new, secular cults of beauty and 'the Spirit' of which he is popularly thought to be an uncritical exponent[24]

For an author shortly to write of El Arte, 'Ego sum lux et veritas et vita',[25] such an intuition as Mallarmé's could offer no comfort.

> *Tessera*, which is completion and antithesis. The later poet antithetically completes the precursor, by so reading the parent-poem as to retain its terms but to mean them in an opposite sense, as though the precursor had failed to go far enough.

The terms 'retained' in the Darío poem but meant 'in an opposite sense' are the terms of *absence*: 'impossible embrace'. The sense, however, is that of unfulfilment, of regret, as distinct from the convoked, nay, the desired, non-presence of 'burnt breast'. That is to say, Darío's *clinamen* involves the inability or reluctance to accept *le docte* ('the learned') the core of Mallarméan cerebrality which renders 'equal' absence and presence. Darío's aspiration fuses the aesthetic and the sensual in his opening quatrain (although, as I shall show in discussion of *apophrades*, it does retain, inseparably, an element of the cerebral in the double-sense of *pensamiento* as: 'thought'; 'pansy'). Crucially, his sonnet is constructed not upon a 'missing term',[26] as is Mallarmé's 'dream', but rather on objective correlatives of his own 'reverie', as concrete, in one instance, as 'the boat of dream'. Mallarmé eschews the 'here' in the passage towards 'lack'; Darío never leaves the 'here', or the 'here below'. A Romantic archetype of *seaward* evasion (the 'real') is forever commingled with a Symbolist *mental* evasion (the 'unreal').

In this case, *tessera* operates to the extent that 'the precursor had failed to go far enough' in developing sensuality, elevating the erudite and the cerebral, perhaps even the spirit, above and beyond Darío's equally important 'hunger' for the fruits of sensuality. Hyperaesthesia, far from attainable through a domestic, fireside reading, in the armchair – amusedly – and at will – is pursued, in Darío's case, through an altogether different iconography of synaesthesia – 'rose', 'kiss', 'lips', 'announces itself' and 'embrace' – however unattainably.

> *Daemonization*, or the movement toward a personalized Counter-Sublime, in reaction to the precursor's Sublime. The later poet opens himself to what he believes to be a power in the parent-poem that does not belong to the parent proper, but to a range of being just beyond that precursor. He does this, in his poem, by so stationing its relation to the parent-poem as to generalize away the uniqueness of the earlier work.

Darío's 'personalized Counter-Sublime' derives from 'a movement towards' the vision of a specific form of the God-head:

> The stars have foretold to me the vision of the Goddess

In reaction to the precursor's Sublime –

> I think longer – perhaps with desperation –
> of the other, of the burnt breast of an ancient Amazon

– Darío opens himself to the power of other(ness) not confined to a personal daydream of the absent breast but to 'a range of being beyond' that vision. His Counter-Sublime is at once more cosmic ('the stars') and more traditional ('the Goddess'), although there remains a strong sense of the 'personalized' in the privilege accorded to a poet-seer singled out by fate ('have foretold to me').

Darío 'generalizes away the uniqueness of the earlier work' by the fusion of the religious, the personal and the fatalistic, which *seems* to take his sonnet beyond the mere 'Beauty' of Symbolism, reinitiating the quest for 'the Ideal' early rejected by Mallarmé.[27] Yet can this be the case? I shall reserve my response to this question to my discussion of *kenosis*, pausing first to consider how *daemonization* operates in 'Yo persigo una forma'.

The power which derives from Mallarmé's initial evocation of 'A ruin blessed by a thousand foams' (line 3), certainly suffuses the equivalent construction in Darío's sonnet:

> Green palms adorn the white peristyle (line 5)

Yet Darío's sonnet goes further. Not only does the line provide a possibly impenetrable shrine for the Goddess of Darío's aspiration, but also, the luxuriant foliage adorning and obscuring an *architectural* peristyle – the columns surrounding a temple – is mirrored, in verse, by the very adornment of Darío's own peri(phrastic) style. 'Peristyle', then, evokes not only (an external) content but also (an internal) form, namely that of the *modernista* aesthetic so often equated with Symbolism, yet more accurately to be compared, in its concentration on the freezing of content and form in 'the immobile block of Art', with Théophile Gautier's Parnassianism. As in the case of 'pensamiento', 'peristilo' here operates paronomastically – as a pun – by the fusion of two equivalent *presences*. The resultant conceit operates at a level more comparable with much earlier styles exploiting conceits and wit[28] than with the Mallarméan technique of juxtaposing an imagined *presence* with a convoked *absence*.

It is by thus penetrating a personal 'peristyle' that Darío's poem appears to achieve, as the second quatrain ends, precisely the 'pursued *form*', the 'range of being just beyond that precursor': 'and in my soul the light rests as does the bird of the moon on a tranquil lake'. Such a moment of suspension, of repose, of quasi-mystic levitation before the would-be consummation and resolution of the imminent sestet, is typically conveyed not by the traditional possession of the mystic's soul by the dove of Holy Spirit, the Paraclete, but by the quintessentially *modernista*[29] equivalent, namely the indirectly evoked Swan, Ideal embodiment of spirituality and Art. It remains to be seen, however, whether the sonnet's tercets will sustain and fulfil the expectations raised in its quatrains, the possibility of fusing 'style' and 'form', of attaining the Ideal which Mallarmé's precursor quatrain specifically rejects (I retain the French in this instance to emphasize the point stylistically):

> Je *n'y* hululerai *pas* de *vide nénie*
> Si ce très blanc ébat au ras du sol *dénie*
> A tout site l'honneur du paysage faux.

Triumph derives here from a construction of negativities – negative verbal particles 'n'y/pas/né/nie/dé/nie' – which themselves provide the masking columns, the specifically Mallarméan *peristyle*, surrounding an enshrined *vide* ('void'). In this respect, I would argue, Mallarmé's poem provides its own Counter-Sublime, contains its own *daemonization*, whereas Darío's poem, up to this point, in a classic 'misprision', takes the precursor's temple to the Sublime: in fact, a collapsed presence, 'a ruin'.

> *Kenosis*, which is a breaking-device similar to the defense mechanisms our psyches employ against repetition-compulsions; *kenosis*, then, is a movement toward discontinuity with the precursor. The later poet, apparently emptying himself of his own afflatus, his imaginative godhood, seems to humble himself as though he ceased to be a poet, but this ebbing is so performed in relation to a precursor's poem-of-ebbing that the precursor is emptied out also, and so the later poem of deflation is not as absolute as it seems.

A re-initiation of the quest for the Ideal, a possible counter to the precursor's savouring of a 'learned' absence, as indicated already, is resolved not only in traditional sonnet manner, in the sestet, but also in the Bloomian 'revisionary ratio' of *kenosis*. The 'emptying . . . of his own afflatus', the humbling of Darío's aspiration, takes the form of 'And I find only . . .', counter-balance to 'I pursue . . .'. What *is* available, tauntingly, is 'the word'. Here, it is the word that flees whereas, in Mallarmé's poem, it is the *Idea*, leaving the *Word* – in this case Paphos – to echo long after the book is closed, deprived of any context of presence, abandoned to mere resonant play, the frolic or 'revel' of guaranteed absence.

Yet the later poem does indeed contain 'a breaking-device similar to the defense-mechanisms our psyches employ'. On the one hand there is an aspiration to the state of music habitually accorded to the Word by generations of post-Romantics and, ironically, not least by Mallarmé:

– I know, one wishes to limit the mystery to Music; when writing aspires to that.³⁰

The 'melodic initiation' here serves as an anticipatory salve to yet another instance of defeat, the ultimate failure to marry 'style' with 'form' at the very end of *Prosas profanas*. Darío's poem clings on to Verlaine's imperative – 'music before all else' – just as his aesthetic will develop more in line with the latter's *Sagesse* than in the less-obviously ethical (though infinitely more revolutionary) way of *Un coup de dés*. . . .

On the other hand, this later 'poem of deflation is not as absolute as it seems', nor can it be. For the 'defense-mechanism' shown above in the *aesthetic* context, also operates at the *ethical* level. 'And I find only . . ./the boat of dream which floats in space', constitutes but a half *kenosis*, fails to abandon the echo of suspension and potential illumination of the second quatrain discussed in relation to *daemonization*. Nostalgic for that lost state of receptive tranquillity, that readiness for a quasi-mystical transcendence, however, the dream-vision can evoke but a clichéd correlative of evasion – namely, the seaward as opposed to the mental – broached already in discussion of *tessera* and identified as indelibly Romantic.

In summary, therefore, while *kenosis* does indeed operate here as 'a movement towards discontinuity with the precursor', it is questionable whether the 'humbling' or 'emptying out' which occurs in the first tercet of Darío's sonnet expresses anything more than Darío's reluctance, possibly inability, to accept Mallarmé's refusal to lament, with an empty wail ('nénie'), the loss of escapist transcendence through Art as a vehicle to 'the Ideal'.

> *Askesis*, or a movement of self-purgation which intends the attainment of a state of solitude. The later poet does not, as in *kenosis*, undergo a revisionary movement of emptying, but of curtailing; he yields up part of his own imaginative endowment, so as to separate himself from others, including the precursor, and he does this in his poem by so stationing it in regard to the parent poem as to make that poem undergo an *askesis* also; the precursor's endowment is also truncated.

The final tercet of Darío's sonnet involves both 'a movement of self-purgation' and 'the attainment of a state of solitude'. In the displacement of 'sobbing' from persona to nature, the poem exploits a pathetic fallacy not only archetypally associated with Romanticism, but, in this case, with a specifically *modernista* setting. The domesticity of Mallarmé's fire-side meditation is paralleled in a very different garden contemplation, that of a would-be 'Prince Charming' of the Sleeping Beauty. This state of solitude, therefore, 'yields up part of' Darío's 'own imaginative endowment' both by evoking the fairy-tale tradition and by diffusing personal emotion in a compliant, sympathetic Nature.

The principal figure of this diffusion is one of Darío's most celebrated images:

> . . . the neck of the great white swan which interrogates me.

The line embodies the underlying doubt of a Romantic ethic in an iconography of Parnassian fixity. I would argue that the swan-image of frozen interrogation, virtually an analogue of *modernismo* itself, differs from Mallarmé's brand of Symbolism precisely in its reworking of his classic formulation 'to paint not the thing but the effect that it produces'. In short, Darío's poetry, his 'style', will ever 'paint the thing *and* the effect that it produces', giving rise to perpetual dissatisfaction in his quest for 'a form' – the ineffable.

Whether the second condition of *askesis* is fulfilled is problematical. Mallarmé's endowment, the heritage of Symbolism as many critics, and perhaps Darío, have inadequately understood it, is arguably 'truncated'. That is to say that a series of images – 'croisée' ('crossing'; 'casement'), 'miroir' ('mirror'), 'vol' ('flight'), 'cygne' ('swan') and 'azur' ('azure') – has constituted the strong but misappropriated influence of Mallarmé upon his successors. In short, an *iconography* of the unattainable has masked and supplanted the *methodology* of convoking absence.

Inevitably, the explanation is as theological as the term iconography suggests. For *askesis*, it will be recalled, derives from 'the practice of pre-Socratic shamans'. I have argued already, in my section on *clinamen*, that Darío appeared *initially* unable to accept the non-theological trajectory of Mallarmé. The final tercet of 'Yo persigo una forma' confirms that fact. Yet this poem is not the only instance of a revisionary reading of Mallarmé on the part of Darío; and the echoes are telling:

> Absence of one religion; virtual presence of all, in its relation with mystery, and liturgical pomp, the virtue of signs, the secret force of

words; the musical spell; *the hierarchical in movement* . . . all this traces a new sign, on the lake in silence, the Swan which comprehends.[31]

This final appraisal of Mallarmé by Darío, his obituary, brings me to the last of Bloom's revisionary ratios.

> *Apophrades*, or the return of the dead. The later poet, in his own final phase, already burdened by an imaginative solitude that is almost solipsism, holds his own poem so open again to the precursor's work that at first we might believe the wheel has come full circle, and that we are back in the later poet's flooded apprenticeship, before his strength began to assert itself in the revisionary ratios of *clinamen* and the others. But the poem is now *held* open to the precursor, where once it *was* open, and the uncanny effect is that the new poem's achievement makes it seem to us, not as though the precursor were writing it, but as though the later poet himself had written the precursor's characteristic work.

It should now be obvious that the thesis of this study of Darío's response to Mallarmé is that the 'burdened' later poet challengingly *misreads* the precursor. Darío chooses to read Mallarmé as *le Cygne* rather than *le signe*.

In 'Yo persigo una forma', Darío 'holds open' his poem, from the very first quatrain, to the work of Mallarmé. The insufficiency of his own style prompts the pursuit of a major influence of 'the later poet's flooded apprenticeship, before his strength began to assert itself in the revisionary ratios of *clinamen* and the others'. Thus, initially, Darío's

> pansy-bud which seeks to be the rose

was open, in a humble, *kenosis*-linked way, to Mallarmé's 'I say: a flower . . .'. In retrospect, according to the application of Bloom's ratios, Darío's poem is *held* open to 'the uncanny effect' of achieving 'otherness' ('l'autre'), momentarily, by its capacity to evoke Mallarmé's poem in a revisionary reading or 'misreading'.

Two transformations are at issue. First, the humble *flower* aspiring to the consummate beauty of the rose; second, the equally humble, embryonic *thought* opening itself daringly, but in ultimate failure, to Mallarmé's monumental achievement of 'l'absente de tous bouquets' ('the [idea] absent from all bouquets'). Darío's sonnet begins on the very note of 'I think . . .' on which Mallarmé's sonnet ends. It is not prepared, however, to risk 'éperdument' – distractedly or 'with desperation', that is to say, both in joy and even unto madness – the implications of that aesthetic of consummation *not* achievable here ('ici'), nor in any physical passion ('where our love stirs the fire'). Though transcending Mallarméan domesticity (marriage?), Darío's flirtation with the mythical 'Goddess' and 'Sleeping Beauty' underlines his but *partial* rewriting of 'the precursor's characteristic work'. It merely displaces the love-object into versions of the Romantically unavailable; it fails to opt for the empty space left by the blazing *non*-consummation of 'the other love', the 'burnt breast' of an inexistent myth. If Darío's poem takes further its Mallarméan heritage, it merely re-inscribes an interrogative on the 'empty paper which whiteness defends'. Yet this is no condemnation, for Darío is not alone in his uneasiness towards Mallarmé's invitation to silence.

It has not so far been my intention in this discussion to generalize and extend the insights afforded by Bloomian analysis to the realm of literary history. My concern has been less the question of whether Darío is Parnassian or Symbolist than to show how poetic influence works *technically*. For this reason I have chosen to concentrate on the intricate play of Harold Bloom's ratios rather than on the psychoanalytic speculation in which they occur. I have not pursued Darío as a case-study of a poet living anxiously in the shadow of the 'strong' Mallarmé, let alone locked in Oedipal rivalry with a castrating precursor. Much less have I sought to psychoanalyse Mallarmé the father-figure himself in, say, his Kleinian preference for the 'good' but absent breast of a quintessentially *literary* mother figure, 'the ancient Amazon', in rejection of the 'bad' but threateningly present ('fruits d'*ici*') breast. Rather has my own (anxious) reading sought, needed, to confront Rubén Darío – traditionally regarded as the classic ephebe – as 'the author-in-crisis, belated, wounded and mortal . . . [for whom] there is always a prior plenitude of meaning to struggle against';[32] to confront, in turn, Darío's confrontation of Mallarmé, for whom such a plenitude can only be absence itself.

In order to problematize further not only Darío's misreading of Mallarmé but also the poetics of influence elaborated by Harold Bloom, I shall examine a poem by César Vallejo. In this case, avoiding a repetition of the application of Bloom's ratios, I wish to encompass those aspects of literary history and of psychoanalysis previously relegated to the margins of this discussion. In the process, Barbara Johnson's challenge to read Mallarmé's poetics as the 'construction of a systematic set of self-emptying, non-intuitive meanings' will be taken up.

Firstly, the question of the 'self'. As Elizabeth Wright has objected:

> there is something oddly self-validating about [Bloom's] practice. . . . The crisis-poem takes for granted a unique self, always there, however divided . . . Bloom writes as if his poet-poet confrontation were *sui generis*. . . . The firm presupposition of a-historical single selves, with their past crystallized around them, makes Bloom's critical practice self-validating in a trivial way, for he thereby keeps out meanings that cannot be directly lodged upon these selves.[33]

Bloom, of course, is far from alone in being locked, still, into a decidedly Romantic discourse of the self, and it is worth pausing, for a moment, to consider this legacy.

M.H. Abrams's binary of the *mirror* and the *lamp*, though deploying images of reflection and projection respectively, nonetheless situates the mind in but one, whole – or potentially unified – space. The artistic process of the mind's contents and aspirations, indeed of its *dis*contents and frustrations, is shown to involve a *framing*, a delimitation of total space, wherein the self both explores and is explored. On the grand scale, for the Romantics, 'Nature's vast frame' (Shelley) serves as the analogue of mind in what has come to be known as 'organicism', namely, that Coleridge-derived 'description of mind in terms of the organic processes of a living plant', subject to 'growth', 'continuity' and 'exfoliation'. As Abrams points out, organicism stems from a theological model. God creates and expresses his 'mind' in and through nature: similarly, the poet creates and expresses his 'mind' in and through the poem – fostering 'the doctrine . . . that a poem is a disguised self-revelation, in which its creator, "visibily invisible", at the same time expresses and conceals himself'.[34] Since the poet, however, imitates but never can be God . . . the highest aspiration is a 'divine' revelation of the self. (In passing, it might be said that Mallarmé's own, early phase of 'angelism' followed such a trajectory.)

In retrospect, then, can one summarize the impact of such 'theocritical' thinking not only on Darío but on Bloom, too? Mallarmé's contemplation of the absent leads to a momentary loss of self in otherness, a *jouissance* (and I use the French term to underline the sublimated sexual activity) which permits the possible 'breaking out' from conceptual frames of time and space limitations, towards the contemplation of the mythical breast *in its absence*. 'Consummation' by possession is replaced by 'consummation' by *fire* . . . the element which destroys the delimiting shape and structures of an object of the poetic imagination clearly defined in *words* ('les mots') though not easily accessible via any framework of thought ('les idées').

When Rubén Darío comes to confront the iconography of absence posed by Mallarmé, the epistemological problem of the relationship between words and ideas is immediately reflected only to be deflected. In pursuit of that 'totalizing' vision directly descended from the conflation poet = God – Bloom's 'prior plenitude of meaning' – Darío's theologically oriented vision of the God(ess) head is literally 'framed' within his own peri(phrastic) style. Consequently, since in this discourse the ethic is obscured by the aesthetic, the sonnet's trajectory is one of encapsulated doubt, the framing within the lake not of the open-ended 'signe'/'signif*ier*' but of the closed symbol – a mere 'cygne'/'signif*ied*'. Whereas Mallarmé's sonnet exploited the creative-destructive element of fire to destroy delimiting and limiting linguistic closure, Darío's sonnet comes to rest on the becalming (stagnant?) element of water and the Swan Lake image, only to reinforce the 'framing' of linguistic interrogation.

As I come to the final part of my discussion and the breaking up of the *modernista* discourse, I borrow and adapt from Michel Foucault's contribution to our understanding of the discursive practices which constitute, in this case, not history but 'literary' history. Rather aptly, Foucault's emphasis falls on that very epistemological challenge which, though ultimately daunting for Darío, is taken up more successfully by César Vallejo. In short, Vallejo is confronted, in his early poetry in particular, not only with the *general* epistemological problem of a 'rebellious, mean language'[35] – or even with the psychological implications of the discourse of the other – but also with the culturally specific 'inheritance' of Darío's Hispano-American *modernismo*. To follow Vallejo's transition from *Los heraldos negros* (1918) to *Trilce* (1922) is to witness his struggling emergence from the straitjacket of a received poetic discourse yet, at the same time, to realize the impossibility of writing outside a conceptual framework (*épistemé*) of the literary history of the *fin de siècle*. Far from being a chronological continuity, a causality, much less a succession of metaphysical or philosophical 'fashions' or adherences, the *épistemé* (basically a structural conceptualization of inter-related, sometimes complementary, sometimes conflictual layers of meaning) is characterized by discursive *discontinuity* and *resistance*.

The 'archaeology' of Vallejo's knowledge in poem XXXVI of *Trilce* 'Pugnamos por ensartarnos por un ojo de aguja' – encompasses past, present and future struggle, both intensely physical and, teleologically speaking, divinatory and eschatological.

>Pugnamos ensartarnos por un ojo de aguja,
>enfrentados, a las ganadas.
>Amoniácase casi el cuarto ángulo del círculo.
>¡Hembra se continúa el macho, a raiz
>de probables senos, y precisamente
>a raiz de cuanto no florece!
>
>¿Por ahí estás, Venus de Milo?
>Tú manqueas apenas, pululando
>entrañada en los brazos plenarios de la existencia,
>de esta existencia que todaviiza
>perenne imperfección.
>Venus de Milo, cuyo cercenado, increado
>brazo revuélvese y trata de encodarse
>a través de verdeantes guijarros gagos,
>ortivos nautilos, aunes que gatean
>recién, vísperas inmortales.
>Laceadora de inminencias, laceadora
>del paréntesis.
>
>Rehusad, y vosotros, a posar las plantas
>en la seguridad dupla de la Armonía.
>Rehusad la simetría a buen seguro.
>Intervenid en el conflicto
>de puntas que se disputan
>en la más torionda de las justas
>el salto por el ojo de la aguja!

Tal siento ahora al meñique
demás en la siniestra. Lo veo y creo
no debe serme, o por lo menos que está
en sitio donde no debe.
Y me inspira rabia y me azarea
y no hay cómo salir de él, sino haciendo
la cuenta de que hoy es jueves.
  ¡Ceded al nuevo impar
               potente de orfandad!

(We strive to thread ourselves through a needle's eye
face to face, taking a chance.
The fourth angle of the circle almost *ammonias* itself.
Female continues male, as a result
of probable breasts, and precisely
as a result of what does not flower.
Are you there, Venus de Milo?
You are scarcely maimed, pullulating
entrailed in the plenary arms
of existence,
of this existence which *yets*
perennial imperfection.
Venus de Milo, whose amputated, uncreated
arm turns round and tries to *enelbow* itself
across greening, stammering pebbles,
dawning nautili, *yets* which cat-creep
recently, immortal eves.
Bow-tier of imminences, bow-tier
of parentheses.
Refuse, and you, to place the soles
on the double security of Harmony.
Refuse symmetry with safety.
Intervene in the conflict
of points which dispute
in the most on-heat of jousts
the jump through the needle's eye!
So I feel now the little finger
too much on the left hand. I see it and I believe
it ought [must] not be me, or at least that it is
in a place where it ought not.
And it inspires rage and alarms me
and there is no way to get out of it, but by making
the reckoning that today is Thursday.

Cede to the new odd number
potent with orphanhood!)

As a consequence of the pervasive, historically unavoidable heritage of *modernismo* – and the Judaeo-Christian intertext of 'the eye of the needle' – the opening verse re-writes (as it echoes) 'Yo persigo una forma . . .'. The strong erotic, specifically coital, image of full-frontal desire for conquest ('face to face, gambling') re-enacts but sexualizes Darío's pursuit of the God(ess)head rather than as a confrontation of the maidenhead. That physical attraction is 'chemical' is a cliché explored in the powerful disruption of geometry threatened by that (orgasmic) moment of 'reaction' ('the fourth angle of the circle ammonias itself') when the fusion of male and female difference is abolished, not in the Mallarméan echo of absent ('burnt') breast, but in the coming together of (burning?) nipples . . . whereby the male's absent but potential breasts are made – verbally – to flower.

This transformation, this virtualization of the inexistent, overtly re-evokes the Darío precursor-poem: 'Are you there, Venus de Milo?'. The vocative 'Tú' ('you' singular), addressed at once to both present lover and to the 'enshrined' Goddess of an inherited poetic discourse, calls upon no one person but a 'fused' persona, now – literally – embraced not just in a single lover's arms but in the clasp of existence itself. Yet this embrace is not 'framing', limiting . . . for it partakes of the imperfection, or the incompleteness, of time, conveyed by the neologism 'yets' – 'a word', but hardly 'an idea'!

A clear shift from second to third person, from vocative to description, initiates further virtualizations, in words, of 'impossible' ideas. Whether the Venus's arms were cut off or never even created, one of them is deemed to turn round and to attempt to *lean* (though *'encodarse'* is another neologism which might call on *'encodigarse'* ['to encode'] as much as on *'acodarse'*). Not that there can ever be a stable surface, a secure support: only greenish, stammering pebbles, sun-rise molluscs (nautili), creeping, cat-like 'aunes', another 'ungrammaticality' which forces time, momentarily, into a substantive (i.e. noun) frame, as if to encapsulate the very eve of immortalities. 'Imminence', then, is 'parenthesized' ('tied in a double bow') in a rather more Mallarméan than Rubén Daríán feminine construction – ('laceadora . . . laceadora').

In brief, the reader is implicated now directly in 'Rehusad' – the plural vocative. We are invited to 'refuse' the security (ever duplicitous) of Harmony – as the *modernista* discourse breaks up, is rendered a-symmetrical. By *our* intervention in the constricting frame of the jousting-lists of the rutting lovers' embrace, we might just (joust) break through, make the (conceptually) impossible leap 'through the needle's eye'.

The final section of *Trilce* XXXVI constitutes an interior monologue, though the first *person* grammatical category is exploited to express dissatisfaction with the *space*, or *frame*, of a notional, limiting (post-coital?) solitary persona. The *mirror-stage* of self-perception – after the assaults on uni-vocality and the frame-breaking which have gone before – leaves uni-corporality as an 'improper' perception ('it ought not be me'), an infuriating, shameful, *casting of the die*: and deliberately I re-echo the echo of 'Un coup de dés jamais n'abolira le hasard' to be found in '*az*a*r*ea'. The paradoxical dependence on the 'institutionality' of the Mallarméan ethic, on the part of Vallejo, seeking a personal 'space' or 'margin' in which to perform, has thrown up that knowledge, in anticipation of Michel Foucault, that the *poem* only 'becomes effective to the degree that it introduces discontinuity into our very being'.

> The traditional devices for constructing a comprehensive view of history and for retracing the past as patient and continuous development must be systematically dismantled. Necessarily, we must dismiss those tendencies that encourage the consoling play of recognitions. . . . History becomes effective to the degree that it introduces discontinuity into our very being . . .[36]

If *I* listen to that imperative, *I* must not have the final (closing) word. Rather I, and you, may hear Vallejo's poem in its *parting* injunction: its highlighting of differentiality rather than continuity in the history of institutions. Dare we cede to the uneven, the 'odd' *modernity*, of a poetic text struggling powerfully to shed the restricting paternity – or maternity – of the discourse of *modernismo*? Try!

. . . Cede to the potent oddness of orphanhood.

Vallejo's exploitation of the vocative plural raises – apart from, indeed, as part of, the other complexities of this poem – the question of *voice*. Who (what) speaks in the poem? Almost inexplicably, the proliferation of literary theories of the last two decades has thrown up *narrative* but little *poetic* critical methodology to cope with, to explain, to situate, a literary discourse laden with multivoicedness, citation, intertextuality and modes of defamiliarization. Lyric poetry has had to 'make do' with useful but rather limiting notions such as Riffaterre's 'ungrammaticality' or Todorov's poetics of discontinuity. For some reason, criticism has been content either to struggle to pull back lyric poetry, generically, to univocal (authorial) control or to label, but not to accept, the more subversive implications of the non-controlled vocality of modern poetry by using such terms as 'Dada', 'Surrealism', 'postmodernism' . . . and so on. Mikhail Bakhtin's notion of the dialogic imagination, so fruitfully applied to the novel, nonetheless bears – bares? – a blind-spot concerning poetry, the concession of a peculiarly 'unstructured', idealized autonomy to the originary, 'monologic' voice of the poet. The notion of *heteroglossia*, however, seems to fit a poetic discourse of multivoicedness, be it Guillaume Apollinaire's 'Zone', T.S. Eliot's *The Wasteland*, Fernando Pessoa's 'Tabacaria' . . . or Vallejo's *Trilce* XXXVI. Though terms such as 'poème-conversation' have been applied to such poetry, all too rapidly 'voices' which seek to restore a so-called coherence, or unity, of view-point re-emerge; instance the role of Tiresias, in *The Wasteland*, whose transhistorical, multi-spatial, bisexual 'voicings' are re-assembled, admittedly at that 'voice's' own instigation:

These fragments I have shored against my ruin.

That presence will always seek to re-assert its own metaphysics is one of Jacques Derrida's most basic insights; that criticism has too often aided and abetted such restorative harmonies is no reason for the reader of Vallejo's poem to overlook, to fail to hear, glaring and resonant absences. For the poem states that such 'security' is 'double' . . . duplicitous and different from itself. The poem commands the frame-breaking of *intervention* . . . against safe symmetries, such as those found in criticism's insistence on *self-presence*. Here I refer not to a theological model of self but to a psychological model of the *subject* and it should be noted that I opt for a 'grammatical' rather than an 'essential' term in order to stress that, even for the purpose of academic presentation, the distinction between models of the self and models of meaning is but provisional and artificial. In Darío's poetry – and implied in Bloom's

Romantically-derived poetics of influence – the process of self-reflection/projection within a (God-derived) 'Nature's vast frame', was identified as consistently narcissistic. In the process of equating 'self' with 'other', all signs become 'signifié'; that is, the signifying 'other' is framed, or enclosed, according to the dictates or desire of the reflector/projector. We might say that such a model of construction of the self fixes identity in a *mirror-state*. And I play here with 'state'/'stasis'/'stability' as being notions consistent with the theologically orthodox tenet that man is made in God's own image and likeness. What is more, a theologically oriented or conditioned subject might well be content, feel whole, unified, at one, with his image and his Maker. In a post-theological, and a post-Saussurian, perspective, however – and certainly, within a Vallejo text not notably anxiety-ridden in its playful fragmentation of 'recognitions', its 'introduction of discontinuities', its 'effectiveness' (Foucault's terms) – such unity, such 'presence', may be insufficient, indeed, thrown into question. When Saussure writes that, in language 'there are only differences without positive terms', he affords the removal not only of the linguistic 'positive term' ('le signifié'), but also of the positive certainty of a *term*inal, teleologically viable guarantor (God) of man's image. We are confronted then with the possibility of an image-construction, image-desire, *not* satisfied with 'state'/'stasis'/'stability', but rather restless, unfulfilled, active, performative; subjects constructing identity on and in a *mirror-stage*. A further complication arises insofar as this 'performance' is by no means often, if ever, conducted *consciously*.

This is not the place for more than the briefest incursion into psychoanalysis. Nonetheless, that is precisely the 'frame' – perhaps a displaced theology – wherein we encounter subjects notoriously restless, unfulfilled, performative . . . even subjects seeking to construct a 'new' identity, to break the frame, to engage with difference. And it is at this point, the point of (*Trilce* XXXVI's) engaging with difference, that the Lacanian notion of the 'Symbolic Order' intrudes:

> The absence of a gap . . . between a concept and its application is a proof of the concept's inadequacy . . . . The gap appears with the initiation . . . into the order of language, what Lacan calls 'the Symbolic Order'. The structures of language are marked with social imperatives . . . . Society's injunction that desire must wait, that it must formulate in the constricting word whatever demand it may speak,

is what effects the split between conscious and unconscious, the repression that is the tax enacted by the use of language.[37]

That 'desire must wait', always subject to 'the constricting word', takes up, but goes well beyond, Mallarmé's intuition of the need to cede the initiative to words, now echoed by Vallejo's text's final injunction. And to demonstrate the implications of the inseparability of desire and language, I turn, once again, to French models, namely Mallarmé and Rimbaud. Unfortunately, Mallarmé's legacy has been rather one-sided; the earlier seeker of 'the Ideal' – with all the theocentric implications I have already discussed – is preferred to the more threatening author of 'after having found Nothingness, I found Beauty'.[38] The 'most trenchantly agnostic' Mallarmé whose 'powers of doubt played not only upon the time-honoured theologies and theodicies' of Western thought (Bowie) anticipates Lacan's intersection of the 'desire' (for Beauty) and the 'constricting word' (of non-referentiality, of the non-*signifié*). Most famously in the *sonnet en* '*x*', wherein the ineffable (since non-existent) *word*, but not the *idea*, 'ptyx', is not only spoken but – 'nul ptyx' ('no ptyx') – negated. An absent absence! In the case of Rimbaud, again, the powerfully anti-essentialist 'split' not only between conscious and unconscious, but between plural poetic voices, has been overlooked. JE EST UN AUTRE states plainly that grammatical subjectivity is ever other; never author. Vallejo's reading (which is misreading under erasure) of Mallarmé through Darío *may* be interpreted not as struggle but as play . . . a shift from the notion of poetic 'voicing' as subject (self)-centred orality to a non-subject (lack)-centred writing. A textual performance.

> Play is the disruption of presence. . . . Play is always play of absence and presence, but if it is to be thought radically, play must be conceived of before the alternative of presence and absence. Being must be conceived as presence or absence on the basis of play and not the other way round.[39]

Further Reading

Good introductions to recent critical theory are to be found in Ann Jefferson and David Robey (eds.), *Modern Literary Theory: A Comparative Introduction*, London, Batsford, 2nd edition, 1986, and Douglas Tallack, ed., *Literary Theory at Work*, London, Batsford, 1987. As both of these also have useful bibliographies, I shall confine myself here to poetry criticism.

For a general introduction which sets poetry criticism in a broader critical context, Jonathan Culler, *Structuralist Poetics*, Ithaca, Cornell UP, 1975, is still a good place to start. Anthony Easthope, *Poetry as Discourse*, London and New York, Methuen, 1983, is a particularly incisive and tightly argued introduction, and is unusual in its concern to demonstrate the historical context and political function of the development of poetic discourse. Richard Makin and Christopher Norris (eds.), *Post-Structuralist Readings of English Poetry*, Cambridge, CUP, 1987, and Chaviva Hosek and Patricia Parker (eds.), *Lyric Poetry: Beyond New Criticism*, Ithaca and London, Cornell UP, 1985, are excellent collections of essays by many of the leading critics in the field, though their emphasis is pre-twentieth century.

One area where the debate over deconstruction has been particularly intense, is Romantic poetry, where Paul de Man's essays, reprinted in *Blindness and Insight: Essays in the Rhetoric of Contemporary Criticism*, 2nd edition, revised, London, Methuen, 1983, and J. Hillis Miller's, some of which are reprinted in *The Linguistic Moment: From Wordsworth to Stevens*, Princeton, Princeton UP, 1985, have been especially influential. Miller's debates with another critic of American writing, Joseph Riddel, in *Diacritics*, Summer 1975, pp. 24–31, and Fall 1975, pp. 56–65, and with the distinguished traditional critic, M.H. Abrams in Morris

Evans and Michael Fischer (eds.), *Romanticism and Contemporary Criticism*, Ithaca and London, Cornell UP, 1986, give a good insight into what is at stake. In *Deconstruction and Criticism*, London, Routledge and Kegan Paul, 1979, Harold Bloom, Paul de Man, Jacques Derrida, Geoffrey H. Hartman and J. Hillis Miller demonstrate their own brands of deconstruction, with the focus on English Romantic poetry.

Another area where the issues are joined in illuminating ways is that of French poetry. T. Todorov's essay 'A Complication of Text: the *Illuminations*' in *French Literary Theory: A Reader*, Cambridge CUP, 1982, pp. 223–37, is a brief survey of approaches, and Barbara Johnson's essays on French poetry in, *The Critical Difference: Essays in the Contemporary Rhetoric of Reading*, Baltimore and London, Johns Hopkins UP, 1980, are clear and accessible examples of deconstructive reading. Michael Riffaterre offers detailed readings of modern French poets, and a theoretical approach of much wider reference in *Semiotics of Poetry*, London, Methuen, 1978, and *Text Production*, New York, Columbia UP, 1983. Other useful accounts, chosen from a wide field are, Paul A. Bove, *Destructive Poetics: Heidegger and Modern American Poetry*, New York, Columbia UP, 1980, Veronica Forrest-Thomson, *Poetic Artifice: A Theory of Twentieth Century Poetry*, New York, St Martin's Press, 1978, and Sandra M. Gilbert and Susan Gubar (eds.), *Shakespeare's Sisters: Feminist Essays on Women Poets*, Bloomington, Indiana UP, 1979.

Notes and References

Chapter 1 pp. 4–22

1 Confusingly, New Criticism needs to be distinguished from later developments in criticism. It is now used to refer exclusively to an extremely influential method which can be represented by Cleanth Brooks, *The Well Wrought Urn*, London, Dobson, 1949, and W.K. Wimsatt, *The Verbal Icon: Studies in the Meaning of Poetry*, Lexington, Kentucky UP, 1954. Cleanth Brooks and Robert Penn Warren's *Understanding Poetry* (3rd edition), New York, Holt, Rinehart & Winston, 1960, has probably been more influential on the teaching of poetry than any other book. For a useful account of New Criticism in general, see Ann Jefferson and David Robey (eds.), *Modern Literary Theory: A Comparative Introduction*, 2nd edition, London, Batsford, 1986, pp. 65–83.

2 Frank Kermode's *Romantic Image,* London, Routledge & Kegan Paul, 1957, is a particularly clear account of the way Romantic organicism continues into this century. For a sceptical re-examination of Romantic claims for the symbol, see particularly Paul de Man, 'The Rhetoric of Temporality' in C.S. Singleton (ed.), *Interpretation: Theory and Practice*, Baltimore, Johns Hopkins UP, 1969, and 'Intentional Structure of the Romantic Image' in Harold Bloom (ed.), *Romanticism and Consciousness*, New York, Norton, 1970, both reprinted in Paul de Man, *Blindness and Insight: Essays in the Rhetoric of Contemporary Criticism*, 2nd edition, London, Methuen, 1983.

3 For a clear demonstration, see Michael Riffaterre, 'Describing Poetic Structures: Two Approaches to Baudelaire's "Les Chats" ', in Jacques Ehrmann (ed.), *Structuralism*, New York, Doubleday, 1970, pp. 188–230. Jonathan Culler's *Structuralist Poetics: Structuralism, Linguistics and the Study of Literature*, London, Routledge & Kegan Paul, 1975, gives a clear account of the issues in chapters 3 and 8.

4 Jacques Derrida, 'Structure, Sign and Play in the Discourse of the Human Sciences', in *Writing and Difference*, trs. Alan Bass, London, Routledge & Kegan Paul, 1978.

5 Jacques Derrida, *Positions*, trs. Alan Bass, Chicago UP, 1981, p. 26.
6 See, for instance, J. Hillis Miller, 'Williams' *Spring and All* And The Progress of Poetry', *Daedalus*, Spring 1970, pp. 405–34.
7 Barbara Johnson, 'Teaching Deconstructively' in G.D. Atkins and M.L. Johnson (eds.), *Writing and Reading Differently: Deconstruction and the Teaching of Composition and Literature*, Lawrence, Kansas UP, 1985, p. 140.
8 For a brief account of this development see Jonathan Culler, *The Pursuit of Signs: Semiotics, Literature, Deconstruction*, London, Routledge & Kegan Paul, 1981, pp. 188–209. For a fuller account see Sheldon Sacks (ed.), *On Metaphor*, Chicago & London, Chicago UP, 1979.
9 In 'The Semantics of Metaphor', in *The Role of the Reader*, Bloomington, Indiana UP, 1979, Umberto Eco has also demonstrated how the recognition of the similarity which seems to be at the heart of metaphor can equally be seen as based on contiguity; in doing so, he challenges Roman Jakobson's influential dislocation between metaphor and metonymy in 'Closing Statement: Linguistic and Poetics', in Thomas A. Sebeok (ed.), *Style in Language*, Cambridge, Mass., MIT, 1960.
10 William Carlos Williams, *Selected Essays*, New York, New Directions, 1954, p. 16.
11 William Carlos Williams, *Selected Poems*, Harmondsworth, Penguin, 1976, p. 31.
12 Francis Ponge, *The Voice of Things*, New York, McGraw Hill, 1974, p. 107.
13 See the interesting exchange between M.H. Abrams and J. Hillis Miller over the merits of New Critical or deconstructive readings of a Wordsworth poem, in Morris Eaves and Michael Fischer (eds.), *Romanticism and Contemporary Criticism*, Ithaca and London, Cornell UP, 1986, pp. 96–182. For a very simple account, see Andrew P. Debicki, 'New Criticism and Deconstruction: Two Attitudes in Teaching Poetry', in Atkins and Johnson, op. cit., pp. 169–84.
14 Jacques Derrida, *Signéponge/Signsponge*, trs. Richard Rand, New York, Columbia UP, 1984.
15 William Carlos Williams, *Paterson*, New York, New Directions, 1963, p. 30.
16 Ernest Fenollosa's *The Chinese Written Character As A Medium For Poetry*, which Pound edited and had published from the author's notes, has been very influential, but the claims for the ideogram are complex and confusing. On the one hand, it seems to represent the ideal of an unmediated language because of its concreteness and specificity. On the other hand, Fenollosa and Pound imply that it can reveal patterns and unities that are in nature, and to which it corresponds, thus linking it

with the claims made for the Romantic symbol, as a means of effacing the gap between language and nature. These claims for the ideogram as a privileged form of language would seem to embody all the mystifications of language that Derrida has attacked under the name of 'logocentrism'. That is, it seems to argue for a language which can be transparent and, in being so, can reveal or express a reality which is prior to it. Derrida's demonstration of how written language in the West has come to be seen as *secondary* to speech, with the consequent privileging of speech as an unmediated expression of presence, is designed to reverse this assumption by insisting that both speech and writing are alike in being reliant on a system of signs out of which meaning is created. He insists that writing should be our model of how language works, rather than speech, and in an intriguing and very rare reference to Anglo-American writing, he locates Fenollosa and Pound, together with Mallarmé and Nietzsche, as representing a major break with a tradition which effaced the role of language. This breakthrough

> destroyed and caused to vacillate the transcendental authority and dominant category of the *episteme*: being. This is the meaning of the work of Fenellosa [sic] whose influence upon Ezra Pound and his poetics is well-known: this irreducibly graphic poetics was, with that of Mallarmé, the first break in the most entrenched Western tradition. The fascination that the Chinese ideogram exercised on Pound's writing may thus be given all its historical significance. (*Of Grammatology*, Baltimore, Johns Hopkins UP, 1976, p. 92).

As I try to demonstrate, Pound ultimately exploits both these contradictory claims for the ideogram in the *Cantos*. For an excellent discussion of what is at stake in these claims for the ideogram, see Joseph Riddel, 'Decentering the Image: The "Project" of "American" Poetics?', in Josue V. Harari (ed.), *Textual Strategies: Perspectives in Post-Structuralist Criticisms*, Ithaca, Cornell UP, 1979, pp. 322–58.

17 Gregory Ulmer, *Applied Grammatology: Post(e)-Pedagogy from Jacques Derrida to Joseph Beuys*, Baltimore, Johns Hopkins UP, 1985, p. 59.
18 Ezra Pound, *Drafts and Fragments*, London, Faber & Faber, 1970, p. 25.
19 ibid., p. 32.
20 Riddel, op.cit., p. 357.
21 William C. Seitz, *The Art of Assemblage*, New York, Museum of Modern Art, 1961, p. 37. Page references for further quotations from this work will be included in the main text.
22 John Cage, *Silence: Lectures and Writings*, Middletown, Wesleyan UP, 1961, p. 99. Page references for further quotations from this work will be included in the main text.

23 Claude Levi-Strauss, *The Savage Mind*, London, Weidenfeld and Nicolson, 1966, p. 21.
24 Robert Duncan, *Roots and Branches*, New York, New Directions, 1964, pp. 21–2.
25 *Coyote's Journal*, 5/6, 1966, p. 21. For an excellent, authoritative account of the whole issue of form and design in modern poetry, see Eric Mottram, *Towards Design in Poetry*, 2nd edition, London, Writers Forum, 1985.

Chapter 2 pp. 23–41

1 Louis MacNeice, 'Yeats' Epitaph', *New Republic*, no. cii, 26, 24 June 1940, reprinted in Jon Stallworthy (ed.), *Yeats: Last Poems*, London, Macmillan, 1968, p. 45.
2 Richard Ellmann, *The Identity of Yeats*, New York, OUP, 1964, p. 188. T.R. Henn, 'The Mill of the Mind', in Stallworthy, op.cit., p. 106. C. Bradford, 'On Yeats' Last Poems', in Stallworthy, op.cit., p. 81.
3 Mikhail Bakhtin, *The Dialogic Imagination*, Austin, Texas UP, 1981, p. 293.
4 ibid., p. 399.
5 Edward Said, *Orientalism*, Harmondsworth, Penguin, 1985, pp. 203.
6 E.M. Forster, *A Passage to India*, Harmondsworth, Penguin, 1973, p. 275.
7 W.B. Yeats, *Collected Poems*, New York, Macmillan, 1956, p. 322.
8 D.G. Boyce, 'The Marginal Britons: The Irish', in P. Dodds and R. Colls (eds.), *Englishness*, London, Croom Helm, 1986, p. 248.
9 Ellmann, op.cit., p. 143.
10 Yeats, *Letters*, A. Wade (ed.), London, Hart-Davis, 1954, p. 910.
11 F.A.C. Wilson, 'The Statues', in Stallworthy, op.cit., p. 167.
12 ibid., p. 167.
13 ibid., pp. 167–8 and 180, emphasis in the original.
14 Martin Bernal, *Black Athena*, London, Free Association Books, 1987. The tenor of my argument is at points indebted to Bernal.
15 Valentin Voloshinov, *Marxism and the Philosophy of Language*, New York and London, Seminar Press, 1973, Part II, Chapter 2. Although this was published under the name of Bakhtin's friend, Voloshinov, I follow the current consensus in attributing it to Bakhtin.
16 Ernest Gellner, *Nations and Nationalism*, Oxford, Blackwell, 1983, p. 100.
17 Wilson, op.cit., p. 175.
18 See his introduction to 'Fighting the Waves' in *Explorations*, London, Macmillan, 1962.
19 Pam Slaughter, 'Feminist Discourse: The Presence of the M/Other', Paper given at the University of Strathclyde, 26 January 1988.

20 Ellmann, op.cit., p. 233.
21 Yeats, *Collected Poems*, op.cit., p. 342.
22 Yeats, *Explorations*, op.cit., p. 451.
23 Peter Stallybrass and Allon White, *The Politics and Poetics of Transgression*, London, Methuen, 1986, pp. 21–2.
24 Yeats, 'Tomorrow's Revolution', in *Explorations*, op.cit., p. 426.
25 ibid., p. 425.
26 See Jeffrey Weeks, *Sex, Politics and Society*, Harlow, Longman, 1981, p. 133.
27 See Ellmann, op.cit., p. 190.

Chapter 3 pp. 42–61

1 Mikhail Bakhtin, *The Dialogic Imagination*, trs. Caryl Emerson and Michael Holquist, Austin, Texas UP, 1981, p. 297.
2 Stephen Coote, *The Waste Land: Penguin Masterstudies*, Harmondsworth, Penguin, 1985, p. 26.
3 For a convenient summary see William Spanos, 'Repetition in The Waste Land: a phenomenological destruction' *Boundary 2*, 1979, pp. 227–8.
4 Umberto Eco, *A Theory of Semiotics*, Indiana UP, 1976, p. 141.
5 Roland Barthes, 'Theory of the text', Robert Young (ed.), *Untying the Text*, London, Routledge & Kegan Paul, 1981, p. 38.
6 ibid., p. 39.
7 Mikhail Bakhtin, 'The aesthetics of verbal creation', in Tzvetan Todorov, *The Dialogical Principle*, Manchester UP, 1984, p. 109.
8 Spanos, op.cit., passim.
9 Martin Heidegger, cited in Spanos, op.cit., p. 225.
10 ibid., p. 266.
11 ibid., p. 284.
12 ibid., p. 262.
13 ibid., p. 229.
14 Maud Ellmann, *The Poetics of Impersonality*, London, Harvester Press, 1987, p. 92.
15 ibid., p. 92.
16 ibid., p. 92.
17 ibid., p. 95.
18 Genesis, 3,22 (Authorized Version).
19 See Eliot's 'Ulysses, Order and Myth', reprinted in William O'Connor (ed.), *Forms of Modern Fiction*, Indiana, Indiana UP, 1959, pp. 123–4.
20 See Anthony Easthope, *Poetry as Discourse*, London, Methuen, 1983, pp. 40–47.
21 Michel Foucault, 'The Order of Discourse', reprinted in Young (ed.), op.cit., p. 56.

22 ibid., pp. 61–2.
23 'Whispers of Immortality', in T.S. Eliot, *Collected Poems 1909–1962*, London, Faber & Faber, 1985.
24 ibid., p. 82.
25 William Spanos, 'Hermeneutics and Memory: Destroying T.S. Eliot's Four Quartets', *Genre*, 11, 1978, p. 524.
26 Martin Heidegger, *Being and Time*, trs. J. Macquarrie and E. Robinson, Oxford, Blackwell, 1967, pp. 55–6.
27 St Luke, 6,41 (Authorized Version).
28 For a discussion of metaphor and metonymy in reference to language and the unconscious see Jacques Lacan, *Ecrits*, trs. Alan Sheridan, London, Tavistock, 1977, pp. 146–66.
29 Paul De Man, 'Semiology and Rhetoric', reprinted in Josue Harari (ed.), *Textual Strategies*, London, Methuen, 1979, p. 139.
30 Thomas Carlyle, *Sartor Resartus* 2,9, London, Chapman and Hall, 1890.
31 Jacques Derrida, *Of Grammatology*, trs. Gayatri Spivak, Baltimore, John Hopkins UP, 1976, p. 309.
32 ibid., p. 309.
33 ibid., p. 310.
34 Harari, op.cit., p. 117.
35 Derrida, op.cit., pp. 144–5.
36 ibid., p. 145.
37 Lacan, op.cit., p. 311.
38 ibid., p. 284.
39 Bernard Sharratt, *The Literary Labyrinth*, London, Harvester Press, 1984, p. 63.
40 Young (ed.), op.cit., p. 63.
41 Harari (ed.), op.cit., p. 188.
42 Mikhail Bakhtin, 'Concerning methodology in the human sciences', in Todorov, op.cit., p. 110.

Chapter 4 pp. 62–84

1 Thomas H. Johnson (ed.), *Emily Dickinson: The Complete Poems*, London, Faber & Faber, 1970, p. 238.
2 Frank Smith, *Psycholinguistics and Reading*, New York, Holt, Rinehart & Winston, 1973.
3 Stanley Fish, *Is there a Text in This Class? The Authority of Interpretive Communities*, Cambridge, Mass., 1980.
4 Jonathan Culler, *Structuralist Poetics: Structuralism, Linguistics and the Study of Literature*, London, Routledge & Kegan Paul, 1981, pp. 113–30.
5 Terry Eagleton, *Literary Theory: An Introduction*, Oxford, Blackwell, 1983, p. 76.

6 Kate Millett, *Sexual Politics*, London, Virago, 1977, pp. 3–9.
7 For a useful analysis of this difference, see Catherine Belsey, *Critical Practice*, London, Methuen, 1980, pp. 15–20.
8 For a good general introduction to Barthes's work, see Jonathan Culler, *Barthes*, London, Fontana, 1983.
9 Roland Barthes, *Image, Music, Text*, trs. Stephen Heath, London, Fontana, 1977, p. 146.
10 Sandra M. Gilbert and Susan Gubar, *The Madwoman in the Attic*, New Haven, Yale UP, 1979, pp. 542–3. It is obvious that Ransom is about to defend Dickinson against these charges. However, male criticism continually uses this strategy of playing on what are 'accepted' views, thereby serving to reinforce the negative view. See also Lowell's comments on Sylvia Plath quoted in Joanna Russ, *How To Suppress Women's Writing*, London, Women's Press, 1984, p. 30.
11 Tom Paulin (ed.), *The Faber Book of Political Verse*, London, Faber & Faber, 1986, p. 49.
12 Cora Kaplan, *Sea Changes: Culture and Feminism*, London, Verso, 1986, p. 80.
13 Jeni Couzyn, *The Bloodaxe Book of Contemporary Women Poets*, Newcastle upon Tyne, Bloodaxe, 1985, p. 15.
14 Gilbert and Gubar, op.cit., p. 68.
15 Juliet Mitchell, 'Women: The Longest Revolution', in Mary Eagleton (ed.), *Feminist Literary Theory: A Reader*, Oxford, Basil Blackwell, p. 102.
16 Toril Moi (ed.), *The Kristeva Reader*, Oxford, Basil Blackwell, 1986, pp. 156–7.
17 Kaplan, op.cit., pp. 77–8.
18 Thomas Johnson and Theodora Ward (eds.), *The Letters of Emily Dickinson*, Cambridge, Mass., Harvard UP, 1958, p. 412.
19 Ted Hughes, Introduction to *Selected Poems of Emily Dickinson*, London, Faber & Faber, 1968, p. 11.
20 See Lillian Faderman, 'Emily Dickinson's Homoerotic Poetry' in *Higginson Journal*, no. 18, 1978, and Adelaide Morris, 'The Love of Three – A Prism Be: Men and Women in the Bridal Poems of Emily Dickinson', in Susan Juhasz (ed.), *Feminist Critics Read Emily Dickinson*, Bloomington, Indiana UP, 1983, pp. 98–113.
21 Adrienne Rich, 'Vesuvius at Home: The Power of Emily Dickinson', in *On Lies, Secrets and Silences, Selected Prose 1966–1978*, London, Virago, 1980, p. 163.
22 Kaplan, op.cit., p. 98.
23 Thomas H. Johnson (ed.), *Emily Dickinson: The Complete Poems*, London, Faber & Faber, 1970, p. 283.
24 ibid., p. 555.

25 ibid., p. 29.
26 Higginson, 'An Open Portfolio', in C.R. Blake and C.F. Wells (eds.), *The Recognition of Emily Dickinson*, Ann Arbor, Michigan UP, 1964, p. 3.
27 Jan Montefiore, *Feminism and Poetry*, London, Pandora Press, 1987. See particularly the argument centred on the exclusion of women from the literary history of the thirties, pp. 22–5.
28 David Holbrook, 'Sylvia Plath, Pathological Morality, and the Avant-Garde' in Boris Ford (ed.), *The Modern Age*, Harmondsworth, Penguin, 1973, p. 446.
29 Peter Ackroyd, *T.S. Eliot*, Harmondsworth, Penguin, 1988. See in particular pp. 192–211. In fact, Eliot actively suppressed such details.
30 See Luce Irigaray, *This Sex Which is Not One*, trs. Catherine Porter, Ithaca, Cornell UP, p. 220. Jan Montefiore gives an interesting account of her relevance to the theorizing of women's identity and sexuality through language, op.cit., pp. 140–52.
31 Ted Hughes (ed.), *Sylvia Plath, Collected Poems*, London, Faber & Faber, 1981, pp. 203, 116, 271.
32 ibid., p. 231.
33 T.S. Eliot in Charles Tomlinson (ed.), *Marianne Moore: A Collection of Critical Essays*, Englewood, Prentice-Hall, 1969, p. 60.
34 See, for example, Malcolm Bradbury and James McFarlane (eds.), *Modernism*, Harmondsworth, Penguin, 1976, where she is included in their introduction as 'contributing to a very modern sensibility', but omitted from the brief biographies of key figures in the appendix.
35 Quoted in Charles Tomlinson (ed.), *Marianne Moore: A Collection of Critical Essays*, Englewood, Prentice-Hall, 1969, p. 3.
36 ibid., p. 46.
37 ibid., p. 139.
38 ibid., p. 52.
39 ibid., p. 173.
40 Plath, op.cit., p. 269.
41 Dickinson, op.cit., p. 247.
42 *Marianne Moore: Complete Poems*, London, Faber & Faber, 1967, pp. 62–70.
43 See Roland Barthes, *S/Z*, trs. Richard Miller, New York, Hill and Wang, 1974, pp. 20–21.
44 Tomlinson, op.cit., p. 57.
45 Moore, op.cit., p. 262.
46 Kaplan, op.cit., p. 97.

Chapter 5 pp. 85–107
1 Julia Kristeva, in Toril Moi (ed.), *The Kristeva Reader*, Oxford, Blackwell, 1987, p. 86.

2 Julia Kristeva, from 'Recherches pour une semanalyse', cited by Philip Lewis in 'Revolutionary Semiotics', *Diacritics*, no. 4, 3, 1974, p. 83.
3 Claire Pajaczkowska, 'Introduction to Kristeva', in *m/f*, 1981, p. 149.
4 James Joyce, cited by Sandra Gilbert and Susan Gubar, *The War of the Words*, vol. 1: *No Man's Land*, New Haven, Yale UP, 1988, p. 156.
5 Moi, op.cit., p. 90.
6 For a discussion of the Kleinian emphasis in Kristeva see Ann Rosalind Jones, 'Julia Kristeva on Femininity: The Limits of a Semiotic Politics', *Feminist Review*, no. 18, November 1984, pp. 56–78.
7 Julia Kristeva, 'Revolution in Poetic Language' in Moi, op.cit., p. 93. All further references to this text will be followed by page numbers after the citation.
8 She alters the Lacanian formulation also by not using capital letters, as Lacan does, for the Symbolic and the Imaginary.
9 Julia Kristeva, 'Woman can never be defined', in E. Marks and I. de Courtivron, *New French Feminisms*, Brighton, Harvester, 1981, pp. 137–41.
10 Roland Barthes, 'From Work to Text', trs. Stephen Heath, *Image Music Text*, London, Fontana, 1977, pp. 155–64.
11 Roman Jakobson, 'Linguistics and Poetics: A Closing Statement', in T. Sebeok, *Style in Language*, Cambridge, Mass., MIT Press, 1960, pp. 350–77.
12 Cited by Ann Rosalind Jones, op.cit., pp. 59 and 136.
13 Fetishism has been discussed at length by Freud and by Marx, but Kristeva's use of the term is quite different from both of their definitions. Freud's definition of fetishism is the fixation of desire on to an object or part-object. For Marx, fetishism refers to the relation between objects; this relationship masks and denies the relations between human beings. Kristeva uses the term to refer to a stasis in signification, where the material word becomes an object in its own right, or where it does not yield up its meaning.
14 Colin McCabe, *James Joyce and the Revolution of the Word*, London, Macmillan, 1979, p. 1. The page numbers of further references from this text will follow the citation.
15 For a discussion of the Marxist debates around the revolutionary potential of modernist writing see Eugene Lunn, *Marxism and Modernism*, London, Verso, 1985.
16 Malcolm Bradbury and James MacFarlane, *Modernism 1890–1930*, Harmondsworth, Penguin, 1976.
17 Jakobson, op.cit.
18 Moi, op.cit., pp. 138–59.
19 Gilliam Hanscombe and Virginia Smyers, *Writing for their Lives: The Modernist Women 1910–1940*, London, The Women's Press, 1987.

20 Carolyn Burke, 'Getting Spliced: Modernism and Sexual Difference', in *American Quarterly*, no. 39, 1987, p. 103. Page numbers of further references will follow the citation in the main text.
21 Consider the short story 'As a wife has a cow a love story', which is discussed by Lilian Faderman, *Surpassing the Love of Men: Romantic Friendship and Love Between Women from the Renaissance to the Present*, New York, William Morrow, 1981, p. 402.
22 Roland Barthes, 'The Death of the Author', in *The Rustle of Language*, Oxford, Blackwell, 1986, pp. 49–55, and Michel Foucault, 'What is an Author?', in Josue V. Harari (ed.), *Textual Strategies: Perspectives in Post-Structuralist Criticism*, London, Methuen, 1980, pp. 141–60. This is not to suggest that Barthes's and Foucault's work is unproblematic, since killing off the author does not enable a feminist theorist to discuss the discriminatory practices against women as authors. However, their work has been a necessary first step in the process of demystifying the production of literature.
23 See Alicia Ostriker, *Stealing the Language*, London, The Women's Press, 1987, for an analysis of this problematic relation.
24 Bradbury and MacFarlane, op.cit., p. 636.
25 Although 'prose-poet' need not necessarily be a belittling term, it is surprising that the term is not used to describe male modernists in the collection.
26 David Lodge, 'The Language of Modernist Fiction: Metaphor and Metonymy', in Bradbury and MacFarlane, op.cit., p. 487.
27 Cited in Burke, op.cit., p. 101.
28 R. Kostelanetz (ed.), *The Yale Gertrude Stein*, New Haven, Yale UP, 1980, p. 120.
29 Allon White, 'Exposition and Critique of Julia Kristeva', Centre for Contemporary Cultural Studies, Stencilled Papers, no. 49, University of Birmingham, undated, p. 15.
30 Cited by Lodges, op.cit., p. 487.
31 Colin McCabe, loc.cit.
32 R. Kostelanetz, 'Dates', op.cit., p. 198.
33 Several of the papers given at the Linguistics of Writing Conference were addressed to the question of the difference to analysis made by a 'perfect' or 'imperfect' model of communication. See for example, Mary Louise Pratt's 'Linguistic Utopias', in Nigel Fabb (ed.), *The Linguistics of Writing: Arguments Between Language and Literature*, Manchester UP, 1987, pp. 48–66.
34 One gets the same feeling with reading Kristeva herself, that although you understand the words and phrases individually, it is the meaning of them when they are juxtaposed which is more problematic.
35 Kathleen Fraser, cited in Burke, op.cit., p. 118.

36 R. Kostelanetz, op.cit., p. 124.
37 Kathy Acker, *Blood and Guts in High School*, London, Pan, 1984, p. 112.

Chapter 6 pp. 108–126
1 Gilles Deleuze and Felix Guattari, 'What is a Minor Literature?', in *Kafka: Towards a Minor Literature*, trs. D. Polan, Minneapolis, Minnesota UP, 1986, p. 19.
2 ibid., p. 18.
3 ibid., p. 16.
4 See, for example, an article in the *Times Higher Educational Supplement* by Ronald Fraser, 13 June 1988, p. 16.
5 Lauretta Ngcobo, 'Editor's note', in Ngcobo (ed.), *Let It Be Told*, London, Virago, 1988, p. vii.
6 Elaine Showalter, 'Critical cross-dressing: Male Feminists and The Woman of the Year', in Alice Jardine and Paul Smith (eds.), *Men in Feminism*, London, Methuen, 1987.
7 This applies equally to the present essay. Though I hope I am aware of the problems involved in writing as a white male on poetry by Black women, that by no means conjures such problems away.
8 See, for example, Chinua Achebe, 'Colonialist Criticism', in *Morning Yet on Creation Day*, London, Heinemann, 1975, and Ngugi wa Thiongo, *Decolonising the Mind*, London, James Currey/Heinemann, 1986.
9 See, for example, Dennis Porter, '*Orientalism* and its problems', in F. Barker *et al* (eds.), *The Politics of Theory*, Proceedings of the Essex Sociology of Literature Conference, Colchester, 1983.
10 Deleuze and Guattari, op.cit., p. 24.
11 Meiling Jin, 'The Knock', in *Gifts from my Grandmother*, London, Sheba, 1985, p. 27.
12 ibid., p. 27.
13 Grace Nichols, 'Island Man', in *The Fat Black Woman's Poems*, London, Virago, 1984, p. 29.
14 Amryl Johnson, 'River and Sea', in *Long Road to Nowhere*, London, Virago, 1985, p. 29.
15 ibid., pp. 12 and 13.
16 T.S. Eliot, 'East Coker' and 'Little Gidding', in *Complete Poems and Plays*, London, Faber & Faber, 1969, pp. 182 and 197.
17 Deleuze and Guattari, op.cit., p. 16.
18 Valerie Bloom, 'Yuh Hear Bout?', in Ngcobo, op.cit., p. 96.
19 Merle Collins, 'No Dialects Please', in Rhonda Cobham and Merle Collins (eds.), *Watchers and Seekers*, London, Women's Press, 1987, pp. 118–19.

20 Fredric Jameson, 'Third World Literature in the Era of Multinational Capitalism', *Social Text*, no. 15, Fall, 1986, p. 69.
21 Maud Sulter, 'As a Black Woman', in Ngcobo, op.cit., p. 67.
22 Jameson, op.cit., pp. 85–6.
23 Ngcobo, 'Introduction' in Ngcobo, op.cit., p. 4.
24 Jameson, op.cit., p. 78.
25 Paul Gilroy, *There Ain't No Black In The Union Jack*, London, Hutchinson, 1987, p. 235.
26 See Edward Said, 'Secular Criticism', in *The World, the Text, the Critic*, London, Faber & Faber, 1984.
27 Johnson, op.cit., p. 54.
28 Gilroy, op.cit., p. 172.
29 See, for example, Vera Kutzinski, *Against the American Grain*, Baltimore, Johns Hopkins UP, 1987.
30 Grace Nichols in Ngcobo, op.cit., p. 105.
31 Gilroy, op.cit., p. 207.
32 Nichols, 'Of course when they ask for poems about the "Realities" of Black women', in Barbara Burford, *et al.*, *A Dangerous Knowing*, London, Sheba, 1985, pp. 48 and 50.
33 Sandra Gilbert and Susan Gubar, *No Man's Land: The Place of the Woman Writer in the Twentieth Century*, New Haven, Yale UP, 1988.
34 Deleuze and Guattari, op.cit., p. 27.

Chapter 7 pp. 127–148

1 Ishmael Reed, *Chattanooga*, New York, Random House, 1973, p. 42. All further references to work from *Chattanooga* are inserted in the text as *C*.
2 The seminal text in this field is, of course, Marcel Mauss, *The Gift*, trs. Ian Cunnison, London, Choen and West, 1970. For a more up-to-date discussion related to literature, see Lewis Hyde's *The Gift: Imagination and the Erotic Life of Property*, New York, Vintage, 1983, which has been helpful for the formulation of many of the ideas in this chapter. I am most indebted, though, to Professor Eric Mottram's lectures on critical theory delivered at King's College, London, during 1986–7. Gift exchange was one of the issues with which he dealt, though he did not examine the work of Jean Baudrillard.
3 Jean Baudrillard, *For a Critique of the Political Economy of the Sign*, trs. Charles Levin, St Louis, Mo., Telos Press, 1981, p. 125.
4 Baudrillard often abbreviates signifier as 'Sr' and signified as 'sd'. For the sake of clarity, I have simply used the full forms of these words wherever they occur. I have done the same with 'EV' (exchange value) and 'UV' (use value).
5 Ishmael Reed, *Conjure: Selected Poems, 1963–1970*, Amherst, Massachusetts UP, 1972, p. 7.

6 *God Made Alaska for the Indians*, New York, Garland, 1982, p. 110.
7 Spellman, one of America's most prominent Catholics, undertook a great deal of social and charity work, but was also a supporter of both McCarthy and the Vietnam War. See also Reed's other poem in *Conjure* 'for cardinal spellman who hated voodoo', p. 58.
8 C.J. Sigler, 'Roman Ritual', *New Catholic Encyclopaedia*, New York, McGraw Hill, 1967, vol. 12, pp. 523–4.
9 Ishmael Reed, *Yellow Back Radio Broke-down*, London, Alison and Busby, 1971, pp. 115 and 129.
10 Ishmael Reed, *Flight to Canada*, New York, Random House, 1972, pp. 82 and 89.
11 See George Hart, *A Dictionary of Egyptian Gods and Goddesses*, London, Routledge & Kegan Paul, 1986, pp. 151–67.
12 See J.M. Linebarger and Monte Atkinson, 'Getting to Whitey: Ishmael Reed's "I am a cowboy . . ." ', *Contemporary Poetry*, no. 2, 1, 1975, p. 10.
13 See M.A. Murray, 'The Battle of Horus', *Ancient Egyptian Legends*, New York, E.P. Dutton & Co., 1913, chapter VIII.
14 Alvin F. Harlow, 'Wells, Fargo and Company', *Dictionary of American History* (rev.ed.), New York, Scribner, 1976, Volume VII, p. 267.
15 C.M. Aherne, 'Fable of Popess Joan', *New Catholic Encyclopaedia*, vol. 7, pp. 991–2.
16 See Robert H. Abel, 'Reed's "I am a cowboy in the boat of Ra" ', *Explicator*, no. 30, 9, 1981, Item 81, n.p.
17 James Clifford, 'On Ethnographic Surrealism', *Comparative Studies in Society and History*, no. 23, 4, 1982, p. 548.
18 James Boon, *Other Tribes, Other Scribes: Symbolic Anthropology in the Comparative Study of Cultures, Histories, Religions and Texts*, Cambridge, CUP, 1982, p. 25.
19 'Pre-Face', in Jerome Rothenberg (ed.), *Shaking the Pumpkin*, New York, Doubleday, 1972, p. xxi.
20 See Ishmael Reed, 'Introduction to *19 Necromancers from Now*', *New Black Voices*, New York, Chapman, 1972, p. 515.
21 From an unpublished essay on Reed's poetry by Vera Kutzinski. My thanks to her for letting me consult her manuscript, and for her suggestions and advice. My comments on 'beware: do not read this poem' follow her lengthier analysis.
22 Chester J. Fontenot, 'Ishmael Reed and the Politics of Aesthetics or, Shake Hands and Come Out Conjuring', *Black American Literature Forum*, no. 12, 1, 1978, pp. 21 and 23.
23 W.E.B. Du Bois, *The Souls of Black Folks,* New York, New American Library, 1969, p. 45.
24 See Leonard Feather and Ira Gitler, *The Encyclopaedia of Jazz in the 1970s*, New York, Horizon, 1976, p. 319.

25 In Walt Shepard, 'When State Magicians Fail – An Interview with Ishmael Reed', *Journal of Black Poetry*, no. 1, 12, 1969, p. 75. The interview was originally published in *Nickel Review*, 28 August 1968, pp. 4–6. 'I am a cowboy . . .' was first published in *Noose*, June, 1968, n.p.
26 In John O'Brien (ed.), *Interviews with Black Writers*, New York, Liverwright, 1973, p. 177.
27 Lorenzo Thomas, 'The Shadow World: New York's Umbra Workshop and Origins of the Black Arts Movement', *Callaloo*, no. 1, 4, 1978, p. 59.
28 See 'Foreword' to *Conjure*, p. vii, and *Shrovetide in Old New Orleans*, New York, Doubleday, 1978, pp. 133–4.
29 Mark Shadle, 'A Bird's Eye View: Ishmael Reed's Unsettling of the Score by Munching and Mooching on the Mumbo Jumbo Work of History', *North Dakota Quarterly*, no. 54, 1, 1986, p. 21.
30 Joachim Berendt, *The Jazz Book*, trs. D. Morgenstern and H. & B. Bredigkeit, Westport, Lawrence Hill, 1975, p. 18. My emphasis.
31 *The Complete Poetry and Prose of William Blake* (rev.ed.), David V. Erdman (ed.), Berkeley, California UP, 1982, p. 95. My thanks to Miles Inada for alerting me to this allusion.
32 John Hollander, *Vision and Resonance: Two Sense of Poetic Form*, New York, OUP, 1975, pp. 208–9.
33 LeRoi Jones, *Blues People*, New York, Morrow Quill, 1963, p. 194.
34 Gunther Schuller, *Early Jazz: Its Roots and Musical Development*, New York, OUP, 1968, p. 8.
35 Gilles Deleuze and Felix Guattari, 'What is a Minor Literature?', *Mississippi Review*, no. 31, 1983, p. 22. My emphasis.
36 See, for instance, Henry Nash Smith, *Virgin Land*, Harvard UP, 1978, pp. 94–5. Reed's second novel, *Yellow Back Radio Broke-Down*, is deeply influenced by the literature of the dime novel.
37 Berndt Ostendorf, *Black Literature in White America*, Sussex, NJ, Harvester, Barnes & Noble, 1982, p. 67.
38 James Clifford, 'Orientalism', *History and Theory*, no. 19, 2, 1980, p. 222.
39 Robert D. Pelton, *The Trickster in West Africa: A Study of Mythic Irony and Sacred Delight*, Berkeley, California UP, 1980, pp. 282–3.

Chapter 8 pp. 149–166

1 Frank O'Hara, *Selected Poems*, New York, Vintage, 1974, p. 112.
2 Gil Ott (ed.), Special Jackson Mac Low issue of *Paper Air*, no. 2, 3, 1980, p. 61.
3 Wendy Steiner, *The Colours of Rhetoric: Problems in the Relation Between Modern Literature and Painting*, Chicago UP, 1982, and

W.J.T. Mitchell, *Iconology: Image, Text and Ideology*, Chicago UP, 1986.
4 See Ferdinand de Saussure, 'The Linguistic Sign', in Robert E. Innis (ed.), *Semiotics*, London, Hutchinson, 1986.
5 One way of approaching the relationship between the two systems (language and visual images), and one that Wendy Steiner employs, is to use C.S. Pierce's categorization of different types of signs. In Pierce's definition a symbol is a sign which is related to its referent only by arbitrary association, and the icon is a sign which resembles or incorporates its referent (which can be objects, events, ideas, or attitudes). One way of distinguishing between poetry and painting, then, is to say that verbal texts are more symbolic while visual images are more iconic, and one way of emphasizing their similarity is to say that both consist of mixed signs. However, since the word icon is sometimes used by theorists to describe an artistic representation, and sometimes used to describe the impression of naturalness that a work of art creates, even when it is non-representational, the term iconic can create a certain amount of confusion, which is why I have avoided using the term in the main text.
6 Steiner, op.cit., pp. 33–50, and Mitchell, op.cit., pp. 95–115.
7 In her opening remarks in *The Critical Difference*, Baltimore, Johns Hopkins UP, 1980, Barbara Johnson makes a related point about the difference between entities actually being differences within them, 'ways in which an entity differs from itself'.
8 Mitchell, op.cit., pp. 95–146.
9 The Abstract Expressionist painter and teacher Hans Hofmann, used the phrase 'push and pull' to describe the dynamic interaction of blocks of colours on a flat surface.
10 Frank O'Hara's strong involvement with painting, collaborations with painters, and work as assistant curator at the Museum of Modern Art in New York, is documented in Marjorie Perloff, *Frank O'Hara: Poet Among Painters*, Chicago UP, 1979, and Bill Berkson/Joe LeSueur, *Homage to Frank O'Hara*, Berkeley, Creative Art Books, 1980. More information about Abstract Expressionism, Pop Art, and the painters of the New York School can be found in Irving Sandler, *The Triumph of American painting: A History of Abstract Expressionism*, New York, Harper and Row, 1970, and Irving Sandler, *The New York School: The Painters and Sculptors of the Fifties*, New York, Harper and Row, 1978. The second section of Francis Frascina (ed.), *Pollock and After: The Critical Debate*, London, Harper and Row, 1985, contains essays on the political manipulation of Abstract Expressionism during the Cold War.
11 For the influence of linguistics, semiotics, and structuralism, on musical analysis see Wendy Steiner (ed.), *The Sign in Music and Literature*,

Texas UP, 1981; Richard Middleton, 'Reading Popular Music', *Form and Meaning (2) Unit 16*, Milton Keynes, Open University Press, 1981; Ian Bent with William Drabkin, *Analysis*, London, Macmillan, 1987, and Jonathan Dunsby and Arnold Whittall, *Music Analysis in Theory and Practice*, London, Faber Music, 1988.

12 Roland Barthes, 'From Work to Text', in *Image-Music-Text*, London, Fontana, 1977, p. 157.

13 Roman Jakobson, 'Closing Statement: Linguistics and Poetics' in Robert E. Innis (ed.), *Semiotics*, London, Hutchinson & Co. Ltd, 1986.

14 See Richard Middleton, 'Reading Popular Music', *Form and Meaning (2) Unit 16*, and two essays: John Blacking, 'The problem of "Ethnic" Perceptions in the Semiotics of Music', and 'A Musical Icon: Power and Meaning in Javanese Gamelan Music', in Wendy Steiner (ed.), *The Sign in Music and Literature*.

15 Richard Kostelanetz (ed.), *Text-Sound Texts*, New York, William Morrow, 1980. In his introduction to the book, 'Text-Sound Art', Kostelanetz says, 'the term "text-sound" characterises language whose principal means of coherence is sound, rather than syntax or semantics . . .'

16 Ian Bent, op.cit., *Analysis*, p. 5.

17 Roland Barthes, op.cit., p. 153.

18 ibid., p. 163.

19 ibid., p. 147.

20 ibid., p. 159.

21 Lysis performance at the Logos Foundation, Ghent, Belgium, October 1986, in the collection of the Logos Foundation (Kongostraat 35 B-9000, Ghent). The Foundation also has tapes of performances by Mac Low of many of his works from performances given at the Foundation.

22 Jackson Mac Low, *Representative Works*, New York, Roof Books, 1986.

23 Anyone interested in the musical considerations involved in the performance of such scores should read Roger Dean, *Creative improvisation: Jazz and Beyond*, Milton Keynes, Open University Press, 1989.

Chapter 9 pp. 167–190

1 Barbara Johnson, *The Critical Difference*, Baltimore, Johns Hopkins UP, 1985, p. 53.

2 ibid., p. 66.

3 See Roger Poole's study of the context of Bloom's psychoanalytical criticism in 'The Yale School as a Theological Enterprise', *Structuralisms, Renaissance and Modern Studies*, no. 27, 1983, p. 24.

4 *Figures of Capable Imagination*, New York, Seabury, 1976, p. XII.

5 Frank Lentricchia, *After the New Criticism*, Chicago UP, 1980, p. 333.

6 Harold Bloom, *The Anxiety of Influence*, New York and London, OUP, 1973, p. 13. Lentricchia is not slow, of course, to counter Bloom's 'humanism' on the grounds of Freudianism: 'Bloom's version of the self denies freedom and individuality as it dooms the subject to one activity – the endless and endlessly evasive expression of father-figure anxieties over which it has no control and which finally it cannot evade', op.cit. p. 336.
7 Tzvetan Todorov, *Mikhail Bakhtin: The Dialogical Principle*, trs. Wlad Godzich, Minneapolis, Minnesota UP, 1984, p. 62.
8 Antoine Compagnon, *La Seconde Main ou le Travail de la Citation*, Paris, Seuil, 1979, p. 34.
9 Jacques Derrida, *Writing and Difference*, trs. A. Bass, London, Routledge & Kegan Paul, 1972, p. 280.
10 Derrida, op.cit., p. 95.
11 Harold Bloom, *Figures of Capable Imagination*, p. 9.
12 Harold Bloom, *The Anxiety of Influence* (see note 6) and *A Map of Misreading*, New York, Toronto and Melbourne, OUP, 1975.
13 *Figures of Capable Imagination*, pp. 9–10. See also here Bloom's definitions of 'Clinamen', 'Tessera', 'Kenosis', 'Daemonization', 'Askesis' and 'Aprophades'.
14 Stéphane Mallarmé, *Oeuvres complètes*, Paris, Pléiade, 1945, p. 76. trs. Anthony Hartley, *Mallarmé*, Harmondsworth, Penguin, 1965, pp. 102–3.
15 Rubén Darío, *Prosas profanas y otros poemas*, Ignacio M. Zuleta (ed.), Madrid, Clásicos Castalia, 1983, p. 177.
16 See Stéphane Mallarmé, *Quant au livre*, Paris, Pléiade, pp. 369–87.
17 Paul Verlaine, 'Art poétique', *Oeuvres complètes*, Paris, Pléiade, 1968, p. 326.
18 Mallarmé, op.cit., pp. 875–6.
19 Malcolm Bowie, *Mallarmé and the Art of Being Difficult*, Cambridge, CUP, 1978, pp. 8 and 16. Bowie refers here to Anton Ehrenzweig, *The Hidden Order of Art*, London, Weidenfeld & Nicolson, 1967.
20 From Mallarmé's letter to Henri Cazalis of October/November 1894, in H. Mondor and J.-P. Richard (eds.), *Corréspondance*, vol. 1, 1862–71, Paris, Gallimard, 1959, p. 137.
21 ibid., p. 869.
22 ibid., p. 857; Hartley, op.cit., p. xxviii.
23 Henri Mondor, *Vie de Mallarmé*, Paris, Gallimard, 1941, p. 684.
24 Bowie, op.cit., p. 4.
25 Rubén Darío, 'Yo soy aquel', *Cantos de vida y esperanza*, pp. 861–5.
26 The notion of 'the missing term' bears some relation, particularly in the context of the play of presence and absence, to the work of Jacques Derrida. In technical terms, however, 'le rêve' as 'le terme absent' refers

directly to the theory of the 'repressed matrix' of Michael Riffaterre, *Semiotics of Poetry*, London, Methuen, 1978, p. 19. See also my 'Undoing the Romantic Discourse: A Case-Study in Post-Structuralist Analysis. Vallejo's *Trilce* I', *Romance Studies*, A Journal of the University of Wales, 5, 1985–5, pp. 91–111.

27 'after having found Nothingness, I found Beauty', *Correspondance*, p. 220.

28 *cf conceptismo*: a witty style, based on complex conceits, reminiscent of the English Metaphysical poets, and one of the principal devices of Spanish Golden Age writers.

29 *modernismo*: not to be confused with other 'modernisms', the Hispanic version, of the turn of the century, is a highly stylized post-Romantic and Decadent style, comparable to the English pre-Raphaelite and the French late-Symbolist.

30 op.cit., p. 385.

31 op.cit., p. 915 and p. 920.

32 Elizabeth Wright, *Psychoanalytical Criticism*, London, Methuen, 1984, p. 155.

33 ibid., pp. 155–6

34 M.H. Abrams, *The Mirror and the Lamp*, New York, OUP, 1953, p. 272. For a full discussion of the organicist model, see Jonathan Culler's 'The Mirror Stage', in *The Pursuit of Signs*, London, Routledge & Kegan Paul, 1981, pp. 155–68.

35 'el rebelde, mezquino idioma' is the legacy of Gustavo Adolfo Bécquer, the foremost of Spanish lyric poets of the nineteenth century and a crucial influence both on Darío and Vallejo.

36 Michel Foucault, 'Nietzche, Genealogy, History', in Paul Rabinow (ed.), *The Foucault Reader*, Harmondsworth, Penguin, 1984, p. 88.

37 Wright, op.cit., p. 109.

38 *Correspondance*, p. 220.

39 Derrida, op.cit., p. 292.

Appendix
Instructions for the performance of a Notated Vocabulary for Eve Rosenthal
by Jackson Mac Low

A Notated Vocabulary for Eve Rosenthal is a 22" × 14" drawing based on 101 words spelled with the letters of Eve Rosenthal's name, 'e' being the only letter used more than once (up to 3 times) in any word. Each word is hand-lettered over a short, hand-drawn, clefless staff on which is placed a series of whole notes corresponding to the letter series spelling the word: The lack of clef indicates that each note group is to be read as if prefixed by a clef chosen by the performer, usually that normal to their instrument. Those playing instruments using more than one clef (e.g., piano) must choose a clef for each note group played. Those playing transposing instruments must both choose clefs and play note groups *at pitch* – not at concert pitch: e.g., a B-flat instrument using treble clef will play a B-flat when playing a note written on the 3rd space from the bottom (treble-clef C). Each word-note group is drawn at a different angle, some being more nearly 'right side up' when one of the drawing's sides is on top, some when another is.

The composition may be performed by any number of speaker–instrumentalists. (Their number may sometimes be augmented by a smaller number who can only speak and/or sing). Starting with any particular word-note group, each moves freely from one group to another, saying the words and/or playing the notes (see below). One may dwell on one particular group, improvising only on its notes and occasionally saying its word, or one may string together words (into phrases, sentences, or nonsyntactical groups) or note groups. Words may be spoken without playing their note groups and note groups may be played without saying their words. *After each few minutes of improvisation, the performer must fall silent and listen attentively for at least 15 seconds* before resuming improvisation, which should be done only when the performer really wants to add new sounds to the aural situation.

Each sequence of notes, reading (in the chosen clef) either from right to left or left to right, may be played any number of times, but must be followed exactly. Each note may be played in any octave, and a variety of octave placements is desirable. Two or more consecutive notes, or a whole sequence, may be played simultaneously, as an interval, chord, or tone cluster. Each tone, interval, chord, or cluster may be repeated one or more times and/ or doubled in two or more octaves. Adjacent notes in a group, as well as adjacent intervals, chords or clusters may be repeated alternatively ('trilled'), and three or more successive notes may be repeated as *ostinati*.

Any word spellable with the letters of Eve Rosenthal's name (only 'e' being used more than once in a word) may be spoken in addition to those already on the drawing. In making sentences, etc., it will often be necessary to add usable structure words and the like. *A*, *an*, *the*, *have*, *are*, *he*, *she*, *that*, *other*, *one*, *three*, *seven*, *ten*, *eleven*, *no*, *to*, *on*, *an'* or *'n'* (for 'and'), *or*, *so*, *here*, *there*, *then*, *than*, *else*, *also*, *never*, *ever*, *tho*, and *altho*, only some of which are on the drawing, are all usable in word strings. An 's' may be added to any noun or verb stem which does not itself include an 's'. Words must be clearly audible, but seldom if ever so loud as to seem to reflect violent feelings. They may be repeated.

The frequent interpolation of silences is necessary and very important. They may occur between tones, chords, words, etc., as well as between periods of improvisation, allowing tones, etc., to be inserted singly among those being produced by other performers. All notes in a series must be played or sung at least once in a forward or reversed order before the series is begun again in either order.

All parameters not fixed by notation or instructions are chosen by performers in relation to the total situation. These include octave placement, simultaneous and/or successive grouping, repetition, duration, rhythm, loudness, tempo, timbre, attack, etc., of tones; ways of using words; and duration and placements of silences.

Performers must listen to, relate with, and respond to each other and to ambient sounds. When they fall silent, they must listen with concentrated attention to the total aural situation and make choices as to further sound production in accord with what they hear.

Sensitivity, tact, and courtesy must be exercised in order to make every performance detail contribute to a total sound sequence the performer would choose to hear. Virtuosity is strongly encouraged but must be exercised with great consciousness of its place in the total aural situation. Performers must be both inventive and sensitive at all times. '*Listen*' and '*Relate*' are the main 'rules'.

A performance may be begun and ended in any convenient manner. Usually it will be best for performers to agree beforehand on an approximate performance duration and for one of them to act as 'leader', signalling the beginning, keeping track of the elapsed time with a watch, and signalling the ending at some point before or slightly after the agreed-upon duration. The leader must be clearly visible to all performers and must exercise judgement as to when, near the agreed-upon and point, the group improvisation can be satisfactorily ended. However, when the situation allows greater latitude, a performance may be allowed to continue until the group reaches an informal consensus to end it.

Jackson Mac Low

Index

Abrams, M. H. 182, 191, 194
Abstract Expressionism 155, 207
accentualism 138–43
Acker, Kathy 107
Ackroyd, Peter 76
Agard, Brenda 118
Alvarez, A. 76
Anyiam-St John, Rita 124
Apollinaire, Guillaume 188
Arnold, Matthew 30
Ashbery, John 5
Augustine, St 46

Bakhtin, Mikhail 24, 25, 30, 32, 33, 34, 37, 38, 40, 41, 42, 43, 48, 60, 61, 188
Barnes, Djuna 95
Barthes, Roland 43, 47, 64, 84, 89, 96, 135, 159, 160, 161, 202
Baudrillard, Jean 128–9, 135, 144, 145
Belsey, Catherine 199
Bernal, Martin 33, 34
Berendt, Joachim 138
Bhabha, Homi K. 111
Bhagavid-Gita 55
Black aesthetic 129–30, 136, 146
Blackmur, R. P. 66
Blake, William 139–40, 142, 143
Bloom, Harold 167–70, 173–83, 188–9, 192, 208
Bloom, Valerie 115–16, 119, 121–2
Boon, James 134, 146–7
Bové, Paul A. 192
Bowie, Malcolm 172
Boyce, D. G. 35
Bradbury, Malcolm 94, 98, 100, 200
Brooks, Cleanth 42, 48, 193
Browning, Elizabeth 67
Burke, Carolyn 96, 97, 99, 103–4
Burroughs, William 135, 146

Cage, John 18
Carlyle, Thomas 55
Chesnutt, Charles 146
citation 64, 168, 188
Clarke, John Cooper 66

Clifford, James 147
Coleridge, S. T. 182
collage 15, 19, 96, 106, 134
Collins, Merle 116, 121
Compagnon, Antoine 168
Concrete poetry 5, 166
Conrad, Joseph 58, 60
Couzyn, Jean 67, 70, 78
Creole 115–16
Cubism 17, 100–1, 106
Culler, Jonathan 63, 191, 199

Dante 58, 59
Darío, Rubén 167, 169, 170–81, 182, 186, 188, 190
Deconstruction 9, 10, 11, 21, 49, 53, 55, 58, 150, 151, 152, 192, 194
Deleuze, Gilles 108, 111–12, 115, 117–19, 123, 144–6
De Man, Paul 54, 191, 192, 193
Derrida, Jacques 9, 12, 15, 17, 21, 50, 56, 57, 58, 122–3, 168, 169, 188, 190, 192, 193, 195, 209
desire 53, 59
Dickinson, Emily 62, 65–6, 67, 68, 72–5, 78, 79, 80, 81, 83
Dixon, Bill 137
Donne, John 49, 118
Dowe, Fyna 121
Du Bois, W. E. B. 135
Duncan, Robert 13, 19, 20

Eagleton, Terry 63
Easthope, Anthony 47, 191
Eaves, Morris 191
Eco, Umberto 43, 194
Ehrmann, Jacques 193
Eliot, T. S. 42–61, 76–8, 86, 95, 114, 188
  The Waste Land 5, 14, 42–8
  Four Quartets 49–61
Ellison, Ralph 135, 146
Ellman, Maud 45
Ellman, Richard 31, 32, 33, 36
Elyot, Sir Thomas 53
Engels, Friedrich 35